Indians

in Unexpected Places

CultureAmerica

ERIKA DOSS

PHILIP J. DELORIA

series editors

KARAL ANN MARLING

editor emerita

Indians

in Unexpected Places

PHILIP J. DELORIA

UNIVERSITY PRESS OF KANSAS

Published by the

University Press of Kansas

(Lawrence, Kansas 66049),

which was organized by the

Kansas Board of Regents and

is operated and funded by

Emporia State University,

Fort Hays State University,

Kansas State University,

Pittsburg State University,

the University of Kansas, and

Wichita State University

Library of Congress
Cataloging-in-Publication Data
Deloria, Philip Joseph.
    Indians in unexpected places / Philip J. Deloria.
        p.   cm. — (CultureAmerica)
    Includes bibliographical references and index.
    ISBN 978-0-7006-1344-7 (cloth : alk. paper)
    ISBN 978-0-7006-1459-2 (pbk. : alk. paper)
    1. Indians of North America—Social conditions.   I. Title.
II. Culture America
    E98.S67D46   2004
    973.04'97—dc22   2004005384

British Library Cataloguing in Publication Data is available.

Printed in the United States of America

10 9 8 7 6 5

The paper used in this publication meets the minimum
requirements of the American National Standard for
Permanence of Paper for Printed Library Materials
Z39.48-1984.

For my mother,

Barbara Nystrom Deloria,

and my father,

Vine V. Deloria Jr.

contents

acknowledgments

When I was young, my grandfather liked to put my brother, sister, and me in his car and race crazily around the neighborhood, crying out, "I'm a New York taxi driver!" He made us laugh, though he also left us a little frightened. In 1990, I recalled those moments wistfully while he dredged up fragmented memories of football glory for a grandson he could no longer call to mind. Only a few months after our last encounter, I found myself sitting by my grandmother's bedside, joining her in a similarly final contemplation of the past. The memories and emotions contained in these encounters led me to start thinking more seriously about Indian athletes and drivers and about the inclination within American culture to insist on the separation of categories like *Indian*, *sports*, *automobiles*, and *New York*. Before writing another word, then, I look back in time, inside myself, and outward to the world to thank my grandfather and my grandmother for the impulses that led to this book. I hope I have done well by them and by other Native people I've placed in the picture. I've incurred many obligations during the writing, and I take great pleasure, at long last, in thanking my family, friends, and colleagues.

Though I've tried to weld them into coherence, these pieces exist primarily as essays, and they've come to life in a variety of contexts. Chapter 4 came first, starting as a short paper delivered at the 1994 Western History Association meeting. John Wunder, Emily Greenwald, Roger Echo-Hawk, and Jennifer Price each offered valuable comments. In 2000, I presented revised versions at a University of Colorado Humanities Center colloquium, at the University of California, Davis, and at the University of Michigan. Among the many helpful listeners at these events, I particularly want to thank Ralph Mann, Gloria Main, Steven Epstein, Louis Warren, Alan Taylor, John Carson, and Chris Talbot. The essay got one final read from some of the fantastic faculty in Native American studies (Gregory Dowd, Andrea Smith, Michael Witgen, Gavin Clarkson) and Asian Pacific Islander–American studies (Amy Stillman and Damon Salesa) at the University of Michigan. Thank you all for your intelligence and generosity.

A version of chapter 3 was previously published as "I Am of the Body: Thoughts on My Grandfather, Sports, and Culture," *South Atlantic Quarterly* 95, no. 2 (spring 1996): 321–38. I am grateful to Jim Fisher, guest editor for the issue "Real Sports," and to Candace Ward, whose editorial admonitions gave me a solid footing for an expansion of the piece. Along the way, I presented the essay at the American Indian Studies Program at the University of Arizona, as a paper at the 1996 conference of the Organization of American Historians (OAH), and as a faculty seminar piece at the University of Colorado. Thanks to Fred Hoxie at the OAH, to K. Tsianina Lomawaima, Kathy Morrisey, and the Arizona crew, and to Fred Anderson, Julie Green, and my colleagues at Colorado.

Chapter 1 was originally a conference paper, delivered at the Western Historical Association conference in 2001. My gratitude goes out to Sasha Harmon for getting me moving on the essay and to Devon Mihesuah and Matthew Dennis for their encouragement and suggestions. Thanks also to my Michigan writing group—Penny Von Eschen, Carroll Smith-Rosenberg, and Sonya Rose—for comments and suggestions on it and chapter 4. Chapter 5 benefited from a number of generous readings that have set me straight on any number of issues. Thanks especially to David Stowe and Amy Stillman on musicological questions, to Susan Dominguez for sharing her deep knowledge of Zitkala-Ša, to Nancy Toff for sending me numerous tidbits, and to K. Tsianina Lomawaima for allowing and helping me to write about her extraordinary aunt Tsianina Redfeather. I presented the essay and received useful commentary at the University of North Carolina, Chapel Hill, in 2002 (thanks especially to Mike Green, Theda Perdue, Joy Kasson, and John Kasson) and from the University of Michigan Native American Studies Group, especially Joe Gone and Tiya Miles. Thank you all.

The introduction and chapter 2 benefited immensely from a workshop session with the faculty and graduate students of the University of Michigan Program in American Culture. Thanks to everyone, especially Vicente Diaz, Paul Anderson, Magdalena Zaborowska, Jesse Hoffnung-Garskof, Carroll Smith-Rosenberg, Maria Cotera, Matthew Wittman, Mary Kelley, Jim McIntosh, Andrea Smith, and Crisca Bierwert. Thanks also to Christina Berndt, Angela Aleiss, and Marc Wanamaker for sharing writings, opinions, and photographs of and about Hollywood Indians. My longtime friend Louis Warren generously offered insights and source material from his extraordinary project on Buffalo Bill Cody.

Along the way, I've had enlightenment and good conversation with friends and colleagues Betty Bell, Tom Biolsi, Constance Clark, Jay Cook, Roger Echo-Hawk, Kevin Gaines, Michael Goldberg, Emily Greenwald, Patty Limerick, Maria Montoya, Gina Morantz-Sanchez, Jeani O'Brien, Willard Rollings, Gerry Ronning, Sonya Rose, Roy Rosenzweig, Suzanne Smith, Carroll Smith-Rosenberg, Robert Warrior, Jace Weaver, Rick Williams, and John Wunder. I have repeatedly discussed most of the ideas in this book with my dear friend Susan K. Kent, who is always watching my back in difficult times. Thank you. Richard White, Erika Doss, and an anonymous reader helped me start the project with an eye for pitfalls and a list of opportunities. And I've relied heavily on several generous souls willing to read the entire manuscript, each of whom helped at a critical stage. Your various promptings have all made their way into the book. Thanks to Greg Dowd, Mary Kelley, Susan Kent, Jenny Price, Carlo Rotella, Gustavo Verdesio, and Penny Von Eschen.

I've been lucky to have research assistance from four talented students. Thanks to Kitty Rasmussen, Ted Chen, Jeana Plas, and Jennifer Holland. I've also had the pleasure of working with a number of dedicated and wonderful archivists and staff members. Thanks, at the Library of Congress, to Jennifer Brathovde, Rosemary Hanes, and Zachary Balian and, at the National Archives, to Maryfrances Morrow. It was my great pleasure to work with Bruce Hanson at the Denver Public Library's Western History Department, Kathryn Hodson at the University of Iowa Special Collections, Paul Eisloeffel and John Carter at the Nebraska State Historical Society, Linda Strauss, Marva Felchlin, and Tori Coutner at the Autry National Center, Marc Wanamaker at Bison Archives, George Miles and Nancy Kuhl at the Beinecke Rare Book Library at Yale, Shelley Howe at the Buffalo Bill Historical Museum in Golden, Colorado, John Powell at the Newberry Library, Jacqueline Eliasson at the Glenbow Museum in Calgary, Alberta, and Kelly Cannon-Miller at the High Desert Museum. The art of Arthur Amiotte has been an inspiration during the last year of this project, and I'm grateful to him for allowing me to use two of his images.

I've been incredibly fortunate to work with a wonderful and talented editor, Nancy Jackson, at the University Press of Kansas. Not only has she been long suffering and patient, as editors should be, but she has also been completely engaged with the project from the beginning. Once or twice a year (and for far too long from her perspective!), Nancy has prompted me to consolidate, articulate, and rethink the project as a whole. Under her intelligent prompting, it has grown, and I owe her my deepest thanks. At the Press, I'd also like to thank Melinda Wirkus,

Larisa Martin, and Susan Schott. I received great copyediting and musicological counsel from Joseph Brown.

Out of all the collaborations one finds in a book such as this, my most valued ones have been those less visible as academic and intellectual genealogy. The best collaboration of my life has been with my extraordinary wife and partner, Peggy Burns, and with my children, Jackson and Lacey, who strive to keep me young in spite of myself. My parents, Vine Deloria Jr. and Barbara Nystrom Deloria, too, have been my lifelong collaborators and partners. I have by turns obsessed about them and taken them for granted but far too infrequently told them how much I appreciate them. I do so now and dedicate this book to them. Thanks Mom! Thanks Dad!

Indians
in Unexpected Places

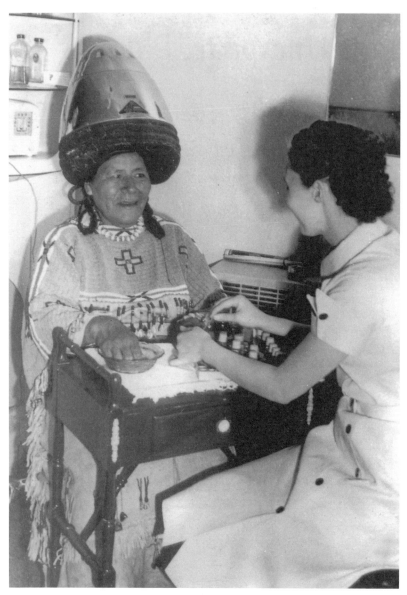

FIGURE 1. Red Cloud Woman in Beauty Shop, Denver 1941.
(Denver Public Library, Western History Department, X-31929.)

generalized title?
→ not her name?
↳ not individualized

introduction

CHUCKLE

I love this image. It's entitled *Red Cloud Woman in Beauty Shop, Denver 1941*. An Indian woman in a beaded buckskin dress sits under a large salon hair dryer. She is receiving a manicure, and one hand soaks in a small dish while a manicurist works on the nails of the other. Glass bottles and an electric timer peer over her near shoulder. A heating unit on the other side and a table in front complete a circle, surrounding her with modern technology. In the upper-right-hand corner, a mirror refuses to reflect the scene, emphasizing instead a single line that segregates darker shades from lighter. I have shown this photograph to many people over the last few years, and, almost always, someone chuckles (see figure 1).[1]

The chuckle is not malicious or hateful or nasty. It's playful, the small laugh that you get when you tell a good, but not great, joke. Where do such chuckles come from? For starters, the silver cone-head hair dryer looks funny on just about anyone. And many people remember a similar-looking old television commercial in which Madge the manicurist pampered her clients by treating their nails with dishwashing soap: "Palmolive? You're soaking in it!" Madge's customer jerks her hand out of the bowl. Dishwashing liquid? That was the last thing she ever expected. The television audience chuckles—and why not? Lots of humor originates with this sort of juxtaposition between the expected and the unexpected.

We might look for the origins of this particular chuckle in the aura of unexpectedness that surrounds Red Cloud Woman. What is *she* doing *there?* Turn the chuckle inside out, and you will see that the laughter that sometimes greets her manicure says a lot about what is expected, about the shared ideologies of "the American grain." Even in the wake of decades of stereotype busting, a beaded buckskin dress and a pair of braids continue to evoke a broad set of cultural expectations about Indian people. Viewers of the photograph may claim not to believe in these *technology*

expectations, but, believed or not, their ghostly presences materialize at critical moments to shape reactions in subtle ways. Such expectations are not hard to name. Indians are primitive, unaccustomed to the modern technology of the 1940s hair dryer. Indians live in the hinterlands, strangers to the urbanity of the manicure. They practice barter or gift economies and are, thus, unprepared for the cash exchange of the beauty parlor. They are solemn and stoic, hardly expected to share a smile with their manicurists. They are subject to familiar assumptions about the relation between race and labor—if in a beauty parlor at all, one expects to find them, not as clients, but as workers. Each of these expectations is laced through with understandings about Red Cloud Woman as an Indian *woman*, for Native women have all too frequently been portrayed as either dominated drudges or feisty natural princesses. This range of expectations is brought to life through Red Cloud Woman's dress, her face, and her hair. But, because the expectations surrounding the notion of the beauty parlor refuse to mesh with those surrounding Red Cloud Woman, her presence in there makes things strange, unfamiliar. The safest response to such strangeness is often laughter, which takes direct aim at the impossibility of the image. A chuckle can reaffirm the rightness of one's broadest cultural expectations, and it reduces Red Cloud Woman's oddly threatening trip to the beauty parlor to a funny, unexpected anomaly.

EXPECTATION AND ANOMALY

If the laughter is not overtly racist in nature, it nonetheless suggests that broad cultural expectations are both the products and the tools of domination and that they are an inheritance that haunts each and every one of us. To chuckle at Red Cloud Woman without malice is perhaps possible. To separate oneself from the history that produced the chuckle is not, and that history contains a full share of malice and misunderstanding. If we ignore the humor of the anomaly and focus instead on *expectations*, we might find the grin wiped from the face of America. Primitivism, technological incompetence, physical distance, and cultural difference—these have been the ways many Americans have imagined Indians like Red Cloud Woman, and such images have remained familiar currency in contemporary dealings with Native people. It is critical, then, that we question expectations and explore their origins, for they created—and they continue to reproduce—social, political, legal, and economic relations that are asymmetrical, sometimes grossly so.

If expectations require our attention, however, so too do anomalies. How does one come to perceive Red Cloud Woman as anomalous? What are the histories of expectation that distinguish that which seems right and natural from that which seems simply bizarre? Does anomaly work to shape expectation itself? We name an event an anomaly in relation to accepted norms and categories. Usually, these categories already exist, and we can easily pigeonhole an anomalous event as something that should fit a certain norm ("Indian women wear buckskin dresses . . .") but does not (". . . and sit under hair dryers").

Even as it defines the unnatural and odd, the naming of an anomaly simultaneously re-creates and empowers the very same categories that it escapes. In other words, we know that Indian women of the 1940s do not belong in beauty parlors because this particular instance is surely the exception. It is so much the exception that we sense the category with more certainty than we did before we confronted the anomalous Red Cloud Woman. Expectations and anomalies are mutually constitutive—they make each other. To assert that a person or an event is anomalous cannot help but serve to create and to reinforce other expectations. Naming Red Cloud Woman an unexpected anomaly, then, helps naturalize categories such as *white, woman, modern, beauty, technology,* and *labor,* among others. Perceived mostly outside each of these categories, Red Cloud Woman helps give them their shape, meaning, and power. A rich cluster of meaning surrounds cultural expectation and its visible manifestation in images, acts, sounds, and texts, to be sure. But, when it comes to naming anomalies, even subtle and contradictory accretions of meaning will work to empower the broad, largely consensual categories that have consistently placed whites over Indians, men over women, capital over labor, and the normative over the exceptional.

Surely not everyone finds Red Cloud Woman odd. I have, in fact, conjured a composite and abstract audience to represent a sensibility within American culture and society. It seems to me a reasonable conjuring. There are other audiences, however, and their responses point in equally important directions. Indigenous viewers of Red Cloud Woman—not just from North America, but from around the world—have rarely been inclined to perceive her as being alien to categories like *woman, modern, beauty, technology,* or *labor.* Though she looks like a client, for instance, Red Cloud Woman might actually have been hard at work, laboring as a model in a long-lived economy built on acting, painting, photography, and other acts of representation (after all, she does have her hair in braids rather than curlers, which suggests that the silver cone-head hair dryer wasn't really functioning!). In that sense, she might be more representative than anomalous. Was she joking around with that economy? Or was she simply getting her nails done? And what would be so weird about that?[2]

As consumers of global mass-mediated culture, we are all subject to expectations. They sneak into our minds and down to our hearts when we aren't looking. That does not mean, however, that they need to rule our thoughts. Why should any audience allow Red Cloud Woman—or any other Indian person engaged in anything unexpected—to be persistently and automatically designated anomalous? What would happen if we were to take a cue from indigenous viewers and question every instance in which Indians are named as anomalies? Perhaps it might be more instructive to think about events in terms of their *frequency* (rare, occasional, frequent) rather than reaffirming the categories and values that accompany anomaly and expectation?

This book seeks to explore these and other questions about expectation, most particularly at the turn of the twentieth century. In that moment, according to most American narratives, Indian people, corralled on isolated and impoverished reservations, missed out on modernity—indeed, almost dropped out of history itself. In such narratives, Native Americans would reemerge as largely insignificant political and cultural actors in the reform efforts of the 1920s and 1930s. World War II would force them to engage urbanism, wage labor, and American culture. Though such changes would nudge Indian people toward the modern world, their first and best chances at freedom, reason, equality, and progress had passed them by. I argue, instead, that a significant cohort of Native people engaged the same forces of modernization that were making non-Indians reevaluate their own expectations of themselves and their society. The world we inhabit is the shared creation of all peoples, though the costs and benefits have been parceled out with astonishing inequality, as have the notions about who has been active in that creation and who has been acted on.

In considering these issues, I want to ask, first, how we might revisit the actions of Indian people that have been all too easily branded as anomalous. Considering the lives of indigenous people around the turn of the century, I want to make a hard turn from anomaly to frequency and unexpectedness. An important group of Native people embraced a different story about themselves than we are accustomed to hearing. In the book's third essay, "'I Am of the Body,'" for example, I'll suggest that, far from one or two anomalous athletic figures—Jim Thorpe and Billy Mills, for instance—many Native Americans participated in all manner of sports in the early twentieth century. Their presence at multiple levels—professional, semipro, college, and local—and in significant numbers suggests that we ought to rethink a particular history of expectation, in this case that surrounding Indian integration into a wider world of modern athleticism. This book will pursue a number of such "secret" histories of Indian life in the late nineteenth century and the early twentieth, histories that include Indian people driving cars, playing football, traveling in Wild West shows, performing music, and acting and directing in the early years of the film industry.

A second pursuit must necessarily turn on the formation of those ideological frames that have explained and contained Indian actions. Native people have always acted from imperatives formed in the meeting of tribal cultures and the social, political, economic, and environmental wreckage and opportunity generated by colonial encounters. Yet Native actions have all too often been interpreted through the lens of Euro-American expectation formed, in many cases, in ways that furthered the colonial project. This is not to argue the familiar cliché about the winners writing the history. Rather, it is to ask us to consider the kinds of frames that have been placed around a shared past. It is not simply to assert that ideology and domination have made certain histories unable to be spoken. Instead, it is to ask how we came to certain kinds of tellings and not others.

Looking more closely, for example, at the ways Indians and non-Indians imagined Native ability to commit violence, or considering the musical origins of the sound that calls out to us "Indians!" (DUM dum dum dum, DUM dum dum dum), these inquiries are meant, not only to suggest the possibilities of secret Indian histories, but also to consider the ways non-Indians came to reframe their understandings of Indians in the wake of what seemed the final confinement of western Indian people to reservations. Each of these essays attempts to put the making of non-Indian expectations into a dialogue with the lived experiences of certain Native people, those whose actions were, at that very moment, being defined as unexpected.

STEREOTYPE, IDEOLOGY, DISCOURSE, AND POWER

Defining expectation is no easy task, for expectations are amorphous things. Expectations are almost invariably raced, classed, and gendered.

Collective
unit
all the
same

They can be colored by religious practice and by regional location, touched by sexuality, transformed by national difference and global exchange. They take shape in a range of forms, from mass-produced images and literature, to drama, to local folklore, to social behaviors. They recur as popular stereotypes, and they are altered and reused for aesthetic purposes. So what exactly do I mean, in this book, by *expectation*?

Reading the list of expectations surrounding Red Cloud Woman, you may have thought to yourself, "These are just old, familiar stereotypes." And rightly so. The idea of the stereotype has been an important tool for understanding the relation between representations—that is, images, texts, music, and performances—and the concrete exercise of power. I want, in the long run, to argue for a richer understanding than that offered by *stereotype*, but it is worth resting for a moment on the term.

stereotype Originally a word from the printing industry, stereotype referred to a printing plate capable of reproducing copies undistinguished by individual difference. Transferred to human beings, one assumes that it originally meant the idea that all Indians, for example, were exactly alike—just like any given page in every book in a print run. Over time, of course, meanings have been imposed onto the stereotype's sameness: "all Indians are exactly alike . . . in being savage warriors" (a negative stereotype); or "all Indians are exactly alike . . . in being people who live in harmony with nature" (a positive one).

Stereotype also names an intuitive sense that some critical mass of shared images can shape material events. Consider, for example, a familiar analysis of stereotyping in relation to nineteenth-century Indian policy. If all Indians were alike in a certain way (heathen savages, e.g., as portrayed in countless representations), then one could see clearly what was to be done (convert them). Since there was assumed to be no variation among Indian people, church and federal officials were able to formulate coherent policies across the country and put them into operation, changing the lives of Indians and non-Indians alike. That is not—at a broad level—an inaccurate description of how things happened. But can the connection really be so clear? Doesn't the link between image, text, or performance and event have to account both for individuals' subjective experiences (what if a stereotype attracts rather than repulses, or vice versa?) and for the collective consensus that produces action? Are stereotypical meanings coherent enough to wield that kind of power? The stereotype of Indian savagery, for example, worked in a number of different contexts—the "kill or be killed" hatred of the frontiersman, the scientific racism of the intellectual, the evangelical demand of the missionary, the sympathetic disdain of the reformer, the justified expediency of the politician.

The idea of savagery undoubtedly enabled white Americans to exercise multiple kinds of power over multiple kinds of Indians. Yet the existence of so many variations on the savage theme also suggests that *stereotype* might function better as a descriptive shorthand than as an analytic tool. A stereotype, we might say, is a simplified and generalized expectation— savagery, in this case—that comes to rest in an image, text, or utterance. It is a sound bite, a crudely descriptive connection between power, expectation, and representation. To burrow more deeply into the world of expectation, we might try to shift from the simplifying tendencies of *stereotype* to the more complex terms *discourse* and *ideology*.

Ideology is one of those words blessed with a disconcerting fluidity. The literary theorist Terry Eagleton once identified sixteen separate senses of *ideology*, ranging from crass deception to complicated realism. Like stereotypes, ideologies appear somehow untrue, an assertion that is at once correct and incorrect. Ideologies offer both truthful pictures of the world as it exists and falsely prescriptive understandings of the world as it might (or should) be. The untrue of ideology has often been couched in terms of illusion or false consciousness and used to explain how certain groups within a society are able to dominate others with only a minimum use of force. Ideology, in this sense, is a mistaken belief that leads people to act against their own best interests. As outright lies, however, ideologies would hardly be compelling, so untruth is tightly twinned together with pictures of the world as it is. Ideologies, we might say, engage the contradictions of the world and construct of them meaningful systems of belief, held by all manner of people across the spectrum of a society.

But writers and philosophers have also seen ideology differently—as a way of considering the ways in which our thoughts are socially constructed. In this sense, the term helps explain how things that are contingent come to be taken as true in such a way that they give us a template for acting. Ideologies, in other words, are not, in fact, true, but, as things that structure real belief and action in a real world, they might as well be. Ideology is not simply an idea reproduced by individuals in and through systems of representation. Rather, it is a lived experience, something we see and perform on a daily basis. The involuntary chuckle that sometimes accompanies Red Cloud Woman, in other words, might usefully be thought of as an ideological chuckle.

One is brought to chuckle, not through overt and willful racism, but through a thickness of consciousness, layered up over cultural and individual time. And the untrue in ideology is not the falsity of that consciousness but rather its suggestion, as Trevor Purvis and Alan Hunt argue, of *directionality*. Ideology, according to Purvis and Hunt, "always works to favor some and disadvantage others," and it makes that work seem "natural."[3] The key ideologies describing Indian people—inevitable disappearance, primitive purity, and savage violence, to name only a few—have brought exactly this kind of uneven advantage to the social, political, economic, and legal relations lived out between Indians and non-Indian Americans.

The expectations and actions that I have been talking about take explicit cultural shape as *discourse*. How to distinguish ideology from discourse? In truth, the lines are pretty fuzzy. Ideology stems from a Marxist tradition concerned with power, domination, and acquiescence. Discourse, on the other hand, emerged from a linguistic tradition interested in the ways in which our languages impose frameworks that limit what we are capable of experiencing or understanding.[4] Taken as a broadly coherent body of intelligible utterances, thoughts, representations, knowledges, and actions, discourses might be seen in broad terms as *practices*—the chuckle itself, in other words—while ideology helps us understand the *content* of those practices.

And not only that. Even as we see ideology (content) functioning within discourse (practice), we might at the same time see discourse (action) functioning within ideology (consciousness)! Both concepts, in other words, *connect*—to one another, to social acts, to individual consciousness, and to changes in practice and circumstance occurring over time. If ideology and discourse suggest that there are structures—and, indeed, limits—to our own knowledge, it is also true that such things can be readily transformed over time. Ideologies and discourses may change, not only in terms of various kinds of local knowledge, but also in relation to the broader social and cultural situations through which they found their original meaning and power. In this book's opening essay, on Indian violence, for example, I argue this point. One broadly accepted ideology that painted Indians as intrinsically violent gave way to a series of fragmented expectations about Indian violence and, eventually, to another broadly accepted belief—that Indians had been pacified. It is not enough to think of these things only in the simplistic terms of savage or noble stereotypes, though expectations do, in fact, exist in those stereotypical forms. At stake in discursive/ideological formations throughout U.S. history has been the body of accepted knowledge about Indian people, the ways in which knowledge helped constitute individuals and groups as subjects, and the new and old ways in which power was to be applied to Indians and non-Indians alike.

As you may have guessed by now, I've taken this detour into stereotypes, ideologies, and discourses for a reason. When you encounter the word *expectation* in this book, I want you to read it as a shorthand for the dense economies of meaning, representation, and act that have inflected both American culture writ large and individuals, both Indian and non-Indian. I would like for you to think of expectations in terms of the colonial and imperial relations of power and domination existing between Indian people and the United States. You might see in *expectation* the ways in which popular culture works to produce—and sometimes to compromise—racism and misogyny. And I would, finally, like you to distinguish between the anomalous, which reinforces expectations, and the unexpected, which resists categorization and, thereby, questions expectation itself.

ESSAY

By turning to the essay form rather than to the monograph (each of these essays has threatened, at one time or another, to blow up into a monograph), this book aims to address critical problems in the writing of American Indian history. That writing has long confronted a singular paradox: the most effective frame for making general sense of the diverse experiences of hundreds of tribal peoples has been that of federal government policy. In effect, this practice centers Indian history, not on Indian people, but on the U.S. government. The understandable response of many historians and many Indian people has been to turn to the unique particulars of tribal and community histories.[5] Taken together, such community-based histories reveal the stunning breadth and texture of American Indian experiences. They also help fulfill the important obligation of scholars to make their work meaningful to Indian communities. And, by revealing a wide range of Native responses, they effectively render inert the generalizing framework built around federal policy.

Even as they do these things, however, tribal histories also militate against efforts to generalize or synthesize, leaving us to wonder how to do justice to the variation among hundreds of tribal and community histories while at the same time reaching for general patterns concerning such things as colonialism and empire in North America. Only recently have historians turned toward cultural analysis as a possible ground for considering Indian–non-Indian relations in broad terms. This is my project here. Rather than tracking policy changes, I take as my unifying theme the changes and persistences found in the ideological/discursive frames that non-Indians used to generalize their expectations of Indian people. All Native people have had to confront these expectations—whether that meant ignoring them, protesting them, working them, or seeking to prove them wrong.

Rather than engage in community history, I've taken as a touchstone the experiences of Lakota, Dakota, and other Native people of the northern plains, especially as they seem to speak to similar Native experiences elsewhere. I've relied on this touchstone in large part because it matters historically that Lakota people were among the last to resist militarily and among the first to enter modern representational politics in significant numbers, as I hope the first two of these essays will make clear. I'm pursuing, however, not a Lakota community, but a cross-tribal cohort, a group of Native cultural producers—actors, singers, athletes, entrepreneurs, and warriors—who moved within white expectations, usually challenging and reaffirming those expectations at the same time.

Such tensions between the general and the specific also crop up around the question of narrative. I aim to tell stories—lots of small stories that may produce a scaffolding but that will not necessarily add up to a master narrative. The essay form, I hope, serves as a manageable container into which those stories can be placed. I've tried to use it to negotiate the line between precision and breadth, without falling fully into either one or the other. This book, then, plans to suggest histories broad enough to strike familiar chords (if not necessarily perfect harmonies) with a number of Native community and individual experiences. At the same time, I hope to offer enough specific experiences to ground my gestures toward broad framings of the intricacies of cultural interaction. I am aiming for the evocative and provocative rather than for the final word. On each of these topics, there is much, much more to be said. Indeed, one of the senses conveyed by the word *essay* is that of a first attempt, an early glimpse, a preliminary assessment: "He essayed his chances." Here, I would like to essay the chances for new ways of thinking about Indian people in the twentieth century.[6]

The tools that I bring to this task are those of history and of cultural analysis. Tracing changes in expectation across time, I use historical analysis to show the very human roots of ideas that have come to seem natural and essential. Likewise, by paying attention to multiple meanings, contradictions, opportunities, and the shutting down of opportunities, I hope to remain open to the complications inherent in any human society—and doubly present when social groups confront one another on the ground, not only of warfare, trade, or politics, but of culture.

The first essay turns to the question of the history of ideological formations, particularly those clustered around ideas that Indians were invariably violent. These ideological frames shifted in the years following Wounded Knee, until they tended to emphasize, not the possibility of Indian violence, but the near certainty of Indian pacification. As a shared expectation, pacification served to bridge the vanishing-Indian ideology of the nineteenth century with the modernist primitivism of the twentieth. The second essay turns to the question of representation and the place of Indian people in constructing (often negative, but certainly complicated) images of themselves. Even as twentieth-century Indian people came to be seen as pacified, the images of Indians in Wild West shows and many Hollywood films increasingly emphasized nineteenth-century Indian violence. How and why did Indian people come to represent themselves in these media at this specific moment in time? In what ways were they complicit in the perpetuation of negative images? And to what extent can we see their lives in show business as pushing back against the expectations that would define them as savages?

The third essay, on sports, suggests that particular forms of primitivism figured around Indianness might allow Native people to help shape a critical dialogue existing within American modernity. If non-Indians worried about corruption and effeminacy in the industrial city, sports offered a solace based on masculinity, whiteness, and class. Indians, as both historical losers and pure masculine primitives, performed as both objects of white desire and colonized people taking advantage of what some saw as the only fair playing field in the history of white-Indian relations.

The fourth essay deals with Indian automobility and use of technology, and it turns from Indian movements within the urban spaces of the United States (and, indeed, the world) to questions of mobility in Indian country itself. Frameworks of expectation suggested that primitive Native people had to work their way, stage by painful stage, through the developmental hierarchy of social evolution before they were allowed to enter modernity. At the same time, assimilationists insisted that any signifier of modernity was necessarily a sign of progress. In their own local embrace of the automobile, Native people blurred together Indian pasts, presents, and futures as they sallied back and forth across the boundary markers of gender, class, and primitivism. Though mobilized as a marker of social progress and racial difference, automobility was, in truth, a mutual experience.

In a final essay, I pursue the origins of the musical expectation that the "sound of Indian" will have a tom-tom beat, a droning accompaniment of open fifths and minor chords, and certain melodic characteristics. Much of this expectation was set by the film scores of the mid-twentieth-century western, but its origins can be found in the late nineteenth century, in a hybrid exchange of musical sounds, American nationalism, and Native reinvention of self and of musical expression. Here, too, Indian performers used expectations to gain entrée into positions in which they were able to participate in shaping the particular form of the modern. As was the case with athletics and other performing traditions, however, structural changes in the economy, culture, politics, and social relations of the United States ended up limiting the possibilities for Native people. By the later twentieth century, such pursuits came to seem thoroughly anomalous. The final issue raised in this book, then, concerns the closing of that small window of opportunity.

In each of these essays, I try to suggest that there were and are significant numbers of Indian anomalies, enough that we must rethink familiar categories. Taken together, it seems to me, the cumulative experiences of such anomalous Indians point to new kinds of questions concerning the turn of the twentieth century—perhaps toward a reimagining of the contours of modernity itself. They suggest a secret history of the unexpected, of the complex lineaments of personal and cultural identity that can never be captured by dichotomies built around crude notions of difference and assimilation, white and Indian, primitive and advanced. Those secret histories of unexpectedness are, I believe, worth further pursuit, for they can change our sense of the past and lead us quietly, but directly, to the present moment.

violence

LIGHTNING CREEK, 1903

The shadows of late afternoon had fallen over the Lightning Creek road as Hope Clear and Peter White Elk drove the pony herd ahead of the string of wagons. Eighteen years old, Hope Clear was helping eleven-year-old Peter and another boy manage the horses and open the gates that occasionally rose up from the road that headed east, back to the Pine Ridge reservation. Strung out behind them in a long column, their families drove wagons full of antelope meat and hides, some taken in the South Dakota Black Hills, others gotten later in trades with the white ranchers and herders of eastern Wyoming. Many of the wagons contained important medicinal plants. These, along with a variety of root plants, berries, and fruits, could all be found in greater quantities and better quality off the Pine Ridge reservation. Eager to be home, and worried about a Wyoming sheriff who had accused them of illegal hunting, the party had made good time that autumn day, covering over forty miles.

A gate loomed ahead. In 1903, fences and gates defined the Lakota landscape. The Pine Ridge reservation, for example, was entirely contained by a long fence, erected five years earlier. Such fences marked the spatial confinement of the Lakotas and other Indian people; they also marked Indians' complicated place in relation to what non-Indians saw as social and cultural development. On the Lakota side of the fence, conditions (and people) were expected to be primitive—though slowly progressing toward the modern world and eventual assimilation into it. At the same time, however, the reservation fence proclaimed that such "old days"—at least the Lakota version—had already come to an abrupt end. The modern world surrounded Indian reservations, and no fence would stop it from transforming Native cultures.[1]

Some people—especially white Americans—dated the end of the old days to 1890, when U.S. soldiers had surrounded and slaughtered Big

Foot's band at Wounded Knee Creek. According to this logic, eleven-year-old Peter White Elk would be part of the "new days." Wounded Knee helped define the collective tribal memory that he was learning, but it could never be part of his immediate personal past. Hope Clear, who might have been five or six years old at the time of the killing, undoubtedly had memories of the terrible event. Older people, like Charlie Smith, one of the party's two leaders, must have been even more affected by the violence of the past. Indeed, if the reservation fence seemed to mark a boundary in space between contemporary and primitive, Wounded Knee seemed to mark a similar division across time. It split old days apart from new days (even as memory and shared culture stitched them together again) as surely as if one were crossing the reservation fence line.

Wounded Knee quickly became a marker, not only for Lakota people, but for white Americans and Indian people across the country—a sort of global sign of military defeat. Individual tribes, of course, each point to similar moments in their own histories—devastating massacres, betrayals and surrenders, resistances squashed, escapes cut off. These markers have entered our shared histories too: Tecumseh's shattered alliance; the Cherokee Trail of Tears; the flight of Chief Joseph; Geronimo's surrender; Captain Jack's final struggle in the lava beds; and hundreds of other less iconic but equally meaningful moments. But Wounded Knee—ostensibly the last instance of armed resistance and violent betrayal—organizes the big break between the possibility and the impossibility of military struggle, and it does so as a cross-tribal and cross-cultural milepost. For non-Indian Americans, the possibility of nineteenth-century Indian violence existed before Wounded Knee; afterward, it became a thing of representation, perfect for twentieth-century movies and books.

Peter White Elk, Hope Clear, and Charlie Smith—also known as Eagle Feather—helped shape the new Lakota world taking painful and hungry shape on the plains at the turn of the century. That world was cobbled together in the overlaps that occurred and the gaps that opened up between past and present and between Lakotas and others. Take Charlie Smith, for example. Like so many other Indian people, Smith had learned English at the Carlisle Indian Industrial School in Carlisle, Pennsylvania. He served in the white reservation bureaucracy as an "assistant farmer," a supervisor and teacher in charge of one of the reservation districts. For the past year, he had worked as a foreman for the Indian agent, supervising forty or fifty Lakota laborers on the work projects created to force them into a cash economy. Local whites described him as "a peaceable and useful man"; Indian people accepted him as a local leader. The party's other head, William Brown, would have a similarly bicultural career, working (along with his brother Edward) in Buffalo Bill Cody's Wild West show, and serving as translator during the 1908–1909 season.[2]

Another gate to open. The new roads taken by Smith, Brown, Lakotas, and other Indian people at the turn of the century led through all sorts of barriers—poverty, white racism, forced transformations of Native cultures, new conflicts with the law. Treaties, for example, that meant much to Indian people meant little to the Americans who had made them. Congress and the federal Indian bureaucracy did not hesitate to cut promised rations, remove and terrorize Indian children in the name of education, and manage and dictate Lakota behavior. Consider the Treaty of 1868, which promised that Lakota hunters could pursue game as long as it was practicable to do so.[3] Lakotas still believed in that right, and it was galling that Wyoming sheriffs felt that they could hound and harass Indian hunters, especially when the hunters had official passes to be off the reservation.

Ever since the 1896 Supreme Court decision in *Ward v. Racehorse*, however, which invalidated treaty hunting rights for the Bannocks and made Indian people subject to Wyoming law, the state had aggressively pursued Indian hunters.[4] Wyoming residents recognized that they had the beginnings of a tourist economy based on out-of-state hunters, who were already coming to pursue the state's animal riches. Game laws, including the requirement that hunters use a local guide and pay a registration fee for their weapons, aimed to manage both the animal population and the population of hunters, be they tourist, local, or regional. Nonetheless, most officials did not pursue local white hunters with the same vigor as they did Indians. Such was almost certainly the case with Sheriff William Miller of Newcastle, who had established a reputation for going hard after Indian hunters suspected of being in violation of state game laws.

There were plenty of Indian hunters on whom one might cast suspicion. During the preceding decade, Lakotas from Pine Ridge had come to rely on off-reservation resources to supplement the shrinking rations that the federal government often failed to supply. Families traveled to compensate for the starving conditions on the reservation side of the fence, hunting, gathering, and trading beadwork and moccasins for beef, venison, and mutton. This kind of crossing between old and new, primitive and modern, troubled some non-Indians. Whites complained mightily about "lazy" Indians receiving treaty-guaranteed rations: they didn't have to work for a living; they were "government pets," caged up and fed; they lived lives, recalled one local, of "lassitude, under the drooping apathetic discipline of the local resident of the Great White Father."[5]

But non-Indians also complained if Lakotas and other Indian people left the reservations and fed themselves through the work of hunting and trade. In 1901, for example, in the midst of a William Miller crackdown on Indian hunters, the Newcastle paper complained that "pesky redskins under Chief Stinking Bear . . . were again on their way up Main Beaver Creek . . . killing and running the game out of the country."[6] Protecting game from Indian threats mixed together new economic interests and older racial antagonisms with common assumptions about Indians as lazy nomadic hunters. Indian hunting looked too much like primitive nomadism and not enough like the white market and leisure hunting depleting wild game populations across the nation.[7] Like many westerners, Wyoming residents were getting ready to battle among themselves about the meanings of sport and subsistence hunting. Eliminating Indian hunters from the picture simply cleared the ground for the intramural struggles yet to come.

Charlie Smith knew enough about the white world to understand that William Miller, the local sheriff who had threatened them the previous day, had been trying to use a warrant from Weston County, Wyoming, to make an arrest in Converse County. Not only that, but the warrant had named only two people. And, in fact, it didn't cite specific people at all, only "John Doe," the name being meant to stand for two Indians who had allegedly been hunting antelope. Yet the sheriff wanted to use it to apprehend the entire party—some forty Lakotas from two separate groups that had only recently joined together. And the dates on the warrant were all wrong. The Indian "John Doe" hunters (not actually) named in the warrant had been spotted the same day that Smith's group left Pine Ridge, which, for a slow-moving party, was a couple days travel away. Smith's group had gone north, to the Black Hills, before looping west and south into Wyoming. There was no way his people could be the suspected game law violators. Finally, Smith had a good idea what would happen if they turned from the trail home and followed the sheriff north to Newcastle: they would be placed in jail for a time and then released, only to find that their meat and medicines had disappeared. "I know your duty as well as you do, and what they expect of you," Smith had told Sheriff Miller, "but you can't take me." Even as Miller tried to turn the column north, Smith had ridden to the front and kept the people heading home, eastward to Pine Ridge.[8]

It was Halloween evening, and the party had one last gate to open before stopping for the night. Hope Clear hopped from her pony and went to the gate. The shots came without warning from the sheltering bank of Lightning Creek. Hope turned to flee. The initial shot spared her, but it knocked Peter White Elk's horse from underneath him. As he stood up to run, a second shot hit him from behind, tearing off the top of his head and sending the boy plunging forward to the ground, dead. "A bullet went through my shawl," Hope remembered, "and another through my dress, and my horse [was] shot from under me."[9] Her father, Gray Bear, and another man, Black Kettle, retrieved their guns, dropped to the ground, and began to return fire, killing two of the enemy. The wagons in the rear turned around and fled; those in the front careened up the hilly fence line near the gate. Heavy wagons were left behind in favor of lighter ones. Those who could muster horses did so. Charlie Smith rode up from the rear, only to be shot down. Black Kettle's gun eventually fell silent, and he sprawled dead where he lay. Grievously wounded, Gray Bear managed to get a horse and follow the fence line. Hope Clear, her mother, and her aunt—Charlie Smith's wife—had followed this route, only to see Mrs. Smith take a bullet just as they cleared the high ground along the fence. Hope had gotten another horse, and she found her father and led him to the wagon. They fled along a creek bed until about midnight, when he left the wagon, sat down against a bank, and died.

"Maybe there is a war broken out between the white men and the Indians," said Mrs. Gray Bear. "We might as well go back and get killed where the other Indians were killed, because we can't get home anyway." In the predawn chill, the women buried the man who had been their husband and father and then turned back to the place of the attack. Charlie Smith, shot through the legs, was still alive, though he too would die later that evening. He had lain immobile all night and was covered with frost. The women had started a fire to warm him up when their assailants reappeared. Hope Clear recalled: "After we saw those people coming, they started to take aim at us. I walked up toward them and they pointed their guns at me. I got pretty close to them. I told them that there were only women there and if they wanted to kill us they could do it." The episode ended with a strange spectacle: this heroic young woman, who had just buried her father and was presiding over her wounded aunt and uncle, found herself shaking hands with each of the killers, the members of the sheriff's posse of Newcastle, Weston County, Wyoming.[10]

How might we think about—or think *with*—the story of Lightning

Creek? I would like to use the incident to sift out the expectations that white Americans used to make sense of the relation between violence and Indian people, particularly in terms of Wounded Knee and its aftermath. Almost from the beginning, white-Indian contact had been imagined and understood using two contradictory and gendered story lines. In one set of narratives, Indian women, linked to the land itself, gave themselves metaphorically to colonizing white men, engendering a peaceful narrative of cross-cultural harmony in which whites became indigenous owners of the continent through sexualized love and marriage stories such as that of Pocahontas. Another set of narratives—and sometimes the two could be woven together—relied on the masculinist imagery of violent conflict.[11] Murder, massacre, torture, captivity, revenge, squabble, raid, campaign, and, most particularly, "surround" and "last stand"—such images and events underpinned white expressions of Indian difference, even in relation to the very real blendings together found in cross-cultural trade, diplomacy, alliance, conversion, and sex. Thanks to mid-twentieth-century Hollywood, images of Indian violence remain powerful today. Centuries before that, however, writers and painters had sketched out a familiar scene: white people surrounded by Indians, forced to make a gallant but doomed last stand. This imagery helped make sustained American aggression appear as a long defensive conquest of the continent. The culminating moment in this tradition, of course, was Custer's Last Stand at the Little Big Horn, canonized at the turn of the century during the very moment of the killings at Lightning Creek.[12]

Even in the late nineteenth century, when, in the wake of Wounded Knee, Indian military resistance seemed at a clear end, cultural relations continued to be framed around the issue of violence. Who was and was not capable of killing? Who was justified in killing? How were violence and manhood linked together? What were the distinctions between war and murder? What did those distinctions say about the breakdown and reassertion of boundaries between Indians and the United States, a colonizing nation that meant to absorb Native peoples into its legal, political, social, and cultural structures? And, given that the relations involving violence between Indians and whites were changing, how did those changes alter or reshape white expectations and understandings of Indian violence?

I am going to suggest that a relatively old set of expectations—focused on the likelihood, perhaps even the certainty, of Indian violence, and made visible through familiar ideas like the last stand and the surround—

gradually gave way to newer expectations. Post–Civil War western reservations, with their incomplete containment of often-mobile Indian peoples, spurred Americans to name a new, rebellious brand of Indian warfare—the *outbreak*. Wounded Knee existed in a complicated relation to this idea. In the aftermath of the massacre, however, the idea of outbreak gave way to a notion of pacification. This trajectory is, of course, a rough simplification. Expectations dovetailed with, contradicted, and contested with one another throughout the period. Regional geographies of violence and pacification differed. Even in the descriptions of Wounded Knee itself, one can see variations. Nonetheless, expectations changed. At mid-nineteenth century, one might have expected to find the clarity of nation-to-nation warfare represented through the image of the surround and the last stand; by the turn of the twentieth century, last stands were pieces of nostalgia, and Indian pacification was the prevailing expectation.

Outbreak has become a familiar key word in representations of Indian violence, for it helped negotiate the ambiguous period in which the U.S. colonial administration exerted only partial control over Lakotas and other Native peoples. Indian outbreaks—and not simply among the Lakota—became a common fear during the first years of reservation management, when there was, for the first time, something for Native people to break out from. *Outbreak, rebellion, uprising*—such words revealed a fear of Indian people escaping the spatial, economic, political, social, and military restrictions placed on them by the reservation regime. They implied containment (and, ironically, its failure), which, in turn, implied a conquest nearly (but not wholly) complete. Only when defeated Indian opponents were rounded up and successfully contained on reservations could one imagine the state of nation-to-nation war that had characterized the eighteenth and nineteenth centuries no longer existing.[13]

Outbreak, then, suggested a particular kind of armed resistance, a rebellion that would never produce renewed autonomy, a pocket of stubbornness in the midst of the sweep of the American empire. As such, it came to have an intensity of meaning in the years following the campaigns of the 1870s and early 1880s, when the last of the western tribes were rounded up and contained. The idea of outbreak proved particularly relevant at Wounded Knee, which turned out to be both its moment of apogee and the beginning of its obsolescence.[14] We can begin to think with and about Lightning Creek, then, by placing it within the developing trajectory of meanings that defined the possibilities of Indian violence.

The massacre at Wounded Knee, that marker of old and new, conquest and resistance, pathos and murderous violence, offered Americans the ultimate example of Indian outbreak. In the early summer of 1889, Lakotas and other Indian people began hearing word of a prophet, Wovoka, who had been given a powerful vision of social change. A new world was coming "like a whirlwind" to destroy the old world. Dead relatives would be there, and the bison would be replenished. A messiah had come to the whites before, some said, but they had killed him. This time, he would come to the Indians. The earth would be turned over and everything started anew. Marked with sacred red paint and a ghost dance taught by Wovoka, Indians could join this new world, but whites would be left behind.[15]

First, three Lakotas were sent out to Wovoka's home in Nevada to investigate. Then, in the winter of 1889–1890, several more made the journey from the various agencies. Good Thunder, Yellow Breast, Short Bull, and Kicking Bear returned to Pine Ridge that spring with the main elements of the Ghost Dance religion. The dancers formed a circle, held hands, and moved in and out around a red-painted tree. For the Lakota religious leader Black Elk and, no doubt, many others, the dance had meaningful resonances with the sacred Sun Dance ceremony, the most important collective ritual in the Lakota year.[16] At the same time, Lakotas had to be wondering whether they had hit rock bottom. The animals were gone, the government rations were late and insufficient, and they were starving to death. In 1889, they had been forced to sign away still more land. The Ghost Dance offered the kind of hope grasped only by the truly desperate, and it did so in familiar forms.

Some Lakotas altered those forms, making the Ghost Dance dovetail even more tightly with their own culture. Short Bull and Kicking Bear introduced "Ghost Shirts." Decorated with a star and crescent moon and feathers at the shoulders, the shirts were said to be able to stop bullets.[17] While most Lakotas continued to dance the ancestors back to life, some considered making their own contribution to the coming world in the familiar form of violent conflict. Never truly defeated, they refused to see themselves as conquered; refused to accept that war might not be part of their repertoire; refused, in other words, to think that what whites called *outbreak* might not really mean a *war* between nations. But believing in one's capacity and doing something about it are two different things. The more radical among the Ghost Dancers never won a consensus among the Lakota people about the possibility of violence. Indeed, many Lakotas persisted in seeing the dance as an essentially peaceful activity. Lakotas and local whites alike would later testify to that effect. In the end, however, the lack of consensus concerning the use of violence mattered little. If the Ghost Dancers were not prepared to force a war with the U.S. Army, the army was more than willing to come to them.[18]

Though most South Dakota agents did not express much concern over the Ghost Dance, Pine Ridge Agent Daniel Royer was much distressed by what he considered an excess of dancing, possibly warlike. That he—and, later, military and civil authorities—was able to see in Indian dancing imminent violence suggests the degree to which *outbreak* had come to structure white perceptions in the wake of colonial containment. Responding to restrictions on Ghost Dancing, a group of Brule dancers from the Rosebud reservation fled in November to the Badlands midway between their reservation and the Black Hills. At the Standing Rock reservation, Agent James McLaughlin set in motion plans to remove Sitting Bull from the Ghost Dance congregations. (My great-grandfather Philip Deloria, newly arrived as a Native clergyman at Standing Rock, was pressed into service to ride out to Sitting Bull's home and try to convince the leader to come in to the agency. He failed, as others had failed before him.) On December 15, McLaughlin sent his Indian police to arrest Sitting Bull. A fight ensued, and the holy man and several others died. Sitting Bull's people fled their homes and made their way south, to Big Foot's Minneconjou band at the Cheyenne River reservation, and together the groups set out for Pine Ridge, 250 miles to the southwest.

The panicky telegrams sent by Agent Royer (pointedly nicknamed "Young Man Afraid of His Indians") gave General Nelson Miles the opportunity he needed to mobilize the largest gathering of federal troops since the Civil War (which he was happy to do in order to stake the army's claim to effective governance of Indian affairs).[19] The Badlands Ghost Dancers had taken refuge at the Stronghold on Cuny Table, a spot largely inaccessible except for a narrow strip of land that dropped away steeply on either side. Troops were deployed throughout the area, and they intercepted the struggling Big Foot band as it came through the Badlands and headed for Pine Ridge. On December 29, the troops of Custer's old Seventh Cavalry—already muttering darkly about revenge—surrounded Big Foot and his people with Hotchkiss guns and proceeded to disarm them. A shot came, and then the order to fire, and then the guns' rapid-fire cannon shells, which tore the Lakotas to pieces. As always (as it would be at Lightning Creek), it was important to suggest that an Indian had fired the first shot, that the massacre was, in some twisted way, defensive.

But Wounded Knee was not simply an awful mistake, a miscalculation at a moment of extraordinary tension. The troops chased fleeing Lakotas for miles across the plains, hunting down and killing, not only men, but women and children, all of them already half starved and exhausted. The official report listed 153 Lakotas dead that day, with 44 wounded. Since there were well over 300 people in the group, it is likely that the number reflects a significant undercount, with some of the wounded making their way off the battlefield to die outside the reach of the grisly census takers.

And, while Wounded Knee proved a truly demoralizing event, Lakotas rallied. Young men rode out from Pine Ridge and attacked the troopers the next day at Drexel Mission. Only the timely (and, no doubt, ironic even then) arrival of black "buffalo soldiers" prevented retaliatory killings. Then, as the wounded streamed into the Pine Ridge agency, the two sides parleyed. General Miles alternated threats and shows of military force with promises and diplomacy; the Lakota leaders insisted alternately that they could not control their young men and that the two sides might be able to come to terms.

The Lakotas had been completely surrounded from the very beginning, so it was appropriate that whites understood the event as an Indian outbreak. The New York Times, for example, painted the dead Sitting Bull's life as a series of outbreaks, all leading up to Wounded Knee. "To prevent a general outbreak," the paper recalled, Sitting Bull had been ordered to the agency in 1876. "In 1879, he broke out again and commenced depredations upon the settlers." After his death, the paper insisted that "he never assented to the control of the United States Government over his people, but persistently fought the troops whenever they came his way."[20]

As John Coward, a media historian, points out, syndicate news dispatches shared among major city papers helped create familiar "news frames" for the representation of Indian-white violence. Wounded Knee—which required the mobilization of half the available army infantry and cavalry units—captured the nation's front pages for almost two months. A significant number of those papers adopted the lurid accounts of the Omaha Bee reporter Charles Cressey, whose paper generated stories for the Associated Press. Cressey did not hesitate to speculate wildly: "There are about 1,500 arms-bearing male Indians here on the Pine Ridge Agency. It is carefully estimated that only one-third of the number are for peace, and that the remaining 1,000 are anxious for blood. But 1,000 is but a handful of the force that the troops here anticipate encountering for there are thousands of others . . . who will surely join the Pine Ridge devils." Similar stories in Detroit, Chicago, Philadelphia, and New York shared similar detail and emphases, though each paper published slightly different variations on the familiar news frames.[21]

The most unexpected of these variations came from the pens of Suzette "Bright Eyes" Tibbles, the daughter of the mixed-blood Omaha leader Joseph La Flesche, and her husband, Thomas Tibbles, an Indian reform advocate. The Tibbleses wrote for the *Omaha World-Herald*, which presented the most critical views of the agency regime and played a lead role in hounding Daniel Royer from his position. They accused the press corps of hanging around the local boardinghouse day after day and then inventing conflicts "out of whole cloth." Suzette and Thomas Tibbles, on the other hand, chose to live with a Lakota family in order to approximate more closely a Native point of view.[22]

Nor were the Tibbleses alone in their criticism. The Santee Sioux physician Dr. Charles Eastman, newly arrived at Pine Ridge, claimed that newsmen were fabricating much of their news. Senator Henry Dawes, invested in protecting his 1887 General Allotment Act, insisted that reporters were poisoning the situation. And South Dakota Senator Richard Pettigrew carped that reporters saw "an outbreak in every breeze, a bloody encounter in every rustling bough." These critical voices—two of them Native—were part of the cacophony surrounding the event. Out of a cacophony, however, can emerge certain dominant themes—and that which emerged from Wounded Knee tended to emphasize the violence of outbreak. Reporters speculated frequently on the bloody battle the next day might bring. The number of warriors, the flight to the Badlands, the uncertainties surrounding the massacre—often these mirrored and repeated one another, sometimes (thanks to wire service reporting) down to the very same sentences. The military did not hesitate to confirm the possibility of Indian violence, with General Miles suggesting a multitribe conspiracy across the west, a "more comprehensive plot than anything ever inspired by the prophet Tecumseh, or even Pontiac." Taken together, these utterances helped define expectations on a national scale, and those expectations centered on the idea of outbreak.[23]

Lakota people from the Rosebud and Pine Ridge reservations had broken out in multiple ways, and it was, perhaps, not the armed retreat of the Brule Ghost Dancers that mattered most. Reservation administrators had long sought to transform Indian people from conquered enemies into colonial subjects, people who were—and who saw themselves as—part of the American state. As Ann Laura Stoler has detailed with regard to Dutch colonial systems, what administrators sought were, "not imitation Europeans, but perfected Natives."[24] Consider some of the basic institutions and technologies through which Indian enemies became known as American subjects. Tribal rolls standardized names, often translating them into English. They recorded individuals, along with pertinent demographic information. Church records noted parents, godparents, dates of baptism, confirmation, and death. Ration-disbursement records quantified the amount of food provided an individual and his or her family. Agency records noted infractions, property, character, education, employment, and all manner of other information. Later, allotment records would map individuals and families in space.

This knowledge could be translated into power over Indian people. To be known by name, date and location of baptism, rations drawn, and enrollment number was to be intimately visible to the colonial bureaucracy. It made it easy to locate a particular person in time and in space and to determine the need for education, discipline, containment, or shunning. Agents and missionaries also reached out to the next generations, with churches and schools focused on the critical moments in which Indian children were coming into their culture. They sought to attenuate children's sense of Indian difference and to make them part of the American polity—albeit without citizenship or significant rights. All these things made the acquisition of knowledge central to the exercise of power, and they did so by attempting to manage sentiment, sexual and marital practice, reproduction, subsistence, deportment, and identification.[25]

The space within and around a reservation was contained and controlled in order to manage Indian people. Fencing projects began to enclose many reservations, and Indian police rode the fence lines and manned the gates. Even from the earliest days of the western reservations, travelers like Charlie Smith's hunting party had to obtain passes and testimonials of friendliness and good conduct when they left the reservation. Reservation space was itself divided into multiple districts. Agency districts each had a central meeting point and a boss farmer or assistant agent in charge. Food forced Indian people to recognize the primacy of this division since the ration-distribution point inevitably became a local center. Likewise, each religious denomination split reservations into chapel districts. At Pine Ridge, for example, the Episcopalians had two districts, with subdivisions clustered around chapels, many of which were built to serve the small—and now relatively immobile—communities that characterized the landscape. Episcopalian districts overlapped with those of other denominations as well as with the school districts. Religious schools and day schools drew students to central locations—often the new communities themselves, but not always. Lakota people, used to moving as they chose, found themselves in the 1880s and 1890s confronting a far more static life, one in which they lived within a bounded landscape, among a web of centers established by church and state, in ways that could be tracked and restricted.[26]

These structures represented a colonial dream of fixity, control, visibility, productivity, and, most important, docility. Such a dream could, of course, be only partially realized. Family camps and reunions, political meetings, hunting trips, church gatherings, local dance lodges—these all represented opportunities for Indian mobility through a landscape that simultaneously remained and was reasserted as Indian. As Frederick Hoxie and others have pointed out, reservation spaces could shift in Indian eyes from "prison to homeland" in a relatively short time. Such a change was partially the product of new Indian understandings of selves, understandings that no doubt reflected the power of colonizing efforts. But it is as much the case that Native people remade the landscapes in their own ways at the same time. This new space, a hybrid landscape, both constrained Native people and created new senses of Indian selfhood, which were, in turn, attuned to new forms of resistance.[27]

It should probably come as no surprise that dancing and hunting offered particularly loaded points of contest between Indians and administrators, for these activities took Indian people beyond the visible eyes of church and state. They represented mobility and, thus, resonated with the fear of outbreak. If one supplied one's own food—as Charlie Smith and his party had attempted to do—then the ration station ceased to exercise its hold. Likewise, social dances asserted a particularly Indian form of leisure that stood in opposition to the agricultural production insisted on by white society. Religious dances offered an even more visible threat, for they suggested a willful breaking away from the hold of church and civilization. And, when, as in the case of the Ghost Dance, dancing appeared to threaten, not only the church, but also the state, and to do so violently, the idea of an Indian outbreak acquired multiple dangerous meanings—not simply physical and military, but social and cultural as well.

As a white fear and expectation, then, *outbreak* offered a new understanding of violence, one poised to replace *the surround* and *the last stand.*

Outbreak was more rebellion than war, as much social and cultural as military, and intimately concerned with the extent to which Indians had or had not been assimilated or forcibly incorporated into American civil society. It entered minds at the moment when it was clear that the war was over but not yet perfectly clear that all the battles had yet been fought.

WHITE CLAY CREEK, 1891

Perhaps nowhere are the issues surrounding outbreak so evocative as in the case of Plenty Horses, like Charlie Smith a young graduate of the Carlisle Indian School. Plenty Horses attended Carlisle for five years between 1883 and 1888. This was a decade earlier than Smith, and it made a difference. Where Smith was able to find a place for himself within the more highly developed Indian service bureaucracy of the early twentieth century, Plenty Horses returned to the Rosebud reservation to find that the training he had received at Carlisle—mostly vocational and mostly out-of-date in an industrial economy—proved particularly useless. "I found that the education I had received was of no benefit to me," he explained. "There was no chance to get employment, nothing for me to do whereby I could earn my board and clothes, no opportunity to learn more and remain with the whites. It disheartened me and I went back to live as I had before going to school."[28]

Plenty Horses was molded as a person in large part through the mechanisms of the state, which tried to substitute a firmly codified white Victorian culture for an equally codified Lakota culture. He embodied the kind of social transformations that would, in theory, lead Indian people to a state of *similarity* rather than *sameness*. That is, the varied efforts to reshape Indian people so as to assimilate them had nothing to do with the sameness that might have characterized social or political equality. Rather, they had everything to do with the practice of perfecting conquered people into similarity—ghost forms of the white conqueror, coexistent but not equal. Americans meant to bring Indian people within social and cultural boundaries only to the extent that they could be shaped using the same institutions and ideologies that made white citizens into subjects—schools, churches, wage labor, and literacy, among others. The greatest threat to the reservation program, then, was not the cross-cultural competence of a Charlie Smith; rather, it was the disciplined Indian who refused the gift of civilization and went "back to the blanket," as Plenty Horses tried. Such blanket Indians seemed a spiteful return to an earlier stage of social development. They rejected the gift of colonial similarity for a reassertion of social and cultural difference.[29]

If Plenty Horses thought he could turn back the page, however, many Lakotas were less certain. Five years away was a long time, and, even if Carlisle had failed to remake Plenty Horses, he had missed a critical period of education into Lakota culture—the years between fourteen and nineteen. Indeed, in the period immediately following the move to the South Dakota reservations in 1877–1878, Lakota culture was itself undergoing a series of transformations, some forced, some the products of resistance and adaptation. Plenty Horses was not around to participate in these reshapings. Even worse, he had missed the most critical years when Lakota boys became men, which left his gender status ill determined and proved disastrous in the end. Even though he literally went back to blankets, moccasins, and long hair, Plenty Horses's welcome among his people was partial at best. In fact, his mixed cultural identity proved threatening to Indian people, whose efforts to fend off the reservation order meant rejecting such overt signs of hybridity, culture crossing, and colonial similarity (see figure 2).[30]

Still, Plenty Horses embraced the Ghost Dance, and, when soldiers showed up at Pine Ridge and Rosebud in November 1890, he had already fled with Two Strike's band into the Badlands. A month later, Two Strike's people decided, after much carrot-and-stick diplomacy on the part of General John Brooke, to come in to the Pine Ridge agency, and they were there on December 29 when the Seventh Cavalry massacred Big Foot's people at Wounded Knee. For Plenty Horses, however, the next day was equally important, for he joined the young men who attacked the Seventh Cavalry at Drexel Mission. The foray made Plenty Horses part of a real war party, and he must have had mixed emotions as he rode down White Clay Valley to join No Water's large camp of Ghost Dancers. He had taken a step toward validating himself as a Lakota man within an older cultural framework. But he was worried about his family and his future. "Of course I was in a bad frame of mind," he would later recall. "Our home was destroyed, our family separated, and all hope of good times was gone. There was nothing to live for."[31]

Yet Plenty Horses did, in fact, have one thing to live for—cultural redemption, a personal outbreak that would repudiate his white education and make him a man and a Lakota once again. And, of all the different ways he might once have sought social recognition—a medicine vision,

FIGURE 2. *Tasunka Ota (Plenty Horses). Photograph by J. C. H. Grabill. Plenty Horses is wrapped in "the blanket," which signaled opposition to assimilation. At the same time, however, he is also boxed in physically—one might say partially contained—by a piece of field artillery. (Denver Public Library, Western History Department, X-31496.)*

hunting skill, bravery in battle—the warfare that surrounded him offered an opportunity to shift his cultural position radically. Drexel Mission had been a beginning. Now, on January 7, Plenty Horses was out with some forty warriors who met up with Lieutenant Edward Casey and two Cheyenne scouts. A soldier with vast experience and a promising future, Casey had been talking with some of the Lakotas who were slipping in and out of the Ghost Dancers' camp, and he thought he saw a diplomatic opening. The word from the camp was that some of the old leaders were amenable to a parley. If Casey could detach Red Cloud and some other leaders from the Ghost Dance camp, the entire movement might simply collapse for lack of numbers and support.

The two groups met that day, not in armed conflict, but in diplomatic pleasantry. Most of the Lakotas moved off, but Plenty Horses and a few others stayed to hear what Casey had to say. He asked if someone would serve as a messenger to ride into the camp to see if Red Cloud or any other of the leaders would be willing to come out for a talk. As the messenger galloped off, Casey followed slowly toward the village, conversing in English with Plenty Horses. As it turns out, Casey's solo effort had duplicated that of General Miles. Red Cloud and the others had just agreed to come in to the agency and parley with Miles when Casey's messenger rode up with the lieutenant's offer. The chief sent him back, along with a messenger of his own, Pete Richard, his mixed-blood son-in-law. Red Cloud was already planning to parley, Richard said, but, more important, Casey should leave immediately. The entire area was full of angry young men. They could not be controlled, and the soldier's life was in danger.

Even as the warning was being relayed, however, the scene was being played out. Plenty Horses backed his horse from the circle, positioned himself behind Casey, pulled out his rifle, and fired a single shot into the back of the lieutenant's head. The bullet exited through the face, the horse reared, and Casey fell dead. Plenty Horses turned and rode slowly back toward camp, no longer (he hoped) a culturally ambiguous figure, having proved himself a man. He had used violence to redraw a boundary of difference between white and Indian and to place himself squarely on the Indian side.

Warfare or murder? Were Lakotas American subjects in rebellious outbreak, a distinct nation engaged in war, or something in between? A little over a month later, the army seized Plenty Horses and imprisoned him at Fort Meade, on the northern edge of the Black Hills. Plenty Horses had shot Casey from behind. Casey had been on a diplomatic mission. Plenty

Horses had conversed with him using English, a language acquired during a five-year period when he was supposed to have become civilized and acculturated. A Carlisle education, tepid though it may have been, set expectations: an educated individual was obligated to follow civil conventions understood in American society. Even as a rebellious Ghost Dancer and a noncitizen, then, Plenty Horses might, nonetheless, be considered a colonized subject bound by the law. Plenty Horses, who had sought to escape American civil boundaries, had, in fact, triggered them. And, according to their logic, he was guilty of the murder of a fellow citizen (see figure 3).

Yet, when the case came to trial, the logic also pointed his accusers to an unpleasant set of corollaries. If Indians were a part of American society . . . if Plenty Horses's action was civil rather than military . . . then the soldiers who had gunned down Big Foot's band at Wounded Knee were equally guilty of the civil crime of murder—and on a larger and more heinous scale. Over the course of the next months, as Plenty Horses sat through two trials, it became clear that the prosecution would hinge on the question of whether a state of war could still exist between the United States and an Indian tribe in the throes of outbreak. Did a national or quasi-national distinction still exist? Or was the event an outbreak of internal people subject to the laws of the state? Plenty Horses's case served as a referendum on the status of assimilation and the related questions of violence and social evolution. Its conclusion would demonstrate both the currency and the inadequacy of outbreak as a way of describing Indian-white violence.

In the first trial, Plenty Horses's lawyers succeeded in demonstrating that the Lakotas considered themselves to be a distinct people at war. The jury deadlocked, not on the question of guilt or innocence, however, but on the question of whether the crime was murder or manslaughter. The jurors easily viewed Plenty Horses as falling within the bounds of American civil justice—at least in the context of punishment. During the second trial, the lawyers sought to bolster their case by including the army perspective. Would General Miles care to appear in court to testify that there had been no war? When the prosecuting attorney raised the issue, Miles responded testily: "It was a war. You do not suppose that I am going to reduce my campaign to a dress-parade affair?"[32] He sent a staff officer to testify to that effect, completely undermining a prosecution that he himself had set in motion. It took only a lunch recess after that testimony for the judge to issue a summary judgment in the case. It had been clearly

FIGURE 3. Trial of Plenty Horses. Seated, left to right: He Dog, Jack Red Cloud, Plenty Horses, Plenty Horses's father, Living Bear. Standing, left to right: Rock Road and White Moon (Cheyenne scouts attached to Casey's unit), Bear Lying Down, Broken Arm. Plenty Horses's clothing marks him as distinct from his companions. Where the others wear jackets, vests, ties, and hats or scout uniforms, he carries a blanket, wears blanket trousers, moccasins, and a shirt only. (Denver Public Library, Western History Department, X-31902.)

shown that a state of war existed and, therefore, that Plenty Horses's action—as murderous as it might seem—counted as an act of war.

The trial bore witness to the conflicted meanings of Wounded Knee. Today, we regard the event as a massacre, a wanton killing of prisoners and noncombatants. Perhaps because it was so obviously criminal, the army took great pains to insist that the outbreak was, in fact, a war—and a heroic one at that. Perhaps the most embarrassing evidence of this propaganda effort lies with the eighteen Medals of Honor distributed in the wake of the killings. The number is so radically disproportionate as to scream, "Whitewash!"—as many have and continue to do. The South Dakota historian Will G. Robinson once pointed out that sixty-four thousand South Dakotans participated in World War II over a period of four years and emerged with only three congressional Medals of Honor. At Wounded Knee, six times that number were handed out for a conflict that lasted barely two weeks.[33]

Plenty Horses's act stood in the same relation to war as murder stood in relation to a massacre of American citizens. If the military's treacherous killings did not qualify as a killing within the bounds of American society, then Plenty Horses's treacherous act could not be a murder. In the end, Americans would justify their violence on two grounds. First, despite previous conquest and a decade of civilizing efforts, the Lakotas remained radically different, culturally, socially, and nationally. Treacherous, they were wholly capable of any kind of violence. Second, Americans suggested that the viciousness demonstrated at Wounded Knee would make the long conquest truly complete. The grand review of troops held by General Miles as he departed the agency performed American power, and it held forth the promise of a bloody future should the Lakotas—or any other tribe—be so foolish as to contemplate violent outbreak ever again.

Almost everything said about Wounded Knee, whether sympathetic or not, reflected a doubled edge. On the one hand, it was clear that, despite various policies aimed at assimilation, Indians—at least the Lakotas, and potentially everyone else—had retained and rebuilt a sense of their own uniqueness. They saw themselves as distinct, not simply in terms of culture, but also in the political sense necessary to the waging of war. Likewise, it was equally apparent that many white Americans saw them in similar terms. Indian outbreaks like Wounded Knee represented a conquest still incomplete. And, because it was incomplete, Indians could not truly be regarded as pacified. They retained the potential for violent action.[34]

On the other hand, Wounded Knee simultaneously made it clear to everyone involved that Indians *had* been pacified. Some might continue to fear outbreaks, but it was difficult to imagine any tribal group being able to muster enough warriors to repeat even the failed mobilization that accompanied Wounded Knee. As the very notion of outbreak was being codified in the reporting of Wounded Knee and taken as a way of thinking about Indians and reservations, it was simultaneously being rendered obsolete. Wounded Knee and Plenty Horses's act both signified a set of simultaneous contradictions: of the lingering possibility and the new impossibility of violent outbreak; of the possibility and impossibility of the remaking of Indian individuals on the personal level; of the fact of cross-cultural hybridity and of continual assertions of Indian difference.

Such contradictions undermined both Indian and American cultural fantasies. For Lakotas, the Ghost Shirts represented a collective cultural fantasy of empowerment and distinctiveness. Plenty Horses's sense of his own accomplishment—remaking himself as a Lakota man—proved equally fantastic. He survived the American court, but many Lakotas could credit neither the action—a shot from behind during a parley—nor the choice of victim. The Lakota leader Young Man Afraid of His Horses had been willing to execute Plenty Horses as part of a cross-cultural exchange of justice, categorizing him, not with Lakotas, but with "bad men." Congratulating Plenty Horses after his liberation, American Horse construed his act, not as distinctly Lakota, but as just the opposite, as insanity: "You killed Casey; that was bad. He was a brave man and a good one. He did much for the Indian, but the whites cruelly starved us into such a condition that the young men were crazy and you did not know what you did."[35]

If violence and spiritual redemption served Indian dreams of social wholeness, whites had their own fantasy world as well. One of the most familiar figures in that world had been the savage Indian warrior, an image that stood at a crossroads in 1890. As long as there remained a real possibility of Indian violence, the imagery of last stands and Indian surrounds helped justify the violence wreaked on Indians during the conquest of the American landscape. In the wake of the final conflicts and the imposition of the reservation administrative structure, there grew a sense that the potential for Indian violence was fading rapidly.

Indeed, in the years preceding Wounded Knee, the images surrounding Indian violence were beginning a transformation, as their material underpinnings supposedly disappeared. Along with warriors, one also found images of docile, pacified Indians started out on the road to civilization. Luther Standing Bear, for example, recounts numerous occasions on which Carlisle students were displayed as docile and educable Indians. The Carlisle band played at the opening of the Brooklyn Bridge in 1883 and then toured several churches. Students were carted around East Coast cities. Standing Bear himself was placed on display in Wanamaker's Philadelphia department store, locked in a glass cell in the center of the store and set to sorting and pricing jewelry.[36] Carlisle, like many other Indian schools, took pains to demonstrate its success in Indian assimilation through strategic public displays—music, Indian labor, and football and other sports.

As the quintessential Indian outbreak, Wounded Knee reinvigorated the imagery of Indian violence by refreshing the belief that it had the potential to be real—at least for a few more years. At the same time, however, it rendered outbreak obsolete and pointed, instead, to Indian pacification. By looking at a slightly later act of violence, we can begin to trace the shifts and similarities between the ideas of nation-to-nation war, rebellious outbreak, and post–Wounded Knee pacification.

PAHA CANWEKNAYANKA, 1893

William Kelley and James Bacon lived near one another, on farms midway between the Pine Ridge agency and Chadron, Nebraska. Sixteen and thirteen years old, they were comfortable enough in the now-pacified landscape of 1893 to be riding the reservation in early February, hunting stray horses. It hadn't snowed much that year, but it had been bitterly cold. As night came on, they decided to stop at a cattle camp, a small cabin with a pair of green haystacks, nestled in a horseshoe bend of the White River. Nearby rose Paha Canweknayanka, Hill-in-the-Timber Butte. George Hadaway and William Underwood, cowboys working for the beef contractor that supplied cattle for the reservation's ration stations, welcomed them. Hadaway and Underwood had beds, but they let the boys spread their blankets on the floor near a wood stove. Perhaps they talked, played cards, shared a bottle and some food. At some point, they drifted off to sleep.

That night, February 2, 1893, four young Indian men opened the door to the cabin, stole quietly inside, and took positions over each of the cowboys. When their leader gave a low cough, they opened fire. Death was almost immediate. Bacon took a shot to the body, while Kelley was shot through the arm, breast, and mouth. One of the cowboys never made it

FIGURE 4. Amos Bad Heart Bull. Translation: "These are the cowboys that Two Sticks killed. This is the way they were lying dead." The image shows the four young men walking away from the cabin, which sits next to two haystacks (to the right) and at the foot of Paha Canweknayanka. To the left, an insert shows the four bodies lying sprawled around a wood-burning stove. (Helen H. Blish, A Pictographic History of the Oglala Sioux, with drawings by Amos Bad Heart Bull [Lincoln: Univ. of Nebraska Press])

from his bed; the other tried to take brief refuge underneath. They were found the next morning, blood gushed from their mouths and heads. One man was still alive but unconscious, and he died that day. The killers—the two sons of the Minneconjou leader Two Sticks, and two companions—fled southwest on the White River and then south along White Clay Creek—the same White Clay Creek down which Plenty Horses had ridden after killing Lieutenant Casey (see figure 4).[37]

The White Clay district meant home territory to Two Sticks's sons and perhaps a sympathetic reception from friends and neighbors. According to the acting agent at Pine Ridge, William Brown, White Clay housed the reservation's largest population of malcontents. "I have been very uneasy in regard to these people for some time past," he observed in one report, "although no overt act has been committed by them." It mattered that the Two Sticks family was Minneconjou, for the people of this band occupied the Cheyenne River reservation to the north, the home of Big Foot. While Pine Ridge's Oglalas and Rosebud's Brules most certainly had connections to Big Foot's band, a party of Minneconjous might be expected to carry deeper emotional ties to the victims of Wounded Knee and, thus, even greater reason for discontent. Agent Brown pinpointed the Minneconjous as the source of his troubles, specifically blaming the camp of Bear Eagle, "a renegade Indian from Cheyenne River agency who insisted upon being transferred to this agency last spring. He has a band of about one hundred and fifty in number who are non-progressive, discontented people."[38] In other words, Bear Eagle and his people continued to resist the colonial order and were, therefore, able to be seen in terms of outbreak.

Others had also perceived that certain reservation spaces had still not fallen under the sway of the state and, in fact, remained open to Ghost Dance theology. The *Rocky Mountain News*, for example, noted on multiple occasions the presence of No Water—to whose camp Plenty Horses had retreated after killing Casey—in the entire affair. On February 5, the paper suggested that No Water had earlier been sent on a secret mission to unite with the Crows for a war in the spring. The next day, it reported that he had flown into a rage and tried to rally his followers to an attack. "A prime mover among the Ghost Dancers and one of the worst Indians on this reservation," the paper said, noting also that Short Bull and Kicking Bear, Ghost Dance leaders from 1890, were back on the reservation, following a tour with Buffalo Bill and the Wild West.[39]

Indeed, bitter memories of Wounded Knee seemed high on the list of possible reasons for the killings. Beatrice A. R. Stocker, a missionary teacher at Porcupine, about twenty-five miles northeast of the agency, saw the killings as both revenge and the beginning of an outbreak. "A good many Indians who lost friends brood upon revenge," she reported to her sister. "Some swear to take a white man's life for each friend they lost, some say they will kill women and children for their women and children. One half-crazy man has begun, and we hear that three white men have been killed. Some say, and a woman and boy."[40]

Others saw revenge mingled with a continued commitment to the Ghost Dance. Some had argued that the Ghost Dance messiah would come after two springs had passed, and there was anticipation that the spring of 1893 would see the earth remade as the original visions had promised. So argued Valentine McGillycuddy, a former agent at Pine Ridge. "The messiah spirit is not dead," he warned, "and whites must not depend on the statement that the Indians are no longer considering the promises made by old Sitting Bull and the other medicine men who led the trouble two years ago. While there is no open dancing, there is quiet discussion of the topic." McGillycuddy saw great potential for an outbreak, for the spring was coming and, with it, the Lakota time for war. "The battle of Wounded Knee and its horrors is still a topic of conversation among the Sioux at and around Pine Ridge," he insisted, "and they won't want much coaxing to give the soldiers plenty of work next summer."[41] While few Lakotas seriously considered the possibility of full and organized war in 1893, Ghost Dance beliefs continued to matter, not simply as a collective memory, but as an important personal experience.

Indeed, Agent Brown's interpretation tended to emphasize the importance of personal ceremonies and visions. According to Brown, Two Sticks, his two sons, and three friends, Comes Crawling, Hunkpapa Boy, and White Faced Horse, had made a sweat lodge on the fateful evening. A blanket-covered willow frame heated by red-hot stones, the sweat was a common form of purification, in both physical and spiritual senses. Brown reported that Bear Eagle and Comes Crawling had seen Two Sticks and the others "come out of the sweat house where they had been going through Ghost Dance ceremonies and declare their intention to go on the warpath as the time for the extermination of the whites had come."[42] The Lakota artist and historian Amos Bad Heart Bull, who discovered the bodies of the cowboys, drew a series of images illustrating the affair in which he took pains to show at least two of the killers wearing Ghost Shirts (see figure 5).

Still other explanations turned, not on visions, but on slights. The *Rocky Mountain News* reported from Chadron, Nebraska, that Two Sticks had been fed by the cowboys "until he became a nuisance and was ordered away. Having been refused further board, he entertained a grudge against the cowboys." When the Ghost Dance vision came, Two Sticks had known exactly who the first victims should be.[43] Luther Standing Bear, who was at Pine Ridge at the time, saw it in more immediate terms. According to Standing Bear, Two Sticks and his family had been out on a hunt and were returning home. Unsuccessful in their search for game, they had stopped to see about trading for something to eat. The cowboys had been drinking or were unfamiliar with Indians: "They did not give Two Sticks and his sons any chance to explain their presence, but began cursing them. They abused them in this way for some little time, and finally kicked them outdoors." When Two Sticks's sons reentered the house, it was to kill.[44]

There is no need to pick a singular explanation. It is difficult to imagine any Lakota violence subsequent to Wounded Knee that did not have

FIGURE 5. Amos Bad Heart Bull. Translation: "The killing of young Two Sticks." In this image, Bad Heart Bull shows young Two Sticks bravely charging the line of Indian Police, while, to the rear, his friend White Faced Horse prepares to come to his assistance. In the lower left, the two youngest boys ("striplings") and old Two Sticks attempt to escape. (Helen H. Blish, A Pictographic History of the Oglala Sioux, with drawings by Amos Bad Heart Bull [Lincoln: Univ. of Nebraska Press])

some memory of the massacre behind it, for the mass murder immediately became a critical reference point in the Lakota social dialect. And Bad Heart Bull's report of Ghost Shirts suggests that Ghost Dance beliefs did, in fact, play some role in the killings. Bad Heart Bull certainly knew the cowboys well enough to understand immediately that at least one of the dead had been a guest. In one of his drawings, one of the corpses is labeled *koska tokan tanhi*, "a visiting young man." Another is labeled *hoksila*, "boy." Two Sticks may have been on similarly familiar terms.

What matters as much is the social and cultural context in which the killings took place. In addition to revenge—either social or personal—and the Ghost Dance, these killings represented the first (and the last) war party for these young men and their father. Like Plenty Horses, they used violence to make a statement about themselves as Lakotas and, as important, as men. The purification before battle and the killings themselves would have made complete sense twenty years earlier; that sensibility had hardly disappeared from the people's collective memory. The outbreak to be feared, then, was not so much the promise of widespread violence as it was the eruption of resistant forms of Lakota culture that were both old and new.

When the Indian police confronted them the following day, the young men made it clear that they would die in a culturally appropriate manner. Bad Heart Bull's drawings show young Two Sticks bravely charging the Indian police, inviting his own death. White Faced Horse, his friend, prepares to come to his aid, though the odds are insurmountable. Both young men would die in battle at the hands of the Indian police, viewed now not so much as friends and relatives as representatives of the agent and the reservation power structure. In this and other changes, we can begin to see a shift in expectation, from the sense of violent outbreak found at Wounded Knee to the very different understandings at play thirteen years later at Lightning Creek.

In fact, white perceptions and expectations fluctuated wildly in 1893, from Valentine McGillycuddy's warnings of an outbreak that would keep the soldiers busy in springtime warfare to Agent Brown's continual reassurances that the issue was murder, not war, and that there was no possibility of an outbreak. Beatrice Stocker wrote to her sister as if she were already surrounded. Perhaps the letter would be her last: "Trouble has begun among the Indians, and nobody knows where it will end. One of our friendly ones will take this letter tonight if I can get it ready. I want to tell you just what we know already, so, if you never hear any more you'll know that much."[45] While the papers debated the possibility of a larger outbreak—would No Water make a break for the Badlands? how many Indians would he take with him?—Agent Brown worked assiduously to convince people that, as of 1893, outbreak was no longer possible. While newspaper reportage began by emphasizing danger, war, and outbreak, it quickly came around to the position that outbreak was impossible.[46] Multiple voices—western whites, federal government agents, and Lakotas, each speaking multiple languages—entered into a dialogue that transformed all. Yet one particular framing of the event—the one focused on pacification—became the most prominent voice in the dialogue.

On February 4, Brown expressed hope that an arrest would be made soon and observed that he had placed guards around nearby schools, established a police camp near the backsliders of the White River area, and requested additional police. As important as these local dispositions might have been, however, Brown noted that they served an additional purpose— public relations—and he requested help from the commissioner's office in telling the story of the incident. "Trusting that such action as may be proper will be taken to quiet any fears that may arise through newspaper reports concerning this affair" is how he signed off his letter. The next day, he insisted that there was "no reason for undue excitement" and trusted "that sensational excitement may be kept down, as the more quiet matters are kept the better results will be reaped in the future."[47] Again, he closed the letter with a plea for prompt rebuttal to sensational reporting. Brown undoubtedly aimed to deflect criticism of his own management, but control over public perception proved as important to the Indian Office.

The Washington office responded, releasing to the press the text of Brown's February 5 telegram requesting promotions for the Indian police officers who had battled successfully with the killers. Brown would, no doubt, have been gratified to have seen the column heading in the *Rocky Mountain News* that day: "Indian Uprising a Fake. Pine Ridge Troubles Have Been Greatly Exaggerated." The following day, the Indian Office released another short press release noting (incorrectly) that three of the perpetrators had been killed and that "no outbreak of the Indians or further trouble is anticipated."[48]

As important as the assertion of the impossibility of outbreak were the rather convincing arguments supporting it. With highly mobile troops at Fort Robinson (30 miles away) and Fort Meade (150 miles), the Lakotas were quite literally surrounded by military force, physically contained by the threat of violent retribution. Even better, according to observers, they had come to understand the other lesson of Wounded Knee—that the use of force would be absolute. As Beatrice Stocker pointed out: "The American soldiers said before that if ever they should be sent to the Indians again they would not wait for orders but would wipe out the whole tribe[.] (Imagine—soldiers!) The Indians know this. So the more peaceable and prudent among them want to give up the culprits and restrain the others."[49]

Many Lakota people called for restraint. A belief in the likelihood of white violence had already made its way into their hearts and minds, much as Indian violence had once been a dominant expectation of non-

Indian settlers. Internalized expectations joined together with the very real threat of overwhelming violence, leading Indian people to question their own autonomy. Even at a distance, the surrounding soldiers boxed them in mentally and emotionally, insisting that Lakotas address themselves only to the social and political alternatives provided by the American state. Fear and resignation helped shape Indian people's consciousness as colonized subjects while at the same time calling up a durable sense of resentment and resistance. The most visible evidence of these painful new ways of being Lakota appeared in the form of a rising group of Indian leaders. Such negotiators—and they could be found on every reservation and community—presented to their people, not simply the agent's position, but also the cold reality of situations like that of Two Sticks, and they represented Native complaints and needs to the agent. Such leaders often had experience in colonial situations, participating in the Indian police, the ration stations, the schools, stores, and agency offices. Yet they worked hard to retain credibility among those actively hostile to the reservation order. Charles Smith would, a decade hence, be seen as one of these kinds of leaders.[50]

And so, according to Brown, even as Two Sticks and his sons crawled from the sweat lodge, Comes Crawling had tried hard to dissuade them from violence. Failing, he had turned to Bear Eagle, who also begged them not to make trouble. "In reply," recounted Brown, "they fired their guns in front of his face, and it is claimed that one of the shots passed through his coat." When, having gotten word of the Indian police's action, No Water supposedly urged his followers to further violence, Young Man Afraid of His Horses rallied his own people and placed them between No Water and the police. And, indeed, according to one report, far from flying into a rage, No Water had heard the shots, recognized trouble coming, and moved his camp closer to the agency. Brown sensed that he had most of the people on his side: "There seems to be no sympathy on the part of any considerable number of Indians towards the murderers; on the contrary, a number of the most progressive and leading Indians residing on the White Clay district . . . condemn the action of Two Sticks and his four followers and express a willingness to see that they be brought to justice."[51]

Indeed, the list of leaders who accompanied Young Man Afraid, Police Sergeant Running Hawk, and the two remaining killers when they came into the agency on February 9 reads like a who's who of former Lakota resisters—Kicking Bear and Short Bull, Bear Eagle, No Water, Bear Louse,

Iron Bull, and others. These men, of course, were not along for the ride, nor were they present to demand that the killers be brought to the white bar of justice. Rather, they understood that they now needed to work within the civil system in order to beg leniency for the two, who were, according to Amos Bad Heart Bull, "mere striplings." To agent Brown, of course, their presence signified that the assimilation program was working—the most recalcitrant had apparently aligned themselves, not with Two Sticks and his outbreak, but with the Indian police, the agent, and the rule of order. And, in a way, Brown was correct. The presence of the Lakota leaders signified that they had accepted the hegemony of the agent, that they were willing to be complicit in his system in order to advance certain collective goals, in this case the freeing of the two youngest boys. We should never forget, however, that what lay behind their participation in civil and administrative arenas was the threat of force demonstrated so absolutely at Wounded Knee.[52]

The incident had a horrific denouement. Old Two Sticks, who had apparently stood outside the door of the cowboy cabin, advising the young men, was reportedly dying and unable to be brought in with the two remaining killers. Yet, when Brown traveled the White Clay Creek district later in the month, he found that Two Sticks "was not yet dead and that all the disgruntled Indians are visiting him." If No Water and Bear Eagle had cast their lot with the colonial system, Two Sticks was a living example, not simply of rebellion, but of an ongoing oppositional force, doubly empowered by his freedom in the wake of the crime. Faced with the choice of proceeding against the two young boys or against the supposed mastermind, Brown easily decided on the latter, noting that he would "hold him in the [agency] hospital until he is able to travel or dies."[53] Two Sticks did not die and was bound over to the federal court in Deadwood, charged with the murder of the cowboys. He was executed in Deadwood on December 28, 1894, proclaiming his innocence but, like his son and White Faced Horse, facing death unafraid. "My heart is not bad," he said. "I did not kill the cowboys—the Indian boys killed them. I have killed many Indians but never killed a white man. The Great Father and the men under him should talk to me and I would show them that I was innocent. My heart knows I am not guilty and I am happy. I am not afraid to die." To many, the prompt response of the Indian police, the easy containment of any lingering possibilities of outbreak, and the execution of a guilty party through civil channels seemed to suggest that Indians had, indeed, been pacified.[54]

Ten years later, at Lightning Creek, we can see the fruits of such efforts—as well as the lingering of older expectations. The *Newcastle Times,* for example, offered the most archaic of all possible narratives, one in which violent Indians surrounded innocent whites, whose own violence was justified as self-defense. The paper painted Charlie Smith as a redskinned outlaw, insisting that "for more than three years he had openly defied Sheriff Miller and had several times sent word that he couldn't be arrested." According to the paper, the Lakotas had actively resisted arrest the previous day, surrounding the whites, and tossing dirt in the air as a sign of their "bad blood" and eagerness to fight. The sheriff had *not* ambushed the hunters, as it appeared, but rather commanded them to halt and surrender (no explanation was given for shots fired at three women running away). The first shot was, of course, fired by an Indian rather than by a member of the posse. The dead Black Kettle was assigned the blame. The paper painted the Indians as aggressors and the struggle as a defensive one, with echoes, not of the Wounded Knee massacre, but of the Little Big Horn: "The fight raged on and in full view of the enemy were our men. There stood Sheriff Miller with a grim countenance. Like a Custer he held his ground. What matter were the odds two to one in the enemy's favor; what matter were the bullets flying all around?"[55]

Other accounts offered more complex explanations that revealed the tensions surrounding assimilation and violence. The government's assimilation policy, particularly as it was represented vigorously by Pine Ridge Agent John R. Brennan, offered a visible target. In theory, assimilation solved the "Indian problem," turning Indian people into Americans by "killing the Indian and saving the man." In practice, many white Americans—particularly those recently intruded into Indian territory—found the prospect of a too close similarity between Indians and non-Indians disquieting. Charlie Smith's Carlisle education proved a popular sticking point, for it suggested this dark side of assimilation—that a rigorous racial and cultural division between Indian and white might no longer be tenable. Perhaps Smith's troubles were not at all Indian in nature, some mused, but rather the product of cultural mixing itself. One familiar narrative strand had him losing all the good qualities of his Indian heritage at Carlisle, retaining all the bad, and, at the same time, picking up the worst characteristics of the whites. Smith was, in this telling, monstrous, a bicultural mistake who reflected the distillation of all that was evil about the mixing of culture and race.

Another narrative compares Smith to the group's other leader, William Brown, mixed in race, but apparently pure Indian in culture. Brown, the story went, had been docile, willing to accompany Sheriff Miller to Newcastle. Smith's education distinguished him, hinted the *Chadron Times*, and served to explain the incident. It wasn't necessarily that the Carlisle Indian School had made Smith a bicultural bogeyman; it was simply that knowledge itself could be dangerous for an Indian. If Smith had not understood that the sheriff had no jurisdiction over him, he would, like Brown, have given in and followed the posse to Newcastle, and the whole mess could have been avoided.[56] Obeying the law was one thing, appropriate to an Indian; understanding its administration was quite another. As a member of the Indian service bureaucracy, however, Smith had, perhaps, come to understand administration well. Seen in this light, his response to Sheriff Miller—"you can't take me"—looks far more like a legal utterance than a promise of physical defiance. If Americans applauded the white cultural influences that had made Smith a hybrid figure, they had a harder time accepting that those influences might be as empowering as they were supposed to be ennobling. It was easy to expect that assimilated Indians would occupy a separate ghetto space, a kind of inferior modernity. Charlie Smith, who insisted that he shared the same contemporary legal universe and was able to wield the same skills, upset those expectations—at the cost of his life.

The incident at Lightning Creek demonstrates the shifts and unevenness in the white expectations surrounding Indian violence at the turn of the century. Were Indians—as the *Newcastle Times* would have it—as violent as ever, capable of attacking and surrounding whites in dire last-stand situations? Or had assimilation and cultural contact produced hybrid monstrosities, violent mixtures with the most lawless characteristics of both Indian and white? Might assimilation not be seen as an oddly tragic success, producing Charlie Smiths, who sometimes found their competence a liability in a world of white hostility and violence? Racial Other, bicultural outlaw, assimilated cultural broker grown too big for his buckskin britches—the range of interpretations suggests that, in 1903, the field remained open to several layers of meaning, from the archaic last stand to the violent white rejection of Indian equality.[57]

But Lightning Creek also reveals a new expectation, one that would structure relations between Indians and non-Indians for much of the twentieth century. In the courtrooms, newspapers, memos, and investigations that followed the violence at Lightning Creek, one finds a new consensus becoming visible: while most people believed that the Indian hunters were justified in their slight resistance, almost no one believed that they were either capable of killing or empowered to do so. Indians had been pacified. "When the trouble began," Agent Brennan observed, "the Indians tried to get away as fast as possible." "Some of them," he said, in a probable exaggeration, "had not fired a gun in twenty years." A. B. Talkington, of Archer, Nebraska, scorned the posse: "It is a high standard of civilization we are living under when a few of these pitiable ragged heathens are not permitted to pass peaceably through the country . . . without being shot down like coyotes. To read of the posses that were sent out from all the surrounding towns to do battle to this ragged little band of heathens, and to hear that the troops had been ready to move on a moment's notice is enough to make an honest citizen sick."[58]

A Washington, D.C., paper scoffed at the possibility of Indian violence, pointing, instead, to other local motives: "If the authorities at Washington can be deluded into the notion that Indians are dangerous and induced to garrison a fort with two or three companies of soldiers, it gives every rancher in the neighborhood a market for hay, and his wood, and his beef cattle, and anything else he raises that the Government needs to buy." Accordingly, when the posse members argued that they had killed because they were afraid of an Indian attack, most observers saw the claim as self-justifying rather than realistic. Only their hometown newspaper, the Newcastle Times, took the claim seriously. Even regional papers, like the Chadron Times, reported that there had been, not an Indian attack, but rather a "Paleface Outbreak in Wyoming."[59] We can take this curious inversion—small-town western newspapers portraying palefaces as breaking out into savage violence—as the marker of a decisive shift in the ways non-Indians made meaning out of violence, Indians, and assimilation.

Three moments in time. In 1890, at Wounded Knee, it seemed clear to almost everyone that Indians were not pacified, that they maintained the capacity for violence. Plenty Horses's case codified the idea that the conflict had taken place, not within a single unified society, but between two societies distinct enough to declare war on one another. By 1893, the shifts in expectation and practice were in visible transition. Was the Two Sticks killing an outbreak? Not on the order of Wounded Knee, which reflected a conquest and containment that remained incomplete. When Two Sticks's sons killed the cowboys, Indian violence remained a possibility for reservation missionaries and regional newspaper reporters alike. Using the same media that sensationalized the possibilities of violence, Agent Brown and the Indian Office publicly waged a struggle against sensationalism—and, most particularly, the rhetoric of the surround, the last stand, the outbreak, and the idea of Indian social distinctiveness. There could be no more outbreaks, the campaign emphasized, and it was essentially correct. Not only did the material impossibilities militate against violence, but Indian people themselves understood the consequences of resistance. From battle, in the case of Plenty Horses, to murder, in the case of Two Sticks, to a paleface outbreak, in the case of Charlie Smith—the trajectory of a new understanding of the potential for Indian violence can be seen in outline.

By Smith's time, Indian people were no longer perceived by non-Indians as belonging to autonomous societies, though they were still marked as different in any number of ways—race, class, culture, the space of the reservation, the supervision of federal authority. To white Americans, Indian difference no longer included the national, or even the quasi-national, distinctions that would have enabled them to wage war.[60] And it was true as a material fact that, by 1903, war was simply not within the universe of possibility for Indian people. Deprived of ready food or supplies, confined and disciplined by a bureaucratic structure, aware that they were surrounded on all sides by fast-moving troops, mindful of the possibility of the total warfare represented by Wounded Knee, Indian people across the country understood that they were no longer able to wage war.

Perhaps the greater import, however, came, not from the material fact, but from the non-Indian expectations that accompanied it. For with the possibility of war went, for some, the possibility of violence itself. *Pacification*, initially couched in terms of the closing of centuries of Indian war, might also refer to the rendering of Indian people themselves as pacified. In other words, a change in political and military status spoke at the same time to a change in the old perception of Native cultures and characters as fundamentally and violently antagonistic. Anglo-Americans had—with at least some grounds for doing so—long cherished the idea that, if you met Indian warriors in the forest or the prairies, there was a chance that they might try to kill you. Now, there seemed to be something of a reverse assumption: Native people were utterly tamed and safe. The masculine aspect of Indian violence had been essentially domesticated, and dangerous warriors no longer counterbalanced open-armed princesses. Indeed, as unresisting figures out of place beyond reservation fence lines,

Indian men and women alike were open in new ways to white violence. Perhaps this sense, not simply of Indian inferiority, but of Indian pacification, read onto the bodies and into the essential natures of Indians, explains Sheriff Miller's willingness to attack forty or more people with only thirteen men.[61]

American expectations were, of course, uneven. The local differences between eastern Wyoming and western Nebraska, for example, speak to such unevenness. Consider the *Times* of Newcastle and the *Times* of Chadron, for instance, whose reports form mirror images of one another. In Newcastle, a white ambush of Indian families and old people became an Indian attack. Though the posse had, in fact, taken shelter behind a creek bed, the paper showed them fully exposed to Indian aggression. And, though only two Indians actually returned the fire of thirteen men, it was the posse that was surrounded by hot lead, not the Indians. Of course, William Miller had stood like a Custer. Both Custer and Miller had been aggressors and ambushers; both were immediately remade as victims surrounded by violent Indians. Making Miller fit the Custer mold was a natural reflex.

The Chadron paper, however, took a different view. Perhaps it felt obliged to defend the local Indians—Pine Ridge was only thirty miles away. But perhaps it is the case that Chadron, with no local white heroes to defend, reported the incident in ways that would have resonated almost everywhere outside Newcastle. Understood now as contained and disciplined, nonviolent in the fear of a repetition of the awful retribution of Wounded Knee, outnumbered outside the reservation, the Indian hunting and gathering parties of Pine Ridge seemed to pose no threat to anyone. Thus the inversion: if anyone had the potential for violence, it was not Indians but whites, criticized by the paper as "men who think Indians have no right to live."[62]

ONWARD TO THE PAST

These stories—of Wounded Knee and Plenty Horses, of Lightning Creek and Charlie Smith, and of Two Sticks and his sons—helped establish critical contexts for the twentieth-century imagemaking even then beginning to take shape. Literature, film, art, television, and other media have often invoked Indian violence in order to stage extended meditations, justifications, and celebrations of non-Indian, American violence. They have negotiated issues of social and racial difference and the violence that might be performed on Indians and others, but they have done so by continuously positioning white violence as defensive. This particular understanding of violence reflects a long tradition in the setting of American expectations, one stretching back to the seventeenth century.

Why were images of Indian violence locked in a nineteenth-century frontier setting even as they proliferated in the representational forms of the twentieth century, particularly film? The disconnection between the popular culture embrace of (nineteenth-century) Indian violence and the equally widespread expectation of its impossibility in the twentieth century proved critical to American engagements with the world of modernity. Images of Indian violence evoked both a specifically nationalist history of defensive conflict and a general primitivism against which the modern might be measured and made visible. The classic Hollywood Indian-fighting western, then, tended to fetishize the violent potential of the Indian, creating a particular array of racialized images and expectations against which members of an assumed audience might imagine themselves.

Pacification, one might argue, served as a bridging ideology between the most powerful expectations of the eighteenth and nineteenth centuries—violence and Indian disappearance—and those of the twentieth, which clustered around various forms of primitivism. On the one hand, pacification rearticulated the vanishing-Indian ideology of the mid-nineteenth century, which erased white acts of dispossession and generously mourned the fact that Indians were disappearing naturally. Pacification shifted the ground: Indians might not vanish, but they would become invisible, as the very characteristic that had once defined them—the potential for violence—was eradicated. Even if they didn't melt away—as earlier vanishing proponents assumed—they would either melt into American society or sit quietly in the marginal distance, no longer disturbing anyone. On the other hand, pacification also rendered Indians safe, thereby opening up their lives and lands to the visitations of various breeds of primitivists. Pacification laid the cultural conditions for the new expectations of the early twentieth century. Harmlessness and primitive vitality, assimilation replacing Indian national distinctiveness, a white American national memory laced through with conquest, all these things added up to either complete domination, with limitless access to Indian lives and cultures, or a complete freedom to ignore Indian people altogether.

Such expectations invariably made their way back into the world of Indian-white relations. If the possibilities of actual Indian violence were foreclosed in the imagination of twentieth-century non-Indians, the possibilities of white-on-Indian violence were not attenuated or controlled in similar ways. William Miller and his posse were hardly the only white vigilantes to attack Indian people in the twentieth century. In the borderlands surrounding reservation spaces, violent attacks on Native people have continued to range from extraordinary to episodic to habitual—in large part because non-Indians have been able to imagine violence against Indian people without also imagining a significant fear of widespread resistance and retaliation. But, while we can accept that certain forms of Indian violence might well be physically contained by military conquest and colonial surveillance, there are whole genres of violent action open to Native individuals and groups, from threats to bar fights to vigilantism to protest activities to military service. The shock that greeted the Indian takeover of Wounded Knee in 1973 testifies in no small part, however, to the ways in which the imagined possibility of an Indian tradition of physical resistance was swept away—for at least seventy years— by the expectations of Indian containment and pacification that came to characterize the turn of the twentieth century.

INDIAN WARS, THE MOVIE

representation

OPENING SCENE: SOUTH DAKOTA, 1913

What would happen, the young Lakota men wondered, if we were to use real bullets in our guns instead of blanks? Buffalo Bill Cody was even now loping toward them across the October plains; no doubt he made a tempting target. Though Cody had once known regular danger, he had spent the last thirty years riding in front of peaceful, cheering audiences, the best-known showman of the late nineteenth century. Some of these very same Lakota men—pacified, one assumed—had been with him in the Wild West's show arena. Now, in the autumn of 1913, a hearty but fading sixty-seven years old, Cody confronted truly angry Indian warriors once again. Appropriately, perhaps, these last epic charges of his epic career would take place, not in the fever of real battle (he hoped), or even in the arena, but in front of a movie camera—the most powerful representational instrument of the new century.

Cody and the Lakotas were meeting very near the ten-year anniversary of the killing of Charlie Smith, Black Kettle, and Gray Bear at Lightning Creek. Twenty years had passed since Two Sticks's sons had murdered the cowboys and twenty-three years since Wounded Knee itself. But Cody had chosen Pine Ridge for his first venture into filmmaking, not because so many violent conflicts had taken place there, but because that reservation was home to significant numbers of professional Indian actors with Wild West show experience that he hoped would translate easily to film. Cody aimed to make a documentary record of the great battles of the Indian Wars, and he had already finagled the cooperation of the U.S. Army. General Nelson Miles was on location, and a detachment of men from the Twelfth Cavalry had been assigned to the film. The cast and crew of The Indian Wars moved through several fights, among them the relatively obscure battles at War Bonnet Creek and at Summit Springs in which Cody had actually played a role.[1] Then, it came time to film the conflict at Wounded Knee.

Miles and the military preferred that the film show a dangerous battle rather than a massacre, an inclination that ran sharply against the grain of the Lakota actors. Indeed, Miles got so caught up in the replication of his own version of Wounded Knee that he insisted that the filming take place on the actual battlefield itself, which included the site of the mass grave of Indian dead. Several Lakota performers refused to participate, threatening to shut down the production. Caught between his Indian cast and his military one, Cody took the path of least resistance and coerced, cajoled, and paid off the Lakota actors, forfeiting decades of hard-won trust to wring from them one last performance.[2]

Though they reluctantly agreed to the filming, some of the young Lakota men apparently toyed with their own vision of modern moviemaking, namely, the replacement of real lead for the filmmaker's blanks. Blurring together representation and reality, they contemplated (re)making the worst moment in Lakota history into an ironic revenge, with the product being dead soldiers, Ghost Shirts that really did shed bullets, and a film that would encompass both the original massacre and its unanticipated successor. According to the film historian Kevin Brownlow, Cody got wind of the murmurs in the Lakota camp and spent the night before the battle riding between the Lakotas and the army, assuring each of the peaceful designs and blank cartridges of the other. But you can bet that he was worried as he galloped across the plains that day (see figure 6).[3]

Or maybe not. The historian L. G. Moses suggests that the story of bullets for blanks, recounted in Moving Picture World, the leading trade journal of the film industry, was nothing more than public relations hype, and he's probably right. Taken as a work of culture, however, the marketing scam captures perfectly the paradoxes of Indian people—and non-Indian audiences and filmmakers—caught in the curious mix of fiction, memory, realism, actuality, and expectation that came together at this precise moment. Focus your attention on The Indian Wars, and things can get pretty confusing. The very real killings at Wounded Knee in 1890, for instance, surely owed something to the images of Indian violence offered up by the Wild West as early as 1883—a moment when the possibility of outbreak was still very real. The Indian Wars pointed back in time to Wounded Knee itself, but it relied on the stories performed and the actors trained in Cody's show. And the ballyhoo account of live ammunition stood in ironic relation to

FIGURE 6. *U.S. Troops Surrounding the Indians on the Wounded Knee Battlefield.*
Still photograph by James Miller from The Indian Wars *(1914). (Library of Congress LOT 12773.)*

the film, the show, and the event, folding representation back over itself to return to the possibility of actual violence, nineteenth-century style.[4]

When Cody screened the movie in Chicago a few months later for a collection of military men, the Lakota actors were not present. Indeed, most white Americans expected that Indian people, largely out of touch with American popular culture (though integral to it), had little sense of—or say about—the way their images might be used. This broad expectation comes down to us through generations of stories in which supposedly primitive Indians are fearful of cameras, duped or coerced into film appearances, the subjects of photographic jokes, so unsavvy that they refuse to play dead after being shot, and so on.

Some Native people may well have been duped or bribed into some performances, and some may have been astonished by photographic images—but not for very long. These are American myths of modernity more than they are reliable understandings about the pasts of Indian people. It is far from clear that Native Americans in general failed to understand or to think critically about the uses of their images. Indeed, for many Native people in the early twentieth century, the opposite is quite likely the case.[5] Shortly after the filming was complete, for instance, the Lakota reformer (and future film actor) Chauncey Yellow Robe, well aware of the politics of Cody's representations, reminded viewers of one important little detail: neither Cody nor Miles had actually *been* at Wounded Knee in the critical moments. Their presence in the film, he argued—"for their own profit and cheap glory"—contravened the claim to documentary realism. The two, Yellow Robe charged, had gone back and become "heroes for a moving picture machine."[6]

Just as Wounded Knee marked an important transitional moment in the expectations surrounding Indian violence and pacification, so too did *The Indian Wars* stand at a similarly pivotal moment of change and cultural negotiation. On one side lay the nineteenth-century Wild West show, a dramatic live performance that successfully engaged the tensions surrounding violent conflict. On the other side stood the twentieth-century Hollywood film, its technologies of mass production reaching audiences differently and engaging for them a different set of expectations. Films, of course, never repudiated the sensibility of Indian violence found in the Wild West. Indeed, they were key to the shifting of Indian violence from nineteenth-century possibility to twentieth-century titillation and metaphor.[7]

Yet the contemporary fictional films that stood closest to *The Indian Wars* often concerned themselves with issues other than violence or representational fidelity. After decades of effort to pacify, civilize, educate, and assimilate Native people into American culture and society, did one finally have to take Indians seriously as Americans? How was that supposed to work? Were "civilized" Indians really civilized or just playing the part? Were they truly modern? In other words, could you trust that Indian people were culturally malleable—and, thus, ripe for assimilation—when down deep you suspected that they would always remain racially different?

In the midst of these vexed issues of expectation, a surprising number of Indian people carved out lives around the practice of representation, making the shift from Wild West to film, from nineteenth century to twentieth, from South Dakota and Oklahoma to Hollywood and New York. It is not unreasonable to ask how and why this happened. Why would Native people agree to represent themselves, particularly when so many representations cast Indians in a negative light? Some motives, of course, are simply unknowable. Others cluster together in identifiable

FIGURE 7. *Lakota Camp at Inceville Film Studio, Near Santa Monica, Calif., 1914.* (*Marc Wanamaker, Bison Archives.*)

clumps: escape; adventure; economic need; cultural celebration; educational outreach. Taken together, these can help locate and explain the Indian people who appear in the unexpected places where images were made—like a Lakota tipi camp carved into a California canyon on the shores of the Pacific (see figure 7).

Native motivations shifted across time. The earliest Wild West performers were not necessarily of a piece with their Hollywood descendants thirty years later, for the different generations engaged very different histories. To place the motives behind Native performance in relation to transformations in media and expectation, we'll need to trace a line extending back to the Wild West and forward to the earliest days of Hollywood. On that line, *The Indian Wars* sits in between, a curious failure in terms of both the nineteenth century and the twentieth. It points in useful directions, however, for its Wild West ancestor was the first institution to link Indians, cross-cultural performance, ideological expectations, and mass audiences in significant ways. Likewise, its more successful movie contemporaries suggested the degree to which things had changed.

The Wild West has a complex genealogy: protorodeo; theater; the dime novel; and a small but important tradition of traveling Indian performers, most famously those who toured England and France with the artist-showman George Catlin in the 1850s. Indian people of all tribes of course had performance traditions built around dance and religious practice, but these were meant for Indian audiences. First performances for non-Indians most likely came as part of diplomatic protocols. As contact zones became busier and more widely spread, non-Indian visitors increasingly took Native ceremonies as entertaining spectacles. Missouri River traders, for example, visited Arikara camps in order to see "magic shows," in which Arikara medicine societies demonstrated their abilities to overcome death or injury—including arrow wounds, gunshot wounds, and even decapitation. In the nineteenth-century West, non-Indians often watched Indian performances. White travelers, for instance, flocked to watch dances during the 1867 Laramie treaty negotiations. Likewise, Indian people on diplomatic visits to Washington, D.C., would often be asked to perform songs and dances. Louis Warren observes that it took a night of mutual performance in 1869 to help seal the alliance between the Fifth Cavalry and the Pawnee Scouts and that such performances were critical to the genealogy of the Wild West: "Cavalry charges, war dances, songs and poetry—these preliminaries were a Wild West show in their own right and Cody was likely among the large appreciative audience."[8]

In the early nineteenth century, a flurry of "Indian plays" in American cities produced a new tradition, one in which white actors playing Indian explored the possibilities of explicitly theatrical performance. By the mid-nineteenth century, Iroquois, Penobscots, and others had started offering Indian-show performances designed for urban audiences; these would expand in the later nineteenth century and the early twentieth to encompass performers from numerous tribes. Midcentury Indian performers—particularly those who devised and managed their own performances—surely set and reinforced white expectations concerning Indian gesture, custom, and appearance, but, by and large, their material seems to have emerged from Native cultural practice rather than the fictions of the Indian play.[9] Buffalo Bill Cody, in turn, created yet another tradition, paying Indian people to act out dramatic roles in white national narratives, familiar stories of the frontier asserted to be historically accurate. It was not simply that Indians danced, sang, and dressed for white audiences but that they were self-consciously cast as dangerous antagonists, captured now within an Anglo narrative of conquest and settlement.

There exists an industrial-strength scholarly literature on the Wild West, and few writers have failed to comment on the bizarre linkages between the production of images and the production of history that dogged Cody's life. He was, according to many, the first modern celebrity in the United States—and not only because of his performances for millions of people or his instant name recognition. Rather, Cody was a celebrity in the sense that he self-reflectively understood the ways in which he lived his life as an image in motion—and that his image/life was to be lived, not only for himself, but for media consumers in a developing mass market.

Cody's life embodied the transformations of that market. One of the Wild West's lineages surely extends back to the dime novels of the 1860s and 1870s, in which Cody became—unlike so many of his imaginary dime novel peers—a quasi-fictional real character, his legitimate but unexceptional adventures magnified and embellished in outlandish style.[10] In a decade of stage shows beginning in 1873, Cody began to act out these fictions, making them compelling by asserting their truth with his own body. As few commentators have failed to suggest, Cody's killing and scalping of the young Cheyenne Yellow Hand in 1876—during which he pointedly wore, not the work clothes of the frontier scout, but his black velvet stage costume—mark the most visible moment in his deliberate confusion of fiction and action. Taking, as it was celebrated, "the first scalp for Custer" legitimated the authenticity of Cody's stage labor by making its props and costumes key elements in the actual work of violence and conquest. His subsequent costumed performances of "The Killing of Yellow Hand" were inescapably perceived as something authentically different from regular stage acting—after all, he had actually performed the act and in the same clothes he was now wearing onstage, using the same knife. The scalp he held proudly aloft was really that of Yellow Hand (see figure 8).

Cody dared the world to differentiate between two distinct forms of action—historical and representational—embodied in his person. The

FIGURE 8. *The Scalping of Yellow Hand. Still photograph from* The Indian Wars *(1914). Buffalo Bill Cody couldn't resist acting the scene out again, yet the empty surroundings must have stood in contrast to the packed arenas where the reenactment usually took place. His arms-up gesture of triumph, however, makes it clear that he is performing—for the movie camera and for the spectators it promised. (Buffalo Bill Museum and Grave, Lookout Mountain, Golden, Colorado.)*

world refused the dare and learned, with the 1883 beginning of the Wild West, to love the refusal. The show's insistence on its educational value rested on a claim of accuracy that seemed to go beyond theatrical representation. As with the clothing, knife, and scalp of Yellow Hand, the Wild West relied, not simply on the appearance of truth, but on the evocative power of actual western gear, which simultaneously signified *real* and *realistic, historical artifact* and *stage prop.* The stagecoach would be real, a veteran of the Deadwood route. Real bison would charge through the arena. And the ultimate artifacts/props were human beings, who would share in Cody's joyous confusion of the historical and the representational—real cowboys roped and rode real horses using real saddles and lariats.

Most important, real Indians, decked out in real feathers and buckskins, led the attack on the real stagecoaches and homesteads. As violent outsiders seemingly watching for a chance to "break out," Native performers authenticated the Wild West in ways that no mere cowboy could match, and Cody's own power drew from the presence of the show's Indian people. Grafted atop the relentless reality of these props—human and otherwise—were stories, familiar generic narratives of Indian attack and rescue. Not nearly as true as the props themselves, these narratives nonetheless reflected expectations so commonsensical as to have their own natural realism. The combination of expectation, authenticity, and theatrical mimicry proved unstoppable, and, for over thirty years, the formula captivated audiences across Europe and the United States.

The words and deeds spilling out of Wild West performances and public relations materials told three broad stories of expectation about Indian people. First, and most apparent in the show itself, was a story about Indian violence and American character. Underpinning this story was a second one, concerning the pacification that had necessarily preceded the Indian performances found in the Wild West. That story was most frequently on display in the camp area backstage. The show preferred to bury a third set of narratives dealing with Indians as modern people. Even when such stories emerged—and they did so only when strategically necessary—they focused crudely on the Wild West's role as an engine of assimilation and social progress. Nonetheless, stories about Indian people and the contemporary world, cast as anomaly or humor, escaped from behind the veil. Perhaps nowhere were these three narrative trajectories so visibly concentrated as in the media- and culture-fest that accompanied Chicago's 1893 Columbian Exposition.

FOREGROUNDING SCENES:
CHICAGO 1893

The Columbian Exposition, designed to celebrate the four-hundredth anniversary of Columbus's arrival in the Americas, drew over twenty-seven million visitors over the course of six months, making it a true mass audience event and a powerful landmark of American self-representation. The exposition came in the midst of a series of crises of expectation that followed the Civil War. Industrial leaders consolidated economic power and fought viciously with the workers who dared to challenge their supremacy. The resulting anxieties dovetailed nicely with worries about the changing character of European immigration and accompanying changes in the urban social fabric. New racial dynamics played off one another—and not only around the new European immigrants. African Americans confronted racial projects aimed at replacing Reconstruction with Jim Crow segregation. Indian people saw their final military defeats, and Chinese, Japanese, and Mexican immigrant laborers were racialized, excluded, and largely controlled. At the same time, the productivity of modern industrial technology bumped headlong into anxieties surrounding the impending failure of the agrarian ideal, as the western ranch economy went corporate and farmers joined the Populist Party to protest their losing position in the national economy. Content for decades to confine their colonial system to North America, Americans developed global imperial ambitions as they considered the far-flung colonies of Britain, France, and Spain. White colonists had deposed Queen Lili`uokalani and taken control of Hawaii in January 1893, only a few months before the exposition's opening. The violent seizure of Spanish holdings in 1898 was not far off, nor was explicit discussion of a new global order. A catalog of only the most obvious anxieties, these nonetheless implicated Native people at every turn—labor, race, agrarianism, indigeneity, colonialism, and assimilation to an American empire.[11]

At Chicago, the United States tried to take a collective breath and reset the expectations that powered the national imaginary. The White City that made up the exposition's central area evoked the stately classicism that Americans thought befitting of their empire of liberty. Demonstrations of scientific and technical inventiveness would define American modernity through mechanical and industrial prowess. On the Midway, ethnological exhibits explained social evolution and the New World order by displaying and ranking indigenous people from Africa, Asia, the Pacific,

and the Americas. And, as Richard White has persuasively argued, two individuals—the historian Frederick Jackson Turner and Buffalo Bill Cody—
divvied up the story of American history, consolidating two familiar narratives, each of which would define a distinctive national character.[12]

Turner's narrative came in the form of an academic paper, delivered at
a "historical congress" organized by the American Historical Association.
Studying the newly released data from the 1890 census, Turner was struck
by the statement: "There can no longer be said to be a frontier line. . . ."
American history, he argued, was the story of a succession of frontier lines,
moving from the first eastern settlements in a steady pattern of westward
migration. At each new turn, the colonist was plunged from civilization
back into an earlier stage of social development. As frontiers developed,
they rapidly recapitulated social evolution, producing out of the primitive
wilds a new American, both individualistic and democratic. The census
gave Turner a focal point around which to build what would become
known as the *frontier thesis*, but it also suggested yet another moment of
crisis: if encounters between settlers and wild landscape produced American character, democratic institutions, and the present economic order,
what, then, did it mean that the frontier was officially "closed"?[13]

The year 1890 also bounded a story that took Indian people themselves
as the centerpiece in the narration of nation. In Theodore Roosevelt's
Winning of the West (1885–1894), Buffalo Bill's Wild West, and a number
of other writings, images, and performances, American history took
shape, not as a frontiersman's struggle with wild lands, but as one long
Indian war, a violent contest in which Americans were shaped by constant
struggle with a dangerous and challenging adversary.[14] As we have seen,
the massacre at Wounded Knee marked the end of that story of struggle,
making 1890 a doubly powerful sign of change. Around that particular
year, then, the closing of Turner's frontier and the pacification of violent
Indians met in a kind of narrative harmony. That meeting seemed to define an epoch, and it could not help but raise the question of Indian status in a pacified, postfrontier world.

Not surprisingly, Buffalo Bill's Wild West proved a far more effective
popular vehicle than Turner's conference paper. Cody's show occupied a
piece of territory just outside the exposition grounds, and visitors could
move easily among the White City, the Midway, and the Wild West. They
might join the eighteen thousand people in Cody's enormous grand-
stands, viewing one of two shows per day, and taking in linked lessons
about empire, conquest, character, and social order. With its powerful

treatment of history and ideology and its spectacular action, color, and sound, the Wild West set audience expectations so vividly that its vision of an American national narrative remains evocative even today.[15]

The Wild West is every bit as important to the story I want to tell. Across the United States, and for three decades, Cody's show engaged American popular culture in ways that helped manage the tensions created as older stories of violent contest gave way to a new understanding that frontiers had closed and Indians had been—and become—pacified. That management is well demonstrated by the flurry of stories about Wild West Indians pumped out by the Chicago dailies, which offered their readers well-worn narratives of expectation, generally concerned with the potential for—and the containment of—Indian violence. "Red royalty is well represented by the seventy-eight Sioux Indians who arrived yesterday from the Pine Ridge agency," jibed the *Chicago InterOcean* in April when Cody's first performers arrived by train. Yet beneath the mocking lay an undercurrent of fear and fascination, generated by the reality that powered Cody's show (and, perhaps, by events like the Two Sticks killings, barely ten weeks past). The Indians were, according to the paper, "bad-tempered" Brules, members of Big Foot's band, "the defeated forces in the battle of Wounded Knee." The *Times* pictured the group as the most dangerous warriors of the recent uprising and noted that Pine Ridge Agent Brown had sent them purposefully, believing that "the educating contact with civilization that they will receive will effectually prevent them from any further inclinations to put on the war paint."[16]

The *Herald* recounted in detail the violent death of Lieutenant Casey, bemoaning the "cowardly crime" before celebrating the arrival of "a big Indian with his face bedaubed with paint, [who] leaped off the rear platform of a car at the Northwestern railway station at 2:30 o'clock yesterday afternoon. He gathered about his body a blue blanket, which was heavy with its beaded symbols and porcupine quills. Standing straight out from his black hair was an eagle feather and clanking upon the beads on his breast was a medal which bore the face of Columbus. This was Plenty Horses, the cruel but forgiven murderer of Lieutenant Casey, and one of the wildest bucks in the outfit."[17]

The *Herald* went on to describe Wounded Knee survivors, including Plenty Horses's wife, shot five times in the massacre, and young John Burke Low Neck, his orphaning described in prurient detail: "Lying in a draw in the hills were his mother and brothers, all of them piled beneath a bloody covering of dresses and shirts." Such reportage evoked violent histories, teasing readers with the possibility of violent retribution. Indeed, without the lingering possibility of Indian danger, containment lost its meaning and power—and containment was the order of the day. Plenty Horses now wore a Columbus medal. If wild, he was also forgiven and, by virtue of his appearance at the Chicago celebration, rehabilitated. The orphan was equally evocative and received substantial media play. Like Plenty Horses, he too had been incorporated into the nation. His joint adoption by Low Neck, a Standing Rock leader, and John Burke, Cody's manager, suggested an Indian future made possible by Indian partnership with a great white father figure.[18]

All the papers promised the arrival of major Lakota leaders, such as Red Cloud, Two Strike, Young Man Afraid of His Horses, Kicking Bear, and Short Bull. Rain in the Face, the supposed killer of Custer, proved a frequent touchstone, for his camp sat near the cabin in which Sitting Bull had been killed, the dwelling laboriously disassembled and transported from the Grand River in South Dakota. Writers could not resist juxtaposing the deaths of the two opposing leaders, with Custer a compelling symbol of the danger of violent Indians and Sitting Bull an equally violent sign of Indian containment. Violence was the omnipresent theme in these tales, containment the understood reality, and, in this, the coverage echoed the message of the Wild West's performance. In each setting, the presence of Indian leadership served as both threatening titillation and public display of national incorporation. The Tribune made clear who was in control: "Col. Cody with a single sentence ordered the Indians to go to work on their tepees." So pacified, domesticated, and contained was the situation that the InterOcean felt comfortable flirting with the ultimate unexpected, miscegenation: "Suburban passengers crowded into the cars with the Indians, and it was not an exceptional thing to find some gayly dressed Pine Ridge red man sharing a seat with a dainty-looking Hyde Park debutante. The girls enjoyed it, and the Indians did not seem very much annoyed."[19]

If the Wild West told the same stories of violent potential and pacification, it tended to divide them up between arena show and backstage camp. The arena performances traded in obvious ways on ideas of violent Indian threat, fended off by cavalry and Cody. More interesting was the camp, which did the real work of managing ideas of containment and pacification while still laying claim to the authenticity of Indian danger. One of the show's most masterful strategies was its insistent lifting of the curtain between stage and backstage in order to show Indian actors in everyday profile and to blur the line between their performance and their lived lives. Thus, it was necessary that Indians live on the show grounds in tipis and that their camp be open to visitors. Indeed, in most Wild West setups (such as that at Chicago), audiences moved through parts of the Indian camp on their way from the entrance to the grandstand. A constant dialogue unfolded between the show and the camp, with the real of the backstage being fed into the performance's imaginative universe. At the same time, the violence represented in the show defined the experience of a postshow camp visit, which seemed that much more real as the threat of danger lingered in the air with the dissipating smoke.

The dialogue between the historical, the actual, and the representational that characterized the Wild West's social geography was profoundly gendered. If the arena seemed a play space of masculine conflict and domination—the plains of the nineteenth century—the camp was, like the newly pacified reservations, domesticated, with women and children visible and tipis well tended (often with steps and rough porch areas). Directed at an arena full of passive white spectators, show Indians' highly masculine violence could, in fact, be simultaneously empowering (in relation to the hapless audience) and disempowering (in their perpetual defeat at the hands of Cody). Even as audiences quailed before the physical fact of the charging warriors, however, they could take comfort in the knowledge of their own social domination, which became visible as they strolled through the domestic space of the camp after the show. Feminized passivity now characterized the pacified Indians, while the audience took on a masculine authority derived from ethnographic pretense and the difference in status between the paying customer and the performer. Every experience within and around the show, then, helped spectators to a visceral understanding of the expectations surrounding violence and pacification. Native performance itself, not surprisingly, worked to the same ends (see figure 9).

The Wild West's realism was not simply a painstaking simulation of a person, a place, or an event. For Cody, Miles, and the Lakotas—and for many of the other Indian people working as performers at the exposition—acting worked differently than it did in the nation's theaters. Cody believed in a form of representation that was really reenacting. Realistic and accurate representation meant reproducing that which had already happened, using, not substitutes, but the original participants, the original objects, the original script. The representation would be demonstrably original because those doing the reenacting would not be performing

FIGURE 9. Indian Camp, Buffalo Bill's Wild West. Photograph by Nate Salsbury. A single-strand wire fence demarks the Lakota camp but does not prohibit entry. Indeed, the steps and the open tipi flap offer clear points of access for the postperformance visitor. (Denver Public Library, Western History Department, NS-431.)

in a theatrical sense. As the original (historical) actors, they would simply be doing what they had once done . . . over again. Audiences' sense that Indians were not acting but reenacting originated in a series of unspoken dialogues—between their historical actions and their performative ones, between the show's melodramatic narratives and its authenticating details, between the real of the backstage camp and the realism of the performances. These dialogues suggested that Indians were *not* performing, that they were simply reliving a real past in which they remained stuck. From a different angle in the audience, one might also have been able to see something more disturbing: in the smothering omnipresence of a white racial gaze, show Indians were, in fact, *always* performing Indianness, whether they wanted to or not, twenty-four hours a day.

The belief that Indians were historical reenactors foreclosed other stories, including the possibility that Indian people occupied the same space and time as their white audiences. The powerful cultural weight of Cody's claim to reenact suggests exactly why the Wild West downplayed a third story line, one that celebrated the unexpected and did, in fact, place Indians in the contemporary world. Cody mobilized stories of Indian modernity and action only as necessary. As L. G. Moses has detailed, for example, when reformers attacked the shows for holding Indians back, allowing them to relive the old days to excess, Cody and others claimed that the Wild West was educational, not only for audiences, but also for performers. Cody argued, according to Moses, "that traveling would enable the Show Indians to appreciate the inevitability of progress as represented in the numbers, achievements, and technology of 'the white race.' Further, when they returned to their reservations, Show Indians would serve their people as advocates for change."[20] In other words, even as the show reenacted past violence and recent pacification, Cody sometimes argued that Indian people existed in modernity, that they might function as contemporary social and political actors, and that the show helped these things happen.

The Indian modern slipped out in Chicago in 1893, as the dailies peppered their violence/pacification narratives with anecdotes of the unexpected. When an English soldier commented on the rainy weather to the Wild West veteran Rocky Bear with the pidgin "How! Heavy wet," Rocky Bear was said to have responded with his best British accent: "Yes, it's rawther nawsty, me boy." The humorous inversion was, of course, the product of Rocky Bear's eighteen months in Europe, and the paper was quick to point out that, though many of the season's Indian performers had not been a hundred miles from Pine Ridge, a number of them had been to England, Paris, and New York. The *Times* gleefully jested that the wages of Wild West Indians were vanishing in the face of their unexpected love for the fair: "The red warriors are destitute of wampum. They no longer have the wherewithal to buy corn and their noblest braves are broken in spirit and hide their faces in their blankets to conceal the unmanly tears. It is the merry-go-round that has done this thing." On June 16, the *Tribune* told an even better story. Two former members of Cody's Wild West, having left the show while abroad two years before, had popped up in Sydney, Australia, where they had become a public nuisance and were regarded as street-partying vagrants. As Moses reports, American Bear and Eagle Elk became part of a diplomatic negotiation regarding the payment of their transportation home. Who was liable for these world explorers—the American government, the Australian government, or Cody himself, who had committed to his performers' safe return home?[21]

The Wild West left behind a trail of similar stories of Indian modernity. They appeared in images of Indians in the gondolas of Venice or playing Ping-Pong backstage. When Wild West Indians hopped into cars or learned to ride bicycles, the inextricable sameness of the Indian and white worlds reared an unexpected head. When performers, such as Hampa Nespa (who willingly worked in European circuses between 1887 and 1909), abandoned Cody for long-term careers in Europe, or when Wild West–seasoned actors joined up with one of the many groups performing as part of the Kickapoo Medicine Show, Indian people were crafting, not simply their own inferior version of modernity, but a shared global world. When groups of Sioux headed off to camp in a Cincinnati park or a New York exposition for the summer, one could see both a long heritage of cross-cultural performance and the opportunities opened up by the Wild West. American Bear, Eagle Elk, Rocky Bear, the merry-go-round riders, the Ping-Pong players, and others were usually figured as anomalies amid a range of more muscular stories that reaffirmed Americans' familiar expectations. Yet hundreds of Indian people took advantage of Wild West tours in order to adventure around the world, producing the modern through their mobility and their works of representation. Telling funny stories about such anomalous Indians helped white Americans lay claim to a separate world, one from which Indian people were to be excluded. Beneath all the mocking static, however, such tales were, first and foremost, Indian stories about Indian encounters with and actions on a modern world.[22]

Armed with a sense of how the Wild West negotiated American expectations concerning Indians and with a brief counternarrative of Indian modernity, we can now return to an earlier question: Why did Native people decide to join Wild West shows (and, later, film companies) in significant numbers? Reservation regimes, we know, meant to fix Indian subjects in place and make them visible through rolls, inspections, and institutional oversights. For opposition leaders such as Sitting Bull, such scrutiny could prove even more intense. In the midst of reservation fixity, the Wild West promised extraordinary mobility, and commentators have been right to point to it as a form of escape from agency surveillance. Imagine that you are Short Bull or Kicking Bear, Ghost Dance leaders locked up in a Chicago stockade who were offered the chance to join the Wild West on European tour. "For six weeks I have been a dead man," Kicking Bear is reputed to have said to Cody. "Now that I see you I am alive again."[23] Sitting Bull agreed to join the show during the 1885–1886 season at least in part because of the relative freedom it granted him, and he was surely not alone in seeing in the show a measure of liberty.[24] While interpreters exercised some control over actors, Indian performers were not simply confined to the Wild West camp but rather strolled the streets of the world's cities. A celebrity performer, such as Sitting Bull or the subsequent Wild West spokesmen Red Shirt and Rocky Bear, often received invitations to meet social and political elites wherever the show stopped.

And it stopped everywhere. For almost thirty years, Buffalo Bill Indians toured the United States. Between 1887 and 1906, they regularly toured Great Britain and Europe. Each year, between seventy-five and one hundred Indian people, often recruited from Pine Ridge or other South Dakota reservations, joined the show. Indeed, the most significant regular flow of money onto that reservation between 1883 and 1913 may have come from Lakota performers traveling nationally and internationally. The late 1880s and early 1890s in particular were starving times for many Indian communities, and performing represented, not simply escape, but also food and wages for Indian actors from a number of reservations. A host of imitators—Mexican Joe, Pawnee Bill, Frederick Cummins, and the Miller Brothers 101 Ranch, among others—offered Indian travelers of many tribes similar opportunities.

Other Indian people spoke not so much of escape or economics as of cultural prerogatives. Some, for example, felt a sense of mission to serve as scouts charged with finding out about the United States. Luther Standing Bear, who left home for the Carlisle Indian School and later worked for Cody as a translator, recalled his desire to demonstrate bravery by leaving home: "At that time we did not trust the white people very strongly. But the thought of going away with what was to us an enemy, to a place we knew nothing about, just suited me." Black Elk wanted to investigate for himself: "I wanted to see the great water, the great world and the ways of the white men . . . if the white man's ways were better, why I would like to see my people live that way." Some Native people used the shows to recapture remembered lives. Joe Rockboy, a veteran of years of Wild Westing, recalled his enjoyment: "It gave me a chance to get back on a horse and act it out again." A number of Indian people also hoped that, by moving intimately in and among white Americans, they could educate their audiences to the virtues of Indian cultures.[25]

Traveling with the Wild West provided Indian people the chance to craft new visions of themselves, for their performance labor drew on the same blurring of self, history, and image that made Cody a prototypical modern celebrity. Cody set the pattern: realism and authenticity produced cultural authority (with Cody claiming, e.g., that the Wild West was not just a show but one of the nation's premier educational institutions). Indian people stood at the heart of the show's claim to be authentic, and actors like Red Shirt and Rocky Bear shared in Cody's claim to authority, performing not simply as wild Indians but as visiting dignitaries involved in cultural and political exchange.

The handsome, charismatic Red Shirt had a long career with Cody. His 1887 arrival in London for the American Exhibition, timed to coincide with Queen Victoria's Silver Jubilee, occasioned admiring reviews, for he knew how to give a good interview:

> In response to a question put to him Ogalisha replies, "I never saw the ocean or a boat before, but I enjoyed the trip very much. I look forward with pleasure to seeing this country. I should like to make friends among the natives over here." This he enunciated in truly regal fashion. Having finished he inclined his head, and I could well-nigh imagine the rest—"I have spoken, go thy way." The whole action of the man tallied with what we read, the only difference being that we are accustomed to associate this language with the backwoods, while the above took place on the Thames.[26]

Red Shirt and his friends visited Westminster Abbey and other churches, joined Cody at the actor Henry Irving's performances of *Faust*, and entertained in his tipi former (and future) Prime Minister William

Gladstone and the entourage of the Prince of Wales. He spoke with Queen Victoria and, with the other show Indians, shook her hand. Of course, the papers wanted to hear his thoughts on the various meetings, and Red Shirt was unfailingly gracious and diplomatic. As Alan Gallop points out, the British press found him "a warrior, philosopher, and poet rolled into one," and it came to a new appreciation of the ways in which American conquest had adversely affected Indian people—and of what it meant to be so far from home, geographically and culturally. "Red Shirt's impression of the white man's world," wrote one paper, "reads like a fragment of the Odyssey" (see figure 10).[27]

Yet Wild West travel always proved a mixed bag of opportunity and discipline—even without taking into account the ambivalence of the representational work itself. For much of the nineteenth century, for example, Native leaders were brought to Washington, D.C., in part because the long trips served as a primer on the size and power of the United States. Red Jacket, Keokuk, Black Hawk, Lone Wolf, Ouray, Pushmataha—these were only a few of the Indian leaders who traveled East. Some were awed; others were not. Few, however, failed to note the odds against them. An implacable foe in the years leading up to the Treaty of 1868, for example, the Lakota leader Red Cloud was led by an 1870 trip east to craft a more temperate realpolitik that recognized the military, demographic, and industrial power of the United States.[28]

Travel had a long history as a tool for crafting Indian subjects into docility, and the travels of the Wild West were assumed to be no exception. If Sitting Bull's 1885–1886 tour with Buffalo Bill Cody offered freedom, it also seemed likely to teach that most recalcitrant of Sioux leaders not to challenge American authority. And, if Kicking Bear and Short Bull welcomed their release from the stockade, they were sentenced to the Wild West in order that they might suffer placelessness and anomie, learn to fear and respect America's might, and be removed from any position of influence among their people. Indeed, after eleven months, Kicking Bear and other Ghost Dancers had had enough and demanded to go home—even if that meant the stockade.

TURNING POINT: THE INDIAN WARS

The Wild West proved one of the great transitional institutions of the late nineteenth century and the early twentieth. It managed the ideological tensions involving violence and pacification. It introduced large numbers of Indian people to wage labor and to the representation of

FIGURE 10. Red Shirt. With beautiful quillwork, a Ulysses Grant peace medal, and a steady gaze off camera, Red Shirt modeled noble primitivism and containment even as he took the opportunity to travel the world and engage in cultural diplomacy. (Library of Congress LC-USZ62 101337.)

Indianness for non-Indian audiences. It built out of celebratory national history a case for the twentieth century's cult of individual celebrity. Not only did the show perform the end of the American frontier; it quite literally embodied it. Even as Cody and his cast transformed the show's content to keep up with postfrontier empire, they aged visibly before their audiences' eyes—and drew attention to that aging through a series of farewell tours. The farewells were those, not simply of Cody, or of the cast, or even of the thing called *the Wild West*, but of those who claimed to know the real West itself.

At Cody's Chicago screening of *The Indian Wars*, one might have observed both the old of the Wild West and the new distinctions that would mark the world of film. Reporters who attended did not fail to extract the showman's familiar lesson, centered on the uncanny relation between the real and the thing being represented. "There," reported the *New York Times*, "was Gen. Nelson A. Miles in the audience, silent and erect, watching Gen. Nelson A. Miles galloping at the head of his troop into the ravine of Wounded Knee. There was Col. Schunk in the audience, intent and interested, watching Col. Schunk skirmishing over the hills of the Bad Lands."[29] But the lesson of the film was not quite the same as that of the show. The Wild West had long traded on the idea that key historical figures were simply re-performing history, with their bodies and selves guaranteeing the accuracy of the performance. The film, with its original casting, was a bit like that. Now, however, historical figures were *watching* their own reenactments, and the guarantee of truth came from their position, not as actors, but as spectators. Where the Wild West had forced viewers to walk through an Indian camp that proclaimed, "This is not a show," film productions replaced backstage authenticity with audience response. The real Miles in the audience imparted authority to the flickering Miles on the screen. That Schunk watched himself without objection suggested that the camera had gotten it right, that Cody and his crew had made a picture that bordered on the real. This shift in authority, from the real performer to the spectator's judgment and desire, would be key to the move away from Cody's reenactment of nineteenth-century Indian violence and toward the imaginative images of Indian violence that would characterize the twentieth century. With the retirement of Cody's cohort, the reenacting of Miles, Schunk, Red Shirt, Black Elk, Standing Bear, and others—based (at least in theory) on history as authentic memory— would give way to the imaginative acting of those who had *not* been there, whose loyalty was as much to the audience as it was to the self or the past.[30]

The Indian Wars itself, however, suggests that we not draw this line too sharply. The Wild West had been one of the early targets of Thomas Edison's film camera, and nickelodeon shorts of Wild West acts had been popular in the first years of motion picture viewing. The show coalesced out of dime novels, stage theatricals, rodeo contests, and circuses, and, through *The Indian Wars*, it poured its accumulation into the new medium. Film technicians looked to the Wild West for examples of lighting and staging. Its narratives became staples of film storytelling. In important ways, plots, figures, techniques, and personnel connected the Wild West's insistent realism with the developing craft of film, which brought its own argument for realism in the precision of photographic reproduction.

And so, in 1913, Cody went to Pine Ridge to reunite Indian actors from the Wild West and to cobble together histories and images onto nitrate film. Given Cody's status, it is easy to imagine The Indian Wars as a blockbuster hit. Instead, it flopped badly. Obsessed with precision reenactment, the film failed to pay enough attention to dramatic narrative structures and story lines. Indeed, Cody's love of reenactment, fired by Miles's mania for accuracy, may have doomed the picture to be, frankly, boring. By 1914 (when the film was released), Americans were increasingly coming to see Wounded Knee as an unfortunate episode on which it was best not to dwell. But it was not simply that Cody proved unable to translate the excitement of the Wild West to the screen or that the subject was unpopular, though such may have been the case. Rather, the film seems to have lacked many of the visual and narrative strategies already well developed in the mainstream film industry. In duplicating the models and expectations set decades earlier by the Wild West, The Indian Wars failed to grapple with new issues and expectations important to the filmgoers of 1914.[31]

By the early 1910s, the industry had already established a significant track record in the production of Indian and western subjects. "From 1910 to 1913 alone," calculates the film historian Michael Hilger, "one hundred or more films about Indians appeared each year, and throughout most of the silent period the American Indian remained a very popular subject."[32] While frequently paying homage to the Wild West's familiar economy of violence/pacification, early filmmakers also expanded plots, settings, images, and actions. In the process, they both reflected and refigured the changing expectations of audiences. Many viewers no longer need contemplate the moment of pacification. The frontier, and, with it, the possibility of Indian violence, had ceased to be a practical concern. What might have mattered more immediately was the problem resulting from pacification and assimilation: How were non-Indian Americans to think of Indian people who functioned as part of the same social, cultural, and historical moment as they themselves?

Luther Standing Bear had served as interpreter during the Wild West's 1902 season in Great Britain, and he was on his way east for a second year when he was caught up in the show's 1903 Maywood train wreck, in which three Lakota actors died and twenty-seven, Standing Bear among them, were seriously injured.[33] A graduate of the first class at the Carlisle Indian School, Standing Bear had long tried to figure out ways in which he might speak for Indian people while negotiating the new world of modern America. He worked for Cody and others as a translator and go-between, a role he would maintain throughout his life. In 1906, Standing Bear, his brother Henry, and one hundred Pine Ridge Oglalas traveled to New York City to appear at the Hippodrome, in an international show that ran through the winter season. On trips like these, outside the confines of the Wild West, Native performers like Standing Bear came to see that they were part of a national cohort of Indian people working, not just in Wild West shows, but in circuses, traveling medicine shows, urban revues, lecture circuits, and sideshows. The Standing Bear brothers became particularly active in this world (which led the Pine Ridge agent—who would have preferred to see them farming—to characterize the pair as "shocking failures").[34]

The Hippodrome trip—followed up by a season of East Coast lecturing—marks a watershed in Luther Standing Bear's career. As he put it: "I met many people who were really interested in learning the truth in regard to the Indians. I determined that, if I could only get the right sort of people interested, I might be able to do more for my own race off the reservation than to remain there under the iron rule of the white agent."[35] Standing Bear's subsequent career was dedicated to the politics of representation—to getting the "right sort" of people interested in the right way. After stints back at Pine Ridge, Walthill, Nebraska, and Sioux Falls left him seeking a warmer climate, he sought out the Miller Brothers 101 Ranch show. A combination ranch and Wild West show based in Oklahoma but active in California, the Miller Brothers 101 Ranch served in the early twentieth century as a primary bridge between the Wild West tradition and the new media of film.

In 1912, Standing Bear became a prototypical California immigrant, relocating west in order to restore his failing midwestern health. Contemplating the film world's possibilities for someone with his experience as an actor and translator, he wrote the film producer Thomas Ince—already working with the Miller Brothers—and asked him for a job. The producer mailed Standing Bear travel money and brought him to "Inceville," one of the first great location camps of the early film era. There, Standing Bear would work with William S. Hart, Douglas Fairbanks, and others, maintaining an active film career until 1935 and authoring five books before his death in 1939 (see figure 11).

As an author who remains in print today, and, indeed, one who stands as a significant figure in American Indian intellectual history, Standing Bear has become unusually visible to us. He was, however, only one of many Indian people who took up film acting as the Wild West shows went into decline. Another Pine Ridge Oglala, William Eagleshirt, also began a film career in 1912 with Thomas Ince, who contemplated making him a lead actor. A handsome man with a winning smile, Eagleshirt received a few substantial roles and wrote a scenario for *War on the Plains*, one of the many Indian films being cranked out of the Bison 101 studios. Princess Red Wing, a Nebraska Ho-Chunk named Lillian St. Cyr, also worked for Bison, appearing with her husband, the actor-director-writer James Young Deer. William Darkcloud (Elijah Tahamont) arrived in California in 1911 with D. W. Griffith, appearing in many of that director's films. (Griffith, best known for *Birth of a Nation*, churned out a number of Indian films during his early years, as did the future big-name director Cecil B. DeMille.) Darkcloud's daughter Beulah also enjoyed a career working with Griffith. John Big Tree, an Onondaga from New York, came west in 1915 and would eventually act in over a hundred films, including the John Ford classics *Stagecoach* and *She Wore a Yellow Ribbon*. The Cheyenne actor Richard Davis Thunderbird, a veteran of Carlisle and the Miller Brothers 101 Ranch shows, appeared in a number of films during the 1910s. Tote DuCrow worked with Douglas Fairbanks during the 1910s and 1920s. William Eagle Eye was active at the same time, appearing with Lillian Gish and Raoul Walsh.[36]

For many producers, the need for authenticity—inculcated through decades of Wild West shows—led to work for Indian actors. Edison, for example, hyped its 1910 film *Riders of the Plains* with the boast that it took "considerable pride because the participants are not make believe actors . . . the Indians are real Indians."[37] F. E. Moore's 1913 production of *Hiawatha* used all Indian actors. *Moving Picture World* praised their work, noting that it was "a breath of fresh air to see real human Indians enacting before us an old Indian legend."[38] Vitagraph, Selig, Lasky, Bison, and

FIGURE 11. Luther Standing Bear in Hollywood.
(Denver Public Library, Western History Department, X-31857.)

other prominent early companies all had Indian actors on their payrolls. Particularly as producers and audiences realized that the film camera rendered the theatricality of stage acting overblown, naturalism in acting allowed Indians to recapitulate their Wild West performance experience. Indian actors who simply acted like themselves in front of the camera were more believable than white actors in redface—or so some critics asserted.

We should not overestimate the power of Indianness in assisting Native actors in getting roles. Many studios preferred to use white actors in makeup rather than recruit Indians, certainly for starring roles. The early critic Ernest Dench found superior those white actors who had "made a study of Indian life," for Indians themselves regressed before the camera to savagery. (Echoing Buffalo Bill, Dench insisted that Indian actors "occasionally manage to smuggle real bullets into action" and that directors needed armed guards to protect against Indian treachery.) Of his days working for Bison, Standing Bear would recall bitterly: "We real Indians were held back, while white 'imitators' were pushed to the front." Over the course of the twentieth century, many of the same filmmakers who embraced the imagery surrounding Indians proved reluctant to embrace Indian people. As many critics have argued, Hollywood has never been a particularly friendly place for Native Americans.[39]

At the same time, however, we should not underestimate the power of Indianness. Indian identity proved compelling enough that at least one actress, Josephine Workman, was re-created as an Indian, Mona Darkfeather, and appeared in over seventy films, her allure dependent on her Indianness. Certainly, Workman was not alone in edging into some identification as Native. Scholars attempting to craft a picture of the film industry's beginnings usually list some thirty Indian performers who appear in various credits in the movies of the early twentieth century. These include actors such as Big Bear, Blue Eagle, Edward Little, Chief Many Treaties (William Hazlett), Nipo Strongheart, Molly Spotted Elk, Chief Thunder Cloud, Dove Eye Dark Cloud, White Eagle (Jack Miller), Chief Phillippi, Two Feathers, Little Thunder, Big Moon, Daniel Yowlatchie, Standing Bear, Jim Thorpe, and Will Rogers, among others. Given the numbers of Indians who served out shorter and more anonymous careers as extras in places like Inceville, we can reasonably assume that the number of Hollywood Indians ran to several hundred.[40]

In many cases, Hollywood Indians' decisions to pursue performance echoed those of the show Indians in the Wild West. In February 1913, for

FIGURE 12. *Inceville Sioux. Thomas Ince (center right) with William Eagleshirt (left) and Two Lance (right), 1912. (Marc Wanamaker, Bison Archives.)*

instance, *Photoplay* reported that the picture business was "a veritable bonanza" for the western Indian reservations: "Over 100 Sioux Indians from the Pine Ridge reservation are working for [Kay Bee], and with every five a chief is required. The Indians receive from $7 to $10 per week and their expenses, while the chiefs are responsible for their various bands, and are paid from $10 to $12 per week."[41] By 1916, with 121 Indian people working at Inceville, Ince moved to build a school, as the actors were rarely before the camera more than three or four hours each day and he claimed to feel an obligation for their uplift and education. Noting that the Inceville "tribe" contained several Carlisle graduates suitable for instructorships, he commented on the excitement of the actors, including "Chief Two-Lance, the ninety-two year old warrior, who is reputed to be worth approximately a quarter million dollars in property holdings" (see figure 12).[42]

Like earlier Wild West Indians, film actors in places like Inceville—many already sharing reservation, tribal, or family ties—developed new collective identities around their work. The Inceville Sioux, in particular, seem to have brought preexisting relationships forged through Wild West performance (though the roster of performers rotated periodically, and the group was probably not stable enough to be considered a community). By midcentury, there existed a small but coherent Hollywood Indian community, which, according to one report, considered claiming a discrete tribal identity, the product of a decidedly modern ethnogenesis. In 1940, for example, the Cherokee actor Victor Daniels apparently applied to the Bureau of Indian Affairs for federal recognition for a new tribe—what one reporter called the "DeMille Indians" of Hollywood.[43]

TRANSITIONAL SCENE:
FROM WILD WEST TO FILM

In the years prior to 1912, film producers across the country churned out short one-reelers and experimented with location, cast, and plot. In the winter of 1908, producers from the Selig company brought a group of Sioux Wild West actors to Chicago during the off-season. The actors camped near the Selig plant and acted whenever the weather was good, making films showing Indian depredations and the arrival of the cavalry. The experiment proved successful, and, in the fall of 1909, a Selig troupe journeyed to Oklahoma to work with the Miller Brothers 101 Ranch show. Later that year, Selig would contract with another show—Will Dickey's Circle D Ranch—for cowboys, Indians, and props. Film companies, it turns out, fit well into the annual subsistence cycle of the now-declining Wild West shows, which could tour during the summer and film during the off-season. The richness of Wild West shows' prop collections and the experience of their casts, not surprisingly, led to a boom in—and a transformation of—Indian and western pictures beginning in the fall of 1909.[44] As the historian Andrew Smith points out, chase scenes often drove plot structures in the middle of the decade (think of The Great Train Robbery, 1903), when westerns tended to work as crime dramas. By the end of the decade, however, chases had been augmented by action and battle scenes based on Wild West staging, with the surround becoming an image as dominant as the chase. The presence of the Wild West shows helped shift film conventions toward the nineteenth-century frontier violence that would largely define the twentieth-century western genre.[45]

If the Wild West helped establish the structure of much early film, California gave it a coherent base of production, replacing the East Coast as the home of the industry.[46] By 1911, six major studios operated year-round in southern California. All did cowboy and Indian pictures that mixed together the key elements of western film production: outdoor shooting in the fabulous light; complex narrative drama; professional organization and directorial vision; and a stable of actors, including Indian people like Luther Standing Bear. Thomas Ince, for example, moved from New York to California in 1912 to make Bison brand films for the New York Motion Picture Company, quickly establishing the location camp at Inceville, in Santa Ynez Canyon. Along with the camp, New York Motion Picture contracted with the Miller Brothers 101 Ranch Wild West show, which provided horses, bison, cowboys, and Indians and allowed Ince to begin making larger-budget outdoor films.[47] The cost of the deal led Ince to abandon short one-reel films in favor of longer two-reelers, which brought in greater revenue but also required a more nuanced sense of narrative and a change in the structure of distribution and payments. "It was about that time," Ince recalled later, "that Lo, the poor Indian, became an integral part of motion pictures. I must not be considered unduly immodest if I claim most of the credit."[48]

In fact, Ince *was* being unduly immodest. The films coming out of Inceville, with their large casts, ready prop supply, and spacious western landscapes, hewed closely to the Wild West show, with its heavy reliance on Indian action. But they were only one strand in the broader fabric of representations of Indian people. Produced by a clutch of competing studios, these films developed plotlines and characters in a number of other ways. Ince did understand, however, that his films were not frontier variety shows à la Cody and that they therefore required linear story lines, introductions and conclusions, character development, motive, and clear causes and effects. Compare, for example, the cool reception of Cody's *Indian Wars* to the far more positive reviews of one of Ince's first California efforts, *Custer's Last Fight*, a film version of one of the Wild West's perennial acts. The three-page review of *Custer's Last Fight* in *Moving Picture World*, for example, proclaimed the film's greatest virtue to be its "serious attempt . . . to produce an accurate account of Custer's defeat" (see figure 13).[49]

Unlike Cody's "accurate" battle films, however, Ince's films carefully framed the narrative, setting up dramatic motive with the fictional killing of an "innocent botanist" and his helper, and ending with sentimental effect, a little girl placing a wreath on the Custer memorial. Ince introduced character and conflict, most notably between Tom Custer and Rain in the Face. He showed the tender affection between the general and his wife and had Tom Custer die "a soldier's death" in his brother's arms. In fact, if there was anything weak in the film, *Moving Picture World*'s reviewer observed, it was the battle sequences: "The audience in front is often con-

HERE SOON!

A Glorious Epic of America's Last Frontier!

"CUSTER'S Last Fight"

STUPENDOUS
COLOSSAL
GIGANTIC!

ONE YEAR IN THE
MAKING

FIVE MASSIVE
REELS

CUSTER'S SEMI-CENTENNIAL

COMMEMORATING THE 50TH ANNIVERSARY OF THAT TRAGIC DISASTER OF 1876

EDUCATIONAL!
EVERY SCHOOL BOY AND GIRL
SHOULD SEE IT!

TRUE AND AUTHENTIC

THE NEW—BIG AND ORIGINAL VERSION OF THE
FAMOUS MASSACRE OF LITTLE BIG HORN.

WITH A CAST OF 2,000

This is a picture every red-blooded American will want to see. In it the great plainsman and scout, Col. Geo. Custer lives over again, as well as his gallant comrades.

True, authentic and faithful in every detail is the picturization of the great Custer Massacre at Little Big Horn—where the dashing Custer and his command, the Seventh U. S. Cavalry, were led into ambush by thousands of Bloodthirsty Indians under Sitting Bull and slain to the last man.—An event that is written down in history as the very pinnacle of Sublime Heroic effort in the face of doom.

A MONUMENTAL TRIBUTE TO THE DEEDS AND PATRIOTISM OF THE AMERICAN PIONEER—A GIFT TO THE YOUTH OF AMERICA

DEDICATED to the spirit and patriotism of the American Pioneer; that the younger generation of today may know and never forget the hardships and perils of the pioneers who laid the foundation of the great American heroism of today.

General Geo. Custer—America's greatest fighter and plainsman, is gone, but the gallant fight with his comrades at Little Big Horn, which though lost, has inspired and thrilled men of all races ever since.

A PICTURE YOU CANNOT AFFORD TO MISS—SEE IT BY ALL MEANS!

FIGURE 13. Broadside, Custer's Last Fight (1912). The advertisements for the film echoed the Cody tradition, emphasizing educational benefits and authenticity. At the same time, however, Custer's Last Fight engaged new possibilities for film narrative and visual interest. (Museum of the American West collection, Autry National Center.)

fused if not completely bewildered by the movement of troops in a delineation purely historical and very naturally loses interest in what may easily appear to be a meaningless conflict." In other words, the very strength of Cody's film—its historical and military precision—proved the weakness in Ince's because it confused an audience thirsty for story line, sentiment, and expectation, all of which Ince was ready to provide.[50]

PLOT STRUCTURE: THE INDIAN PICTURE

The initial California companies were soon joined by others, and together they created a genre of "Indian pictures," distinct from the early frontier pictures and from the westerns that would follow. Many of these Indian pictures built plots, not around the Wild West spectacular, but around the easily produced domestic melodrama. Tightly contained by its small cast and familial setting, the domestic melodrama was prone to plot repetition, a danger compounded by the need to move films rapidly to distribution. Few producers took the time to innovate, which led critics like W. Stephen Bush to complain of the films' often-formulaic quality:

> Always the same plot, the same scenery, the same impossible Indians, the wicked halfbreed, the beautiful red maidens, the fierce warriors, the heroic cowboys, the flight from the Indian village at night. The last scene, which is hardly ever omitted, is especially diverting. Either the "lovely maiden" or the "faithful squaw" steals out of the tepee, lingers among the sleeping Indians, at least one of whom is a restless sleeper and then making about as much noise as a monkey in a hardware store, escapes and warns the white man or somebody else, it does not really matter much whom.[51]

Along with the complaints launched by critics like Bush, the film summaries published by *Moving Picture World* allow us to identify plot structures that helped set the expectations of Indians that audiences would carry home with them. In a number of films, Indians act only in relation to other Indians. They love, betray, elope, commit suicide, or feign death, à la *Romeo and Juliet*. Most such films offered portrayals not so much of Indian life as of the conventions of noble savagery, with an emotional range characterized more by sympathy than by violence. Brushed by romantic primitivism, these films do not seem nearly as curious and compelling as a second (and larger) set of narratives in which Indians and whites interact across and in terms of racial and cultural boundaries. In these films, Indian racial difference is actively *made* in relation to non-Indians, and it is usually made palpable through cross-race romance.[52]

Romantic race crossing has a long history in American writing and theater, not simply with regard to Indian people, but whenever writers have wished to imagine or engage race and gender relations. Colonial imagery has often paired white European men with Indian women in order to legitimate colonization in relation to the indigenous landscape. In early film, as the historian Andrew Smith has pointed out, there is no underestimating the impact of Edwin Milton Royle's *The Squaw Man*, which used this particular structure in setting expectations for the cross-race film dramas that followed. *The Squaw Man* began as a Broadway stage play but was remade several times as a film, including three versions by Cecil B. DeMille alone.[53]

In *The Squaw Man*, white masculine nobility is richly signified by the British elite James Wynnegate (that extra *n* and *e* tell the tale!), in love with his cousin Henry's wife, Diana. Scandal involving Henry seems to implicate James, who is compelled to flee to the American west, taking on the more prosaic name Jim Carson. There, he rescues the Indian maid Naturich from the clutches of the evil Cash Hawkins. When Hawkins seeks his revenge on Carson, Naturich kills the bad man, saving Jim, not simply from Hawkins, but from having to kill—an act of which Indians are, of course, quite capable.[54] Jim takes up with Naturich, and they have a child and build a life together. Of course, in the west, this relationship makes Jim/James a "squaw man," and, when Diana arrives on the scene bearing, along with her white womanhood, the news of Henry's death and Jim's exoneration, she hardly approves of the situation. Naturich does the right thing, however, killing herself so that her lover and son are free to return to England and reap the benefits of civilization and white-on-white marriage. Suicide proved a necessity in the story, which argued for an essential racial difference: Indians like Naturich simply could not learn the behavioral codes that would allow them to live happily ever after in the civilized world. Naturich's gender matters here as well, for Indian women tended to be the ones most prone to suicide, while Indian men more often turned savage, in a hypermasculine and violent sort of way. A number of early films echoed this story line, with Indian women offering whites access through marriage to their primitive authenticity and their land. Having transformed their white partners, the Native spouses then voluntarily eliminate themselves so that reproductive futures might follow white-on-white marriages.[55]

Even more evocative were films that pondered the possibilities of relationships between Indian men and white women. If the white man–Indian woman match offered New World identities and hybrid vigor, the inverse relationship carried a far more troublesome charge. The standard colonialist structure—white man–Indian woman—matched gender domination (men over women) with social domination (European over indigenous). But the inverse pairing—Indian men with white women—could take place only in a society in which Indians and white women both enjoyed a measure of equality with white men.[56]

Filmmakers worked over the possibility of liaisons between Indian men and white women with surprising frequency. In almost every case, we should note, the Indian man is rejected by the object of his affections. Consider, for example, D. W. Griffith's *Call of the Wild* (Biograph, 1908). Subtitled *The Sad Plight of the Civilized Redman*, the film's tuxedoed hero, George Redfeather, is toasted by high society for his success on the gridiron as a Carlisle football player. Confusing his civilization with equality, he proposes to a white woman, who turns him down. Hearing, in his anger and disappointment, "the call of the wild," Redfeather tears off his fine clothes, beats his chest, grabs a bottle, and returns angrily to his tribe. His warriors capture the woman in the woods, and Redfeather is about to take "savage" vengeance when she appeals to his sense of religion and talks her way out of the jam (see figure 14).[57]

Why this interest in what would have been called *miscegenation* at a time when even the hint of cross-race romance involving African American men would have led to a lynching? Twelve states had miscegenation laws that applied to Indian people—though these laws were not nearly as pervasive as those aimed at African Americans—and romantic, marital, and sexual relationships that crossed Indian and white racial categories were patrolled through less formal social and cultural mechanisms. In the imaginative world of film, however, cross-race relationships gave filmgoers a powerful vocabulary and a story line for thinking about the larger social issues of assimilation and equality in the postfrontier world. What would it mean if assimilated Indians were equal to such a degree that one could contemplate intermarriage? Early-twentieth-century audiences confronted a number of competing ideas swirling around these issues. There was Thomas Jefferson's old admonition that white and red would "form one people": "You will mix with us by marriage, your blood will run in our veins." As with Jefferson, however, saying it and acting on it were quite different things. More familiar was *Call of the Wild*'s opening vision of as-

THE CALL OF THE WILD

Sad Plight of the Civilized Redman

LENGTH, 988 FEET.   PRICE, 14 CENTS PER FOOT.

"Gild the farthing if you will, but it is a farthing still." So it is with the Redman. Civilization and education cannot bleach his tawny epidermis, and that will always prove an unsurmountable barrier to social distinction. He may be lauded and even lionized for deeds of valor and heroism, or excellence in scientifics, but when it comes to the social circle—never. "Lo the poor Indian", and well we may say it, for his condition is indeed deplorable; elevated to intellectual supremacy, only to more fully realize his extreme commonalty. Such was the plight of George Redfeather, the hero of this Biograph subject, upon his return from Carlisle, where he not only graduated with high honors, but was also the star of the college football team. At a reception given in his honor by Lieut. Penrose, and Indian Agent, the civilized brave meets Gladys, the Lieutenant's daughter, and falls desperately in love with her. You may be sure he is indignantly repulsed by Gladys and ordered from the house by her father. With pique he leaves, and we next find him in his own room, crushed and disappointed, for he realizes the truth: "Good enough as a hero, but not as a husband". What was the use of his struggle? As he reasons, his long suppressed nature asserts itself and he hears the call of the wild: "Out there is your sphere, on the boundless plains, careless and free, among your kind and kin, where all is truth". Here he sits; this nostalgic fever growing more intense every second, until in a fury he tears off the conventional clothes he wears, donning in their stead his suit of leather, with blanket and feathered headgear. Thus garbed, and with a bottle of whiskey, he makes his way back to his former associates in the wilds. He plans vengeance and the opportunity presents itself, when he surprises Gladys out horseback riding. He captures her after a spirited chase and intended holding her captive, but she appeals to him, calling to his mind the presence of the All Powerful Master above, who knows and sees all things, and who is even now calling to him to do right. He listens to the call of this Higher Voice and helping her to her saddle, sadly watches her ride off homeward. The film is most thrilling in situations, beautiful in photography and superbly acted.

No. 3482   CODE WORD—Revezado

Produced and Controlled Exclusively by the
American Mutoscope & Biograph Co.
II East 14th Street, New York City.

PACIFIC COAST BRANCH,   312 California Street
Los Angeles, Cal

Licensees { Kleine Optical Co.   American Mutoscope & Biograph Co.
Great Northern Film Co   Williams, Brown & Earle.

We will protect our customers and those of our licensees
against patent litigation in the use of our licensed films.

FIGURE 14. Poster, Call of the Wild (1908). The poster explicitly framed the film's narrative moral: even the most successfully assimilated Indian need not be treated as a social equal, for underneath the civilized facade lurked a savage always ready to respond to the call of the wild. (Library of Congress LC-USZ62 116691.)

similation in which perfected Indians somehow stopped being Indian yet were never to be seen as equal. They would act properly, but that didn't mean you had to let your daughter marry one.[58]

Scattered across the American cultural landscape, however, there were, in fact, readily visible examples of Indian people who had proceeded through the educational system and who participated in contemporary middle-class life. White reformers who believed in cultural transformation were placed in the position of accepting such individuals as equals in whom the Indian had seemingly been killed, leaving behind the man. The marriages to white women of Ely Parker (the first Indian Commissioner of Indian Affairs), the physician Charles Eastman, the Reverend Sherman Coolidge, the writer-activist-physician Carlos Montezuma, or Taos's Antonio Lujan might seem to some to represent the final step in this transformation to civilization. Maybe you did have to let your daughter marry one.

Race mixture, primitivism, cultural but not social equality, the bind of the antiracialist progressive reformer with a marriageable daughter—it all made for a confusing package. So, while Thomas Ince's films hung on the allure of nineteenth-century violence, many others meditated equally seriously on the problems of postconquest social relations. Why shouldn't a civilized Carlisle football player seek a white wife? The answer seemed to be that, as George Redfeather's subsequent behavior demonstrated, even the most acculturated Indian had the potential to hear the call of the wild and (like Plenty Horses in 1891) leave the contemporary world for a return to the racialist blanket. Likewise, though Indians like Naturich could lead whites to the primitivist wellsprings of nature and virtue, they did so with full knowledge that white men and white women belonged together, creating a future in which there was no room for Indians (or anyone else, for that matter).[59]

After evoking the possibilities of cross-race romance, then, miscegenation pictures usually reasserted expectations and propriety. Even such containment did not necessarily stop criticism. "Another feature of this film that will not please a good many," sniped *Moving Picture World* about *Red Deer's Devotion* (Pathé, 1911), is that "it represents a white girl and an Indian falling in love with each other. While such a thing is possible, and undoubtedly has been done many times, still there is a feeling of disgust which cannot be overcome when this sort of thing is depicted as plainly as it is here. . . . The fact that the girl's father shows the Indian away from the house rather hurriedly at the muzzle of a gun is, in a way, a modifier of the tense situation, but it will be admitted by most who see the film that it is not the sort that pleases the average audience."[60]

Expectations for postconquest social relations might also be negotiated through what might be called *race-reciprocity* films, which used models other than romance. Rather than relying on would-be lovers, such films mixed and matched gender, race, and age, with the result that one might have Indian and white women befriending one another, men befriending men, young and old befriending each other. Often in these films, a white person extends the first hand of friendship to an Indian, who later repays the kindness.[61] These films—and they are many—tend to offer generally sympathetic pictures of Indian people, with the possibility for friendship across social lines evoked and celebrated.

Consider the 1912 Selig film *The Saint and the Siwash*, in which an Indian girl repays the kindness of a white couple on the lam by killing the brutal man who would reveal their secret (and who also happens to be beating her!). The film's structure seems to suggest that the exchange of favors (kindness for protective murder) might stand for the even larger favors that might be traded between cultures. The Siwash girl gains the courage to strike back only after having been schooled in bravery by white exemplars. At the same time, however, savage inclinations remain attached to Indians—the courage instilled through her contact with whiteness takes form in a racial willingness to kill, an act from which the white protagonists are, thereby, spared.

The number of race-reciprocity films, and the plentiful variations on the theme, suggest that it was, perhaps, the most compelling way in which early filmmakers worked with the question of postfrontier social relations. These films engaged social and racial crossings without the extra charge carried by sexuality and romance. For the most part, they left white protagonists in control while humanizing Indians and establishing their gratitude, not simply for specific white favors, but for the gift of contact with civilization. Indeed, gratefulness proved a prevailing theme in such films as *Dove Eye's Gratitude* (Bison, 1909), *Red Wing's Gratitude* (Vitagraph, 1909), *The Mesquite's Gratitude* (Kalem, 1911), and, of course, *An Indian's Gratitude* (Selig, 1908).[62]

A smaller, but still significant, number of films took on the question of postfrontier race relations more directly, criticizing the treatment of Indian people and showing white racism, double standards, unfair policies, and corruption. In *A True Indian Brave* (Bison, 1910), for example, white settlers insult an Indian woman. When her husband defends her, the settlers set out to lynch the two. The clarity of the settlers' status as villains led the reviewer for *Moving Picture World* to note that the film's "conclusions will not be wholly flattering to the white man."[63] *The Red Man's Penalty* (Bison, 1911) shows a corrupt Indian agent handing out rotten meat, leading to a skirmish and the capture of two whites. The cavalry arrives, however, and the Indians are, the film makes clear, punished unjustly. A brutal removal program is portrayed in *The Red Man's View* (Biograph, 1909), one of a number of films illustrating Indian endgames as a result of white settlers' greed and ill will.[64]

Still other films tried to do what the Wild West show had refused to do: think about Indians and social relations in the contemporary world. Filmmakers sent imagined Indians off to Harvard and to Carlisle for educations and then brought them back to reservations to see what would happen. One of the most prominent of these films was *Strongheart* (Biograph, 1914), based, like *The Squaw Man*, on a stage play popular after 1905. Written by William DeMille (Cecil B. DeMille's older brother), it tells the story of the Dakota Soangataha (Strongheart), sent by his tribe to New York to study at Columbia and there exposed to all the prejudices of white America. Strongheart finds a safe niche, however, on the football team, and he wins the affection of the sister of one of his teammates. Jealous of his success, a rival steals the team's signals and passes them to an opponent. Strongheart is suspected as the leak but is able to prove himself innocent and win the heart of his temporarily doubtful lover. At the moment of his seeming success in navigating the white world (replete with successful cross-race romance!), word comes that his father has died and he must return to his tribe, which he reluctantly does. *Strongheart* tantalizes with the near success of its Indian protagonist but, in the end, reasserts fundamental racial differences: the pull of the tribal will win out over the opportunity of the modern.

The Red Woman (World 1917) mixed the miscegenation and race-reciprocity figures together, not on the nineteenth-century frontier, but in the contemporary world. Maria Temosach, the daughter of a chief (naturally), wins high honors at an eastern college but is still rejected by white society. She saves the life of a rich white man and bears his child, only to have him leave her. Unlike most cross-race romances, however, this film brings the departed lover back and concludes with a marriage and a future. *The Indian Land Grab* (Champion, 1910) shows a young Indian involved in political lobbying to prevent a crooked white politician from stealing his people's land. The politician's daughter tricks him, however, and he is to be executed by his people for his failure. At the last moment, the woman reappears, having realized both her love for the Indian and the larger social issues involved. The document that she carries will protect the Indian lands, and she herself will marry him and live among his people.

If a few such films played with images encapsulating both modern success and the nobility of tribal life, the majority were not so optimistic about Indians crossing over. In *Lone Star* (1916), an Indian man becomes a famous surgeon . . . but is rejected by whites for being Indian and by Indians for going white. In *The Great Alone* (American, 1922), a half-breed Stanford football star rescues the white woman he loves . . . but eventually takes up with a fellow mixed blood. *Blazing Arrows* (Western, 1922) features a Columbia University student who is rejected by the white woman he loves only to rescue her, marry her, and . . . discover that he is really an adopted white. In *Curse of the Red Man* (Selig, 1911), education plunges an Indian into alcoholism as he struggles disastrously to negotiate cultures. In 1914, William Eagleshirt played yet another drunken college graduate in *Last of the Line* (Bison, 1914). With no place in either society, he breaks the peace made by his father, who is forced to kill him. Even as films such as these allowed cross-race romance, celebrated Native virtues, or allowed Indians to exist as contemporaries, they also set new expectations about the difficulties that Indian people might face in finding a safe space in a modern, yet tribal, world.

FOCUS GROUP: NATIVE CRITIQUE

Critics and reviewers commented frequently on the crudity of many representations of Indians. Producers spoofed Indian dramas, and trade journals made fun of them.[65] Alanson Skinner, a curator at the American Museum of Natural History, took the industry to task on the question of authenticity, showing how far film was drifting from Cody's insistence on representational detail: "From the standpoint of a student, most of the picture plays shown are ethnologically grotesque farces. Delawares are dressed as Sioux, and the Indians of Manhattan Island are shown dwelling in skin tipis of the kind used only by the tribes beyond the Mississippi." Skinner called for a documentary approach, noting many rituals and ceremonies that, if accurately recorded, would interest an audience. (At the same time, he accepted without question Indian romances such as *Hiawatha*; violence and bad ethnography alone set him off.)[66]

Such criticism—focused on details or on lack of sophistication and realism—was not likely to counter the expectations being set by the Indian pictures. Though few expected them to jump into the critical mix, Indian people did not live in a world apart from the movies. At Pine Ridge, for example, an inspector noted in 1913: "A moving picture machine has been installed in the chapel. Shows are given on Friday and Saturday evenings." Nor, it turns out, was that reservation alone. The 1911 Selig film *Curse of the Redman* mobilized critics across Indian country, revealing that Native viewers had a pretty good sense of how they were being portrayed.[67]

Curse of the Redman purported to tell the real-life story that has come down to us as that of Willie Boy, remade in 1969 as *Tell Them Willie Boy Is Here*.[68] The Selig actor-director Hobart Bosworth wrote the *Curse* scenario in order to make moral arguments about the dangers of alcohol and the inability of education and cultural transformation to alter Indians' essential racial nature. The film's antihero, Zerapai, graduates from an Indian boarding school and returns home, only to be shunned by his tribe for his modern, white ways. Caught between two cultures, he begins to drink, murders a fellow tribesman who refuses to let Zerapai marry his daughter, and flees to the desert with his lover. Abandoning her in the midst of a desperate chase, he is finally cornered and commits suicide. While many Indian suicides had been framed as noble self-denials—giving up claims on white lovers in order to grant them futures—Zerapai's suicide is decidedly savage, both a reassertion of an essential Indian nature and the failed result of the effort to educate Indians into white modernity.[69]

Though Selig cut particularly egregious scenes (e.g., Zerapai beating his lover), the film nonetheless generated a storm of protest—and most particularly among Indian people themselves. In February 1911, two delegations of Anishinaabeg from Minnesota arrived in Washington, D.C., to protest against Indian films in general and *Curse of the Redman* in particular. Their criticisms were pointed: white men too often portrayed Indians. Because Indian actors were not always involved, so as to correct or refuse the portrayal, film producers were able to depict "thrilling" scenes that Indians, actors included, found "grossly libelous." Barely a week later, the *Nickelodeon* was reporting the anger of Cheyenne and Arapahoe people, who had seen *Curse* while in Washington, D.C., visiting President William Howard Taft. In March, *Moving Picture World* reported that Indians from western and northwestern reservations were appealing to the Indian Bureau and to President Taft to place restrictions on the "objectionable features" of the filmed portrayals of Indian life. Delegations of Shoshones, Cheyennes, and Arapahoes were on their way to Washington, D.C., to protest. The *Chicago InterOcean* authored (and *Motion Picture World* reprinted) a mocking article in pidgin English that sought to dull the Native critique and reassert familiar expectations about Indian inability: "This show heap bad. Heap big lie. Pictures show Injun men bad men and do heap bad thing all time." And so on. The piece concluded with a plea for the Arapahoes to go ahead and take vengeance on filmmakers—in front of a camera—since "the surest offset to a photo-play which shows 'fake' Indians doing a bad thing is a moving picture showing real Indians doing a praise-worthy act."[70]

The furor reemerged in the autumn. In September, W. H. Stanley, the superintendent of a southern California reservation, observed, first, that Indian people loved the movies but that they did not like the portrayal of Indians. "The Indian of today will spend his last cent on a moving picture show when he visits the city," he wrote. "I have known of several who have visited every moving picture show in town before they returned home, but nevertheless, they were loud in their complaints of what they termed 'the white man's injustice.'" In October, John Standing Horse, a New York actor, wrote indignantly to *Moving Picture World* (of which he was a regular reader) that white actors were a joke: "Have also seen the picture with all the made-up Indian men with big war bonnets on their heads. . . . They should get the real Indian people. There is about a hundred men, women, and children in New York out of work most of the time, from the reservations out West, and only a few of them get any work. Pathé and Biograph use them more than the other companies, as they know just how to act and don't laugh all the time like some of the white men." Standing Horse was writing as an actor ("Have lived all my life in the West and have worked for different picture men") who had a sense of his craft and of his superiority to white actors playing Indian roles. Likewise, Standing Horse understood that he was part of a community of actors, most likely a community feeling the pinch of unemployment as film companies abandoned New York and New Jersey in exactly these years and moved to California.[71]

In December, Red Eagle wrote *Moving Picture World* to protest that the average Indian picture made the Indian out to be a "yelling, paint-bedaubed creature, reeking of barbarism and possessing little or no intelligence," and cautioned that such films were "instilling an antagonistic germ in the mind of the young American against the American Indian that, if continued, may cause a bitterness." Red Eagle proposed an act prohibiting the showing of Indian pictures, noting two particular exemptions. He suggested, first, that tribal rites and ceremonies properly documented would remain valuable and, second, that the people to do the documenting should be, if not specifically Native, deeply sympathetic. Red Eagle claimed the right of Indian people to control, not only film content, but also the means of production—nothing less than the camera itself.[72]

Each of these critiques raised a problem later framed elegantly by Luther Standing Bear. Standing Bear's *My People, the Sioux* ends with a poignant recollection of his attempts to influence the ways in which Indian images were produced. Standing Bear went to directors, stage managers, and writers, telling them that Indian parts were not written, played, or costumed properly; they misrepresented Indian dress and movement. Audiences, he was told, don't know the difference, so why should it matter? At one point, he thought he had reached Thomas Ince: "I told him none of the Indian pictures were made right. He seemed quite surprised at this and began asking me questions. I explained to him in what way his Indian pictures were wrong. We talked for a long time, and when I arose to leave, he said, 'Standing Bear, some day you and I are going to make some real Indian pictures.'"[73]

What would it have meant to have made "real Indian pictures"? Standing Bear's critique called up the specter of Buffalo Bill Cody's *The Indian Wars*, with its real details and reenactments by real historical actors. The Wild West, of course, had grafted faux narratives over authentic props, human and nonhuman. Standing Bear, Red Eagle, and Standing Horse understood the power that such narratives could exercise as films, and they tried to fight that power by working to change the practice of representation. In significant ways, however, they remained hindered by a Wild West model in which correct costuming and (reen)acting would, on their own, lead to more accurate, less damaging pictures. Buffalo Bill's *Indian Wars* suggested, however, that the recommendations of Red Eagle or Standing Bear—to turn to the documentary—were likely to founder on the expectations of the paying audience. If these Native critics focused too much—and, perhaps, mistakenly—on the details of props, behavior, and clothing, they were, nonetheless, working their way toward a more important critique and proposed reform. They wanted to challenge and alter the narratives that floated so naturally above the props, authentic or not. Standing Horse's and Standing Bear's experiences suggested that successful, subversive films might be made within the limits of audience expectation—if one could only get an Indian person behind the camera. And this is exactly what seemed to happen in the case of James Young

Deer, who, in the middle of 1911's campaign of Indian critique, became the head of a major West Coast studio.

CLIMAX: JAMES YOUNG DEER AND
PRINCESS RED WING

James Young Deer was an ambiguous figure, with a shape-shifter's identity and a hazy history. Young Deer had since childhood lived his life, according to *Moving Picture World*, "in amusement channels." He traveled with Barnum and Bailey, among other circuses, and worked for the Miller Brothers 101 Ranch show. Young Deer began his film career with the Kalem and Lubin Companies, where he wrote scenarios, acted in lead and supporting roles, and worked in production. Biograph hired him to appear in the D. W. Griffith film *The Mended Lute* (Biograph, 1909), and, shortly afterward, he worked for Vitagraph, where he was featured in the 1909 film *Red Wing's Gratitude* (Vitagraph, 1909). The star of that film was Lillian St. Cyr, a Nebraska Ho-Chunk graduate of the Carlisle Indian School who performed under the stage name Princess Red Wing (see figure 15). Before *movie star* became an institutionalized identity, Red Wing was a visible presence in American popular culture, the first widely recognized Indian actress. Young Deer and Red Wing married and began working together as a team, questioning dominant expectations while working within plots and narratives familiar to their audiences. In the early years of film, both were able to thrive in a world of small casts and crews. With only a few people responsible for a given film, they had ample opportunities, not only to act, but also to write, direct, design, and edit (see figure 16).[74]

Founded in 1909, the New York Motion Picture Company almost immediately recruited Young Deer and Red Wing, and, in November of that year, the two moved to Los Angeles to work producing Bison brand westerns—almost two years before the arrival of Thomas Ince.[75] In late 1910, they moved again, hired away by the French company Pathé Frères, whose westerns were under attack for their "unwesternness." (Standing Bear was not the only one who cared about details. Pathé's actors were, according to critics, wearing the wrong clothing, using the wrong saddles, and performing in the wrong landscape.) In early 1911, the two set up shop outside Los Angeles, with Young Deer as the head of Pathé's West Coast studio. That spring, *Moving Picture World* observed: "Young Deer has gathered about him a competent organization of professional men and

FIGURE 15. Princess Red Wing (Lillian St. Cyr Johnson), 1915. Every bit the
Hollywood Indian, Red Wing looks almost Grecian in her blanket, unbraided hair, and
pheasant-feather headdress. (Nebraska State Historical Society, RG 2411.ph: 7160.)

FIGURE 16. *James Young Deer and Princess Red Wing with Crew in New Jersey.*
Note Young Deer's trademark hair, long and unbraided, as well as his beaded vest and
gauntlets. Red Wing clasps his arm while around them tower a group of white cowboys
and a New Jersey forest. (Museum of the American West collection, Autry National
Center.)

women, and is sparing neither effort nor expense to make the Pathé
Frères productions topnotchers in the film market."[76]

As Andrew Smith has argued, Young Deer's Pathé films rejected squaw
man story lines—even while remaining cognizant that these narratives
structured the cultural expectations of audiences. In a series of films,
Young Deer and Red Wing set out to rewrite the white man–Indian
woman narrative structure, using inversions that allowed the films to
continue functioning as domestic melodramas.[77] If race and gender made
one another authoritative, with the "natural" dominance of men dove-
tailing and exchanging meanings with the "natural" dominance of white
people over Indians, then inverting either race or gender upset the entire economy of meaning. How, within an audience's expectations, could
the formula "(Indian) man controls (white) woman" make any sense?
Men might control women, but Indians should not control whites. In-

version used the asymmetries of cross-race romance to break down expectations while retaining enough familiarity to hold an audience.

In *The Falling Arrow* (Lubin, 1909), Young Deer and Red Wing made a tentative foray in this direction by pairing the eponymous Young Deer, a male Indian hero, with Red Wing's Felice, a Mexican woman. The idea of race crossing was moderated as *Mexican* signified an existing history of cross-race reproduction and a whiteness that was partial. Consider the structure of *The Falling Arrow* in relation to *The Squaw Man*. The latter begins and ends valuing the white-on-white love of Jim and Diana. An Indian woman kills an evil white man both to protect her father and to protect Jim. Naturich's killing of Cash Hawkins opens the door to cross-race romance between an Indian woman and a white man, with the product being a mixed-blood child. When the chance arises again for white-on-white love, the Indian woman sacrifices herself so that the white lovers might be happy in civilization. Her mixed-blood son, however, will—at least theoretically—be transformed, losing his Native culture and, thus, becoming assimilated. In effect, *The Squaw Man* rehearsed both options held out to Indian people—disappearance and assimilation.

The Falling Arrow, on the other hand, erases *The Squaw Man*'s opening frame, which celebrates love among white people, beginning instead with a gendered inversion: Indian man saves Mexican woman (in this case, from the attentions of Jim, a white outlaw). Unlike in *The Squaw Man*, however, in *The Falling Arrow* this salvation does not open the door to cross-race romance as Young Deer is rejected by the father of Felice, the woman he has saved. But wait. Where *The Squaw Man* offers the redemption of white-on-white romance, here that possibility is—while real— marked as evil. Felice prefers the Indian savior to Jim, the white outlaw kidnapper. In *The Squaw Man*, the decisive act is the suicide of Naturich, which brings white lovers together and grants them a future. In *The Falling Arrow*, it is a second rescue of Felice from the evil Jim and her return to her father's home. Though this second rescue is offered as evidence, not only of the competence, but also of the love of the Indian man, Felice's father would rather pay him for his service in cash. Staying true to the possibility of cross-race romance, Young Deer refuses the money and insists on marrying Felice. If Naturich reflected the expected disappearance of Indians, the marriage at the end of Young Deer's film offers the promise of an Indian future and the willingness of non-Indians to accept Young Deer in their society (see figure 17).[78]

In *An Indian's Bride* (New York Motion Picture, 1909) and *Young Deer's Re-*

FIGURE 17. *James Young Deer and Princess Red Wing. Here we see Young Deer and Red Wing (lower-right-hand corner) with the actress Evelyn Graham, two other Native actors, and a horse emerging from an incredibly fragile tipi. (Museum of the American West collection, Autry National Center.)*

turn (New York Motion Picture, 1910), Young Deer and Red Wing pushed the inversion harder, first making the female lead a true white woman, then, in the latter film, allowing a male Indian character to reject white womanhood, assimilation, civilized dress, and even the memory of cross-race male bonding, all in favor of a return to his own community and a marriage to an Indian woman. *Young Deer's Return* may reflect the partnership's most subtle scripting. In that film, Young Deer saves a prospector, who gives him a watch as a sign of the cross-race exchange of favors. Young Deer attends Carlisle, enters into white society, and falls in love with a white woman. She even brings him home to meet her father, who cannot bear the thought of her marrying an Indian—until Young Deer recognizes him as the prospector and produces the watch, which signifies that a white man might owe his very life to an Indian. Recognizing his obligation, the father gives his consent to the marriage, at which point

Young Deer refuses the offer and returns to his own tribe, where he will marry an Indian woman.

Young Deer's earlier miscegenation films undoubtedly pushed the buttons of white viewers. *Return* allowed the audience to flirt with, but avoid, a cross-race romance. In that sense, it seems less radical. White womanhood will remain intact, and Indians will stay with Indians in an apparent rejection of the cross-race romance. At the same time, however, the film's deep flirtation with such romance—and the acquiescence of the father-prospector to the match—lets Young Deer and Red Wing offer up a devastating critique of white racial prejudice. The father may be willing to respect one Indian, in return for his life, but he fails to respect Indian people in general. He hangs on to race expectations until he is shamed into greater introspection. It is hard to know exactly how it all played out on-screen, but, if one imagines white viewers picturing themselves in the place of the white characters, one finds a collection of messages: a white woman might prefer an Indian man; such a romance exists as a real possibility; a white man acting with prejudice acts shamefully; Indians deserve respect and equal treatment, not simply as individuals, but as a group; from a Native perspective, the rhetoric of equality that surrounds education and assimilation looks fraudulent in the face of continued racism.

Equally important, *Return* escapes the paradox that cropped up when one used cross-race romance as a figure for social equality: Indian-white romance of any sort also implied assimilation and failed to allow a serious future for Indians, which is figured here as red-on-red marriage and reproduction. The film successfully used cross-race romance to attack white racism, but it then transformed the plot structure in order to speak for Indian futures. In *Return*, Young Deer and Red Wing moved outside the structure of the miscegenation drama, setting up *white* approval for cross-race partnering (decidedly unexpected) while letting their Indian protagonist reject such crossing, thus affirming the potency and the future of tribal culture independent of white society.

The two offered an even more pointed rewriting in *The Prospector and the Indian* (Pathé, 1912). Here, they returned to the familiar race/gender structure, with a white prospector marrying an Indian woman, White Star. When the couple is rejected and harassed by the white community, White Star runs away and, à la Naturich, attempts to commit suicide. Expectations would have White Star succeed in her attempt, with the prospector returning to his people, having reaped the benefits of Indian initiation into the world of the frontier. In fact, the film insists that the prospector's primary loyalty is to his Indian wife, not to whiteness. He searches out her people and actively encourages them to destroy the white settlement, which they do. To make his rejection complete, the prospector joins the tribe, thus taking the idea of cross-race marriage—which usually functions in terms of integration into *white* society—and placing it in an Indian society that arguably has a future of its own.

The Squawman's Revenge (Pathé, 1912) takes the colonialist race/gender dynamic one step further. In this film, a white girl found and raised by Indians grows up and finds a white husband. This white-on-white partnership leaves the racial order intact. But the other men in the husband's camp insist on seeing the white girl in cultural terms, as an Indian, and they threaten to ostracize the husband unless she leaves, which she does. Again, however, Young Deer and Red Wing elevate personal loyalty above racial affinities, having the husband join the Indian community and helping them take revenge by destroying the white settlement.[79] Now, not one, but two white people will go Native. Reading through the capsule summaries in the pages of Moving Picture World, one can't help but pull up abruptly on coming across, in the midst of familiar plots, radical inversions and rewritings in which white men and women reject American society for the Indian world and, in fact, assist Indians in destroying white civilization.[80]

Though they seem to have preferred to concentrate on reworking the expectations framed by the miscegenation story, Young Deer and Red Wing did, in fact, turn on occasion to the contemporaneous, perhaps nowhere as tellingly as in Red Eagle, the Lawyer (Pathé, 1912), which features a real Indian hero, modern and educated.[81] With white swindlers plying Chief Iron Claw with liquor in an attempt to get his signature on a land deed, Iron Claw's daughter White Feather turns to the Indian attorney Red Eagle for help. After putting a stop to the swindle, Red Eagle is assaulted by the gang, knocked out, and dumped in the woods. With Red Eagle out of commission, the swindlers succeed in getting the chief's signature, and it looks as if yet another story of Indian dispossession is about to be played out. Instead, Young Deer imagines both the power of the law and that of a government that cared to do the right thing. Rescued by White Feather, Red Eagle presents the story to the government agent, who nullifies the deed and imprisons the swindlers. Red-on-red romance concludes the film, as White Feather and Red Eagle pledge their love and stake an Indian claim to the future.

Red Wing and Young Deer clearly had a sense of the importance of the contemporaneous in representations of Indianness, particularly in relation to larger social contexts. The January 1913 Tournament of Roses parade, for example, followed the example of so many parades in outlining the local social order, in this case, testifying to the arrival en masse of the film industry in the preceding two or three years. "One might have thought," boasted Moving Picture World, "that this years' [event] was a motion picture affair," with cameras, floats, stars, and even the shooting of scenarios built around the parade. James Young Deer had Pathé sponsor a float concerned not so much with the film industry itself as with the general question of the representation of Indian people. At one end of the float, entitled "Indian Life—Past and Present," stood a tipi, with an aged woman, a hunter, a dead deer, and a live wolf, at the other a sharply dressed college graduate. Behind the float trailed the rest of the Pathé Company's studio Indians and cowboys. The representation was threefold. It illustrated, not just one vision of the past (tipi, old woman, wildlife), but also two visions of the present. The first of these latter was a representational vision—of a college graduate, educated and capable. The second was a real backstage vision of Indian people at work in the business of representation. (Nor was Pathé the only studio to display its Indian actors. Thomas Ince's Kay-Bee company sent more than a hundred Sioux actors from Inceville, who demonstrated Indian dances, games, and camping.)[82] One imagines that the images dueled with one another, the familiar primitivism of the past crashing into representations of the present that laid bare the process through which images of the past were produced.

The images of past and present produced by Young Deer and Red Wing offered a politics of Indian representation. If the evidence for such a politics is mostly textual, it is also the case that many of their films were singled out by critics and bypassed by audiences who were not interested in seeing challenges to their familiar expectations. As Andrew Smith recounts, Young Deer was first reined in by Pathé and then marginalized as the studio system took hold during the 1910s. He disappeared from Hollywood in the middle of that decade (see figure 18).[83]

Because Young Deer and Red Wing made their films before the studio structure was truly settled, they were able to exercise a measure of autonomy. The studio system made such unscrutinized autonomy less likely, and it paid increasing attention to the matching of its products to audience likes and dislikes. Young Deer and Red Wing's Pathé films were,

FIGURE 18. James Young Deer and Princess Red Wing in California at Bison Films Cast Dinner. Tracing from figure 16 to figure 18 suggests a narrative that takes the two from the naïve backwoods of New Jersey to the decadent backlots of California. Both Young Deer and Red Wing have pumped up their Indian accoutrements, with sashes, beads, headdress, and apron (note, however, that Young Deer continues to wear the same vest). Together, they frame and foreground the white company, leaning on statuary pedestals that highlight their classic Indian nobility even as they stand (rather than sit) to the front of the picture plane. (Museum of the American West collection, Autry National Center.)

of course, made to seek an audience, and, even as they questioned expectation, they relied on plots and imagery familiar to white viewers. But they were not films that blindly recounted national and racial expectations, and they failed the audience test—which suggests that the pair may well have been up to something.

Red Wing's film career flourished until the mid-1910s. Indeed, for many critics, the highlight of that career came with her performance as Naturich in Cecil B. DeMille's 1914 version of *The Squaw Man* for Paramount. Her appearance led *Moving Picture World* to reaffirm the critique of John Standing Horse: "It is not altogether a pleasing spectacle to see white women impersonating Indian squaws, and they are seldom, if ever, successful at it; on the other hand, Indian girls who can awaken and hold sympathy for their roles are few and far between, but Princess Redwing performs her part with exquisite fidelity and great depth of feeling. The play's highest merit is the opportunity it affords this accomplished actress."[84] When Red Wing's film career flagged, she performed in vaudeville, established herself on the college lecture circuit, created an Indian costume company, and became active in Indian affairs in the eastern United States. Like so many other Indian representations, her performances could not be wholly disentangled from the social and political struggles of Indian people. Indeed, this linkage between Native aspirations for justice and popular media performance suggests a broader view of the "Indian Wars," a panorama that would include, not simply the military, but also the cultural, social, political, legal, and economic struggles waged by Indian people.

DENOUEMENT: NOT SO HAPPY ENDING

In Chicago, 1893, the exposition, the newspaper stories, the academic papers, and Buffalo Bill Cody's popular entertainment all pointed powerfully to the past. Columbus's four hundredth anniversary mattered, for Discovery marked the beginning of the American era. But 1890, the date of the supposed closing of the frontier and of the final killings of the Indian Wars, mattered more. Frederick Jackson Turner and Buffalo Bill Cody meant to draw lines between the epoch of Columbus, now closed, and a modern era opening up. The Columbian period was defined, both coming and going, around contacts with Indians. The fact of the era's closing helped shape a familiar expectation: that Indian people would remain back with Columbus, locked in history, memory, and representation, and excluded from a new social and political world.

Would Indian people have accepted such an assertion? It is not hard to imagine tribes meeting on the Chicago Midway, comparing notes, and concluding that the era of armed military resistance was over. Even amid the onslaught of forced assimilation, allotment, linguistic genocide, and religious suppression, however, one has a much harder time picturing Indian people assuming the absolute end of religions, cultures, and social practices. Imagine an Indian Frederick Jackson Turner or Buffalo Bill Cody, a Native person offering Indian interpretations of the closing of the frontier, of violence and pacification, of modernity. I imagine such a person, not drawing the stark lines of epochs and eras, but rather recognizing that, while military conflict was no longer an option, the struggle between Native people and the United States had not concluded.

Across Indian country, the recognition of military defeat had pushed Native people to develop strategies for continuing the struggle. Treaty organizations, regional political organizations, pan-Indian reform groups, Indian fraternal organizations—all these aimed to seek justice through legal and political channels, a strategy that has dominated much of the twentieth century and that should probably be read in terms of at least partial success. Indian performers such as Standing Bear, Red Wing, and others participated in such organizing. They recognized as well, however, that political and legal struggles are tightly linked to the ideologies and images—the expectations—that non-Indians have built around Native people. In making Indian images, Native actors sought to participate in a struggle waged on the cultural front, particularly through the developing forms of mass media, which promised to reach larger audiences. Literary writing, the Wild West, and the soon-to-be-developed medium of film offered opportunities where the narratives that created expectations about Indians could be subtly contested.

Of course, no Indian Turner arose at Chicago to offer a single coherent meditation on the meanings of Indian history, the recent killings at Wounded Knee, and the path to the future. But the Potawatomi leader Simon Pokagon spoke loudly about the failure to include respectful representations of Indian people at the Columbian Exposition, and he drew on the romanticism of the vanishing Indian to play cultural politics in his "Red Man's Rebuke," published on birchbark. Nor was Pokagon alone. A substantial number of Indian people—linked by their experience of prereservation, reservation, and contemporary contexts—spoke, wrote, and performed in the years surrounding the turn of the century.[85]

If there was no Indian Turner in Chicago, there were many Indian Codys, grabbing media attention, and reflecting white expectations back to the white writers and readers of the mass market dailies while working quietly to challenge those expectations. Many of those men and women would later move to California, swapping the flagging Wild West show for the most powerful imagemaking machinery of the twentieth century. Offering themselves as film fodder for a cultural imagining of the issues surrounding race and culture crossing, many of them set out not simply to make a living—though that mattered a great deal—but to take part in the representation of Indianness. It is true that one might be moved to judge their efforts a failure—James Young Deer was shunted to the margins, Princess Red Wing never made as many films as the faux Indian Mona Darkfeather, Thomas Ince never kept his promise to make "real Indian films" with Luther Standing Bear, and the relatively sympathetic films of the early decades gave way to genre-defining representations of war-whooping Indian savagery that lasted for most of the rest of the century.

What may matter more, however, is the fact that a significant group of early-twentieth-century Indian people—many born to completely different cultures—came rapidly to understand the power of representation and of cultural production. It is no coincidence that imagemakers such as Standing Bear, Red Wing, and Young Deer also thought in social and political terms or that John Big Tree and many other Indian actors continued to push producers like Thomas Ince, refusing to appear in films that denigrated Indian people. During the 1920s, the Chickasaw director Edwin Carewe would carve out a place in the film establishment, and Louis Brave and Humming Bird (also Chickasaw) would advise directors on Indian subjects. By 1936, Jim Thorpe and the Blackfeet actor Many Treaties (William Hazlett) had formed a seventy-five-member Indian Actors Association, attempted (unsuccessfully) to join the Screen Actors Guild, and petitioned the federal government for a film code requiring that Indian roles be played by Indian people. In 1940, Victor Daniels would make his recognition bid for the "DeMille Indians" of Los Angeles. In the 1950s, John War Eagle and Jay Silverheels were devoting full Hollywood careers to questioning the politics of representation. And, by the 1980s and 1990s, things had come full circle, with primarily political Indian activists such as Russell Means, Dennis Banks, and John Trudell turning toward acting and film representation.[86]

Nonetheless, the line tracing the shadow of the twentieth century from Wild West shows to contemporary Indian actors is a shaky one. To think about its uneven quality, I want to return one final time to the transitional moment represented by Cody's *The Indian Wars*. The Wild West experience that underpinned Cody's film project worked well for Indian people. Lakota performers traveled together, as families and friends. Even as the show enabled them to tour the nation and the world, it also offered them a measure of security—good wages, built-in tour guides handling complex travel arrangements, a chance to put deeply rooted skills on display. A film industry casting about for operational business models in its early years turned easily to the Wild West. Show Indians made their way to California, both as individuals and as part of larger troupes of actors, traveling and working together comfortably as they had in the shows.

As the industry developed new aesthetic practices, and as it became clear how different film and show really were, however, Indian people came to seem less essential. The story of Lakota men contemplating putting real lead in their weapons might excite movie public relations agents and worry Ernest Dench, but it would never have had the spine-tingling electricity of the same tale passed about a Wild West show. The Wild West placed its authority in its performers, and it relied on their authenticity to woo its audiences. Film, which interposed celluloid, projected light, time, and physical distance between history, reenactment, and audience, did not need the possibility of Indian violence. It was not General Nelson Miles's appearance on the screen that mattered, then, but rather the affirmation coming from his chair in the audience. Buffalo Bill's key question, Was a performance real? gave way to a different query: Was the spectator-consumer taken with the image? Illusion came to matter more than authenticity—and illusion proved to be one of the great aesthetic joys of both film production and film viewing.

This aesthetic transformation carried with it a market logic. Studios produced a wide range of imagery, but it made economic sense to do so using a constricted pool of actors, each one capable of playing numerous characters. Some followed the lead of Thomas Ince, who set up Inceville as a studio geared to make certain kinds of films (those involving rugged landscapes, horses, and wagons) and not others. In that situation, Native people might find a regular place—as horseback-riding Arabs one day, as cowboys another, and as Indians on a third. Such options grew increasingly constricted, however, as film production turned toward the industrial, with manufactured movie stars and a full-blown studio system.

For that system carried with it a racial logic as well, one in which whiteness served as the color of versatility. Indians and African Americans could represent only those particular identities—which cut them out of leading roles altogether. In contrast, long traditions of blackface and redface authorized white actors to appear in other racial guises. By the mid-1910s, films that had treated contemporary Indian people in a twentieth-century world began giving way to representations focused on the nineteenth century. Restricted to playing a single role—nineteenth-century Indian—Native actors might look like an unnecessary luxury, at least to a studio accountant. White actors, on the other hand, could daub on some makeup, and pull on a black wig, and chalk it up to the illusion of film.

Indian actors continued to make their way in the California film industry, but their numbers necessarily shrank as studios shied away from the Wild West practice of building large, diverse companies. And, of course, even as the number of Indian performers declined, the number of films showing violent, savage Indian opponents increased, especially in the century's middle decades. In effect, these later films skipped over the ambiguities of the early Indian movies—and over the rhetoric of Indian pacification—choosing, instead, to reinvigorate the expectations surrounding the older imagery of the surround and the last stand. And so, even as most Americans expected that Indian people had been pacified, they also came to expect images of nineteenth-century Indian violence on the silver screen. When these expectations functioned simultaneously, the effect was devastating. Contemporary Indian people seemed like pathetic anachronisms—anachronisms because they appeared as primitive and savage as the Indians on-screen; and, worse, pathetic because, as pacified people, they lacked even the screen Indians' determination to resist white conquest. And, thus, the often-repeated assertion among Indian people that, growing up at midcentury, they had identified with the cowboys rather than the Indians.[87]

But there had once been a moment in which other stories were possible. James Young Deer and Princess Red Wing leapt into a gap that opened for a few short years. In that ambiguous, formative moment—before Hollywood, when filmmaking was still inflected by the Wild West tradition—Indian authenticity licensed them to produce films. The economic structure of the industry empowered them to make those films from a particularly Native position. Given the opportunity, they chose, not to pursue the violence and pacification issues so key to the Wild West, but instead to focus attention on the problems of postfrontier modernity: How were Americans to think about contemporary Indian people? And how were Native people to participate in that conversation? Young Deer and Red Wing had it right, I think, for, when it comes to American culture, those are still the questions that matter.

"I AM OF THE BODY"
My Grandfather, Culture, and Sports

athletics

MEMORY

Like his father before him, my grandfather, Vine Deloria Sr., was an Episcopalian minister. A powerful orator, he gave sermons that moved people in extraordinary ways, and he was, by all accounts, beloved by the congregations of the South Dakota reservation parishes he tended. Some claim that the conversion of a majority of Sioux Episcopalians was due to the proselytizing of my grandfather and his father, my namesake, Philip J. Deloria. In a different time, my grandfather would almost certainly have been appointed bishop of South Dakota. Frustrated with racial barriers in the church and difficult conditions in the state, he left for a small town in Iowa, then moved, in 1954, to New York City. There, he confronted a set of equally intractable problems as the first director of the national church's Indian mission programs.[1]

For my grandfather was also Native, born into a Yankton Dakota family, and raised on the Standing Rock reservation. In the 1950s, while in New York, he spoke out forcefully against the federal government's plan to force Indian assimilation by "terminating" tribal governments. He insisted instead that the church nurture and maintain an Indian clergy to serve its Indian adherents. These views won him no friends in the church hierarchy, and he was eventually forced out of his position. Lakota culture tolerates a far greater degree of contradiction than the Episcopal Church, however. If the church demanded that he act and believe as a terminationist because that was what the church hierarchy believed, the Sioux people were content to see him as both a Christian minister and a respected tribal elder. My brother and I used to play anthropologist with him, recording his inexhaustible store of songs and tales on our father's reel-to-reel. And actual anthropologists, as well as linguists and historians, would visit him, seeking to plumb his knowledge of old words and oral history.[2]

For a long time, I saw my grandfather in a similar light, as a minister and an Indian storyteller. I did not pay attention to an equally important third fact about him: he was a man of extraordinary physical vitality. At seventy-one, he had no trouble playing George Mitterwald to my Bert Blyleven (I was a Minnesota Twins fan at the time), bent into a crouch, and holding out his old-fashioned catcher's mitt—a flat, weathered pancake, slightly dented in the middle. He liked to pass the football around too and threw a nice, tight spiral with good distance. While I ran triangle patterns around the yard, he would stand in place, cocking, firing, and invariably parking the ball right in my hands. At eighty-three, when he helped perform my wedding ceremony, his voice boomed throughout the church, distorting the sound system, which was quickly turned off. A few years later, we were walking together on Medicine Knoll Butte, outside Pierre, South Dakota, and we ran into a barbed-wire fence. I pushed down the lower strand with my foot and pulled up the middle strand in order that he might slip through. But, even as I bent down, he grasped a half-rotten post and vaulted over the fence. Marveling, I wondered what he must have been like as a younger man.

My grandfather died of Alzheimer's disease in 1990. As his mind discarded parts of his life and personality, older memories sometimes seemed to acquire new vitality, and one occasionally got a fragmentary peek into his life as a young man seventy years before. I last saw him on a day when—like so many of his last days—a lifetime of significance was broken down to fragments, in this case, a snatch of music, sung over and over, and a story. He loved the song "School Days," and, if you would sing the melody, he had a descant verse that accompanied the song. Where "School Days" spoke of the call of "reading and writing and 'rithmetic," his verse responded with the attractions of the nonacademic curriculum: "domestic-nestics and basketballs." He had learned the song, and the verse, as a boy while attending Kearney Military Academy in Nebraska, where he sharpened his love of both music and basketball. It has served to remind me of how powerful his educational experience was in shaping his life.

The story grew out of the usual, painful preliminaries:

Who are you?
Your eldest grandson, Philip.
Oh. Do you live here?
No. I'm visiting you from Connecticut, where I'm going to school.
Ah. Connecticut . . . Connecticut Aggies, Connecticut Aggies.

FIGURE 19. *Vine Deloria Sr., St. Stephen's College's "Greatest Athletic Hero."*
(Courtesy Vine Deloria Jr.)

> *Suddenly, time is running out, and St. Stephen's College needs a touchdown to beat the Connecticut (Agricultural and Mechanical College) Aggies. Playing full-back, Vine Deloria takes an option lateral, fakes a run, and then heaves the ball fifty-five yards downfield into the waiting arms of a receiver.*

I don't know that my grandfather was really able to pull, out of his shattered memory, a coherent narrative of a game or even a single play. But I hope he did. The pass, in our family's collective memory, not only sealed the victory for St. Stephen's, but also set a record as the longest forward pass in college football that year (see figure 19).[3]

The more I thought about this exchange, the more compelling it became. It made me realize that, even as the Alzheimer's began to take him away, he had started to dwell increasingly on his memories of athletic competition. Indeed, I'd heard the story of the Connecticut Aggies before; it had started creeping back into his repertoire in the mid-1980s. At some primal level, I began to think, my grandfather saw his primary identity, neither as a Christian minister, nor as a Lakota elder, but as an athlete. Could it be that sports were more important to his personal makeup than race or religion?

Perhaps, but he probably never parsed his life so neatly. He came to maturity during a brief moment when sports functioned as a complicated nexus between Indian and Euro-American cultures; for those fifty-odd years, all the confusions of centuries of cultural collision were put on display at ballparks and on gridirons as Indian and non-Indian athletes and audiences called modern sports culture into being. Yet, even as Indian men shared a playing field and a set of sporting rules and cultural understandings with non-Indians, they were able to draw substantially different meanings from athletic competition. For my grandfather, race, religion, culture, and family were inextricably tangled with his feats on the playing field. No doubt many non-Indian athletes encountered similar tangles, but Indian players, like other Indian performers, carried with them specific tribal histories and general Indian histories that rendered their experiences unique.

MY GRANDFATHER'S WORLD: CULTURE

Born at Wakpala, South Dakota, in 1901, my grandfather belonged to that "pacified" generation of Native people who were supposed, once and for all, to be finally assimilating into the American melting pot or simply dying off. The massacre at Wounded Knee was barely a decade past. Charlie Smith had not yet been gunned down in Wyoming. The Dawes General Allotment Act, meant to assimilate Native people by dividing up communal land into individual plots in order to inculcate Jeffersonian agrarianism, was swiftly becoming a corrupt vehicle for the mass dispossession of Indian landholders. The federal government would soon bolster existing restrictions on religious dancing and other cultural practices. The Supreme Court was about to rule, in *Lone Wolf v. Hitchcock*, that Congress exercised plenary power over Indian people and could, thus, abrogate any treaty at any time. Agents and "boss farmers" controlled many aspects of reservation life, and Indian children were torn from their families and sent to boarding schools to be forcibly made white.[4]

It is customary to sum up these policies in terms of domination, resistance, and conflict, though these formulas take on somewhat different forms when we move from social, economic, legal, and military questions to ones focused on culture. Did white Americans successfully erase most or all Native culture? Did a resistant Indianness somehow survive? The questions are the same as those posed by James Young Deer and Princess Red Wing decades ago: How were Americans to think about contemporary Indian people in the context of the modern world? And how were Native people to help shape that thinking?

Any change in Indian practices, of course, can be coded in multiple ways. For those who believed in assimilation, change could be seen as progress toward the eventual erasure of distinct Indian culture. For those who believed in essential racial differences, true change seemed unlikely. Such critics tended to see similarities rather than transformations and to take them as evidence that Indians could exist, on some lower social stratum, within the American nation. For those concerned with the integrity of Native cultural and social practices themselves, change has been almost inevitably coded as decline—as the incremental death of traditional Native culture. Alternatively, others have chosen to celebrate the vitality of *culture* itself as a metaconcept, pointing to the inevitability and legitimacy of its continual refigurings. In that context, cultural change is simply a natural process. When multiple peoples come together, change happens.[5]

My grandfather's world existed someplace in the midst of these understandings. Like all American Indian groups, the Lakota worked hard—and with some measure of success—to retain an essential control over their culture, even in the most transformative moments. In the eighteenth and nineteenth centuries, they had made over their world as they claimed European horses, rifles, and steel trade goods as their own. In fin de siècle America, the descendants of these people hunted cattle as they had once hunted the nearly extinct bison, celebrated the memory and form of the Sun Dance within strategically altered Fourth of July ceremonies and church convocations, remade their warrior societies and women's groups as church sodalities, started a fashion craze for cowboy clothes, and amassed enormous herds of horses. Again and again, they created new Indian worlds, fusing diverse cultures, or fitting themselves into the interstices between a core Native tradition and new practices introduced from the American periphery.[6] My grandfather and great-grandfather, for example, were part of a cohort of Sioux ministers who essentially hijacked their respective denominations (Episcopalian, Congregationalist, Presbyterian) to create the cross-denominational Brotherhood of Christian Unity, which effectively organized South Dakota Sioux Christianity—and put the emphasis on the *Sioux* as much as it did on the *Christianity*.[7]

To celebrate these remakings too uncritically, however, would be to ignore the disparate power relations that existed both on the reservations and in the cities. When Indian people refigured their world, they did so within the constraints of American rules, regulations, expectations, and power. Fourth of July celebrations and Wild West performances were not the same as Sun Dances and war parties. The infrastructure of a missionary church was not the same as tribal social and political institutions. Power cuts many ways, of course, and so the same society that imposed limits on Indians also offered a certain power to Native people who could find and push the right cultural buttons. The Wild West's Indian performers punched those buttons hard; Young Deer and Red Wing did too, seizing their moment in the film industry and seeking to undermine mainstream expectations about Indian-white relations. As we have seen, the intercultural world that took shape in the early twentieth century formed in response to both Indian and non-Indian expectations, imperatives, and constraints.[8]

My grandfather grew up remembering, on the one hand, harsh government agents and missionary proselytizing and, on the other, enormous church convocations where powerful Native men sang the Lakota hymns of the Brotherhood of Christian Unity. His parents raised him to be fluent in the language and the ways of his ancestors yet equally able to move competently through American society. When his mother died in 1915, my grandfather boarded the train to Kearney, Nebraska, to attend an Episcopalian military school. Though he arrived speaking little English, he came to wear a uniform and to study hard, and he rose eventually to the top rank of cadet colonel. He learned English and went by the name Pete, a nickname he preferred for his entire life. At the same time, however, the boys with whom he lived learned to speak small vocabularies of Lakota. Rather than simply assimilating, my grandfather helped create a new, cross-cultural world for himself and his companions.[9]

In this schoolboy grappling with race and culture, it did not hurt that my grandfather was big, strong, tough, fast, and coordinated, with more than a bit of a temper. And he had grown up in a world mixed, not only culturally, but also physically. His father had him swimming in the river or bathing in cold water every morning, and he learned from his family and friends a particularly Indian kind of physicality. At the same time, his love for horses and riding was translated into the cowboy context of many early-twentieth-century western reservations. He was skilled with a rope and had spent his childhood sneaking out at night with friends to ride calves as if they were rodeo steers. These abilities translated easily to the athletic competition so important to military and boarding schools, and, while at Kearney, he lettered in football, baseball, and basketball.[10]

The idea of sport was nothing new to Native people. Lacrosse, a popular but relatively latter-day American pastime, dominated the eastern region of Indian America for centuries, with numerous variations in stick, field, and duration. Colonial commentators noted the presence of "Indian football," which involved kicking and pitching a stuffed deerskin through enormous goals. For plains people, horse racing, speed and endurance running, and many other games in which men and women competed were also ways of training for the exigencies of a demanding physical life. Across the southwest, long-distance and speed running had important physical, social, and spiritual significance, and accounts of multiple-day runs of extreme length are not uncommon. Like American sports, Indian contests had rules, traditions, and multiple layers of cultural meaning, with performances signifying at once status or rank, individual ability, religious observance, and group identity.[11]

Indian athletes may have first started competing formally with non-Indians during a mid-nineteenth-century upsurge of interest in foot-racing. The Lumbee historian Joseph Oxendine recounts a number of well-known Native runners of the period. In 1844, thirty thousand people watched the Seneca racer John Steeprock compete against thirty-seven white runners. Another Seneca runner, Louis "Deerfoot" Bennett, raced throughout the 1850s, before being invited, in 1861, to compete in England, where for two years he won numerous purses, returning home with considerable prize money. After the Civil War, he organized a traveling troupe of runners. In 1876, the Pawnee runner Big Hawk Chief ran an unofficial under-four-minute mile (timed with two stopwatches on a closely measured track). Guided by the Six Nations runner Bill Davis, who in 1909 would finish second in both the Boston and the U.S. Amateur Marathons, the Onondaga runner Tom Longboat blew away the field in

Boston in 1907, beating the previous record by almost five minutes.[12] Indian runners competed with non-Indians less often during the mid-twentieth century—a period nonetheless highlighted by the Lakota runner Billy Mills's 1964 Olympic gold medal in the ten-thousand-meter race.

While running offered a natural venue for Indian–non-Indian competition, many older tribal sporting practices—shinny, lacrosse, stickball, and the like—continued on reservations. At the same time, Native people also welcomed the mid- to late-nineteenth-century introduction of American-style football and baseball, easily enfolding these newcomers into extant cultural traditions.[13] While my grandfather's athletic experience—and that of many other Indian athletes—would rely on the boarding school system of the late nineteenth century and the early twentieth, sports also made their way into Indian country earlier and through other channels. Knocking about in some version as early as the 1820s, and first codified in 1845, baseball owed a substantial debt to the movement of men and the forced leisure time that characterized the Civil War. Unlike football, which has its clearest roots later in the century, baseball was, at least in part, a child of the midcentury military, and, in the wake of the Civil War, it spread quickly to posts across the west, most of which were strategically positioned to supervise and control Indian people.

Baseball, which lacks the allegorical contest over space and the close physical contact of football, may well have been the perfect sport for soldiers and Indians to play together and, out of those encounters, to spread from tribe to tribe. Missionaries, sometimes taken with the ideal of "muscular Christianity" and the civilizing possibilities of structured games, also served as channels for baseball and other sports. Exercise and athletic programs attached to churches gave many Indian boys and girls their first introductions to American sports.

By the late nineteenth century, reservation teams had begun to compete with one another. The Indian boarding school system—institutionalized in 1878, with Hampton Institute's first Indian students, and more famously the following year, with the founding of the Carlisle Indian Industrial School—had become a hotbed of athletic talent, with recruitment ploys and players sometimes raided by non-Indian schools. This new kind of athletic competition could sometimes be seen as part of a refigured warrior tradition, but it also provided an entrée into American society—a chance to beat whites at their own games, an opportunity to get an education, and, even at its most serious, an occasion for fun and sociality.

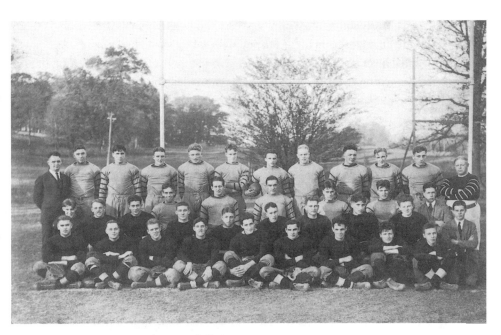

FIGURE 20. *St. Stephen's Football Team, 1922.*
Vine Deloria Sr. (top row, fourth from right). (Courtesy Vine Deloria Jr.)

SPORTS IN MY GRANDFATHER'S WORLD

In 1922, my grandfather won a scholarship to St. Stephen's College in Annandale-on-Hudson, New York, a small school with close ties to the Episcopal Church. (During the 1930s, St. Stephen's became more secular and was renamed Bard College.) For a long time—perhaps even his whole life—my grandfather assumed that the scholarship had materialized from the same church and Indian-targeted philanthropy that had enabled his older sister, Ella, to attend Oberlin College. When local parishioners just happened to drop by with a new suit of clothes, for example, my grandfather saw their generosity in terms of the church's long-standing desire to Christianize Native people and to support its Indian clergy in particular. I suspect, however, that his having lettered in several varsity sports—football, baseball, track, and lacrosse—during every one of his four college years was not incidental (see figure 20). In Bard College's official history, he is listed as "St. Stephen's greatest athletic hero."[14]

If sports were an important part of a new Indian world, they were instrumental to transforming and reshaping modern American culture at the turn of the century. As with Wild West shows and movies, the meanings built around sports helped the contemporary world make sense. As baseball players stared each other down, football players collided in bone-crunching maneuvers, and boxers pummeled one another, they enacted a series of powerful stories for spectators and a burgeoning newspaper readership. Football, as Michael Oriard has pointed out, offered a series of narratives for debating—and reaffirming—any one of several competing understandings of an American masculinity in the midst of a crisis of self-doubt. Debates over the gentlemanly nature of prizefighting and football let fans and critics tell stories that, alternatively, criticized upper-class masculine pretension or denigrated working-class brutalism. At the same time, the unifying power of spectator sports offered a sense of community to those anxious about the rise of an anonymous mass society. As compelling and meaningful performances, then, sporting events rapidly came to function as powerful commodities, offering meanings, collective identity and sense of self, and entertainment, all for the price of a bleacher ticket. As Oriard insists, however, sports functioned differently from other mass market commodities. Unlike literary or artistic representations, football and other sports brought to the spectator a reality factor—something akin to that found in the Wild West. Far from predictable, sports held the potential to surprise spectators with any number of contingent events, including, perhaps, the ultimate reality of players' deaths.[15]

Nowhere were these cultural needs felt so keenly and sated so thoroughly as in colleges and universities. Beginning with the Ivy League athletic programs of the 1870s, intercollegiate sports evolved into a crucial signifier of masculine, class, and race identities.[16] The Yale-Harvard football game, for example, defined and reinforced an elite New England sense of self.[17] While the two sides maintained a pretense of being locked in mortal combat, a discourse of good sportsmanship and the institution of identically posh, crimson and blue–themed proto-tailgate parties sustained their commonalities as (re)producers of the same elite class. At the same time, however, one could make meanings and locate oneself amid other, relatively less important distinctions between Harvard and Yale (we say "boola boola"; you don't!). Upper-crust American manhood, the games suggested, could survive the taming of the frontier, the threat of effeminating urbanism, and the challenges of reorganized family relations and politically and economically active women. As Yale's mascot keepers patrolled the sidelines with Handsome Dan the bulldog (several generations of which were stuffed and displayed in the university gymnasium), players and spectators together experienced a test or performance of crucial values—toughness, tenacity, and (quite literally) good breeding.[18]

Small colleges and state universities emulated the Ivy League example, creating athletic programs in order to boost institutional self-esteem, rally alumni, and establish distinctive identities. In 1919, the new president of St. Stephen's, B. I. Bell, determined to enhance the reputation of his tiny, somewhat stodgy school, instituted an intercollegiate athletic program. Given that the college had barely a hundred students, this move was unquestionably bold. In Bell's first year, St. Stephen's played local high schools, but, by 1922, my grandfather's freshman year, the schedule included games with St. Lawrence, the City College of New York, and Providence College. In 1925, the college's increasingly impressive list of opponents included Trinity, Williams, Middlebury, and Colby as well as St. John's and Norwich. My grandfather captained the football team, whose high point was a decisive win over the University of Rochester in 1925. The basketball team also won major victories that year against Colgate, Hamilton College, and—in a move toward big-time legitimation—Yale.[19]

The success enjoyed by St. Stephen's in the early 1920s was readily available to colleges that were willing to play ringers. In fact, when St. Stephen's hired a new football coach in 1924, he brought with him ten players whose tuition bills were covered by phony promissory notes. The ensuing scandal forced the college to drop football after the 1925 season.[20] The team's previous coach appears to have engaged in a more subtle form of unconventional recruiting, seeking atypical but potentially successful students—like my grandfather. Native men were, indeed, perfect recruits for such college teams. The success of the Carlisle football teams, which began playing the Ivies and other big-time schools in the late nineteenth century, made it clear to coaches and sports fans alike that Indian communities were producing great athletes who could enrich a football or baseball program. And, unlike blacks, Indians had long been enmeshed in the discourse of American assimilation. "Giving the Indian a chance" was a culturally appropriate move, a shouldering of the white man's burden. Often academically underprepared, Indian players invariably walked the fine line between ringer and scholar-athlete.

If these cross-cultural worlds were new, however, older forms of racial discrimination retained much of their power. One of the reasons my grandfather had such keen memories of being given clothing is because he also remembered not being allowed to try on clothes in Annandale stores. At one point, he confronted a mob of hostile students who had translated his opposition to a student strike into racial terms and were howling anti-Indian epithets. The Penobscot baseball phenomenon Louis Sockalexis, who played for Cleveland in the late 1890s, confronted verbal abuse (war whoops, "ki yi yi" calls, insults) and occasional physical harassment. So too did John "Chief" Meyers, who played baseball for the New York Giants and the Brooklyn Dodgers during the first two decades of the twentieth century. As the baseball historian Stephen Thompson points out, "Chief," a nickname applied to almost every Indian baseball player from the 1890s through the 1950s, is a subtle—or not so subtle—indication of the kinds of racism that Indian athletes had to confront.[21]

But it was also the case that Indian athletes, especially those who helped a team win, could receive a surprisingly genuine welcome in many quarters. Meyers, a Cahuilla catcher with a powerful bat and a fourth-grade education, found himself the toast of Dartmouth College for a semester in 1905. He joined a fraternity and won a large following in Hanover before the school discovered his falsified credentials.[22] One of the great Indian novels of the early twentieth century, the Osage author John Joseph Mathews's *Sundown*, treats similar issues of acceptance and rejection through the lens of Indian players and college football, with intense fraternity recruitments of Indian players thought to have a future. My grandfather, too, was simultaneously welcomed and dismissed by his fraternity peers and the school's fans and alumni. But we should not draw the lines too inflexibly, as if race defined only a practice of discrimination and athletic talent produced only appreciation. Spectators might at once value athletic skill and reject the special privileges that accrued to players. And, if Indian identity led to catcalls and racist nicknames, it also called forth real—if often condescending—forms of affection.[23]

EXPECTATION

Indian athletes fit neatly into the nostalgic, antimodern image often attached to professional and collegiate sports. In the early twentieth century's tête-à-tête with cultural primitivism, Indians could be objects, not simply of racial repulsion, but also—as they reflected nostalgia for community, spirituality, and nature—of racial desire.[24] The sportswriter

BENDER

FIGURE 21. *Charles Albert "Chief" Bender, Philadelphia Athletics Pitcher, ca. 1910.* (Library of Congress LC-USZ 62 097857.)

Grantland Rice, in commenting on the Anishinaabe Hall of Famer Charles Albert "Chief" Bender, explicitly identified a set of racial essences that he thought made Indians great natural athletes (see figure 21). The Indian's "heritage is all outdoors," observed Rice. "His reflexes are sharp. He takes the game—in fact every form of life—as it comes to him. He rarely gets excited or off balance. . . . Given the same chance, he has the white man lashed to the Post."[25] Rice could well desire to give Bender "the same chance," for his underlying premise—that Bender was not likely to get it—powerfully marked the world of the ballpark off from the world of social struggle. Rice allowed, and even reveled in, the inversion that would have put Bender in the position of colonial, or even slave, master, lashing (a word that here seems to signify both "tying" and "whipping") the white man to the post. The willingness to concede Bender's superiority signals a deeply rooted desire for, among other things, the primitivist meanings coded onto Indian bodies.

The performances of Bender, Meyers, and my grandfather offered white audiences spectacles of a lost time of natural physicality and strength. Where the Wild West Indians who had toured with Buffalo Bill had (re)enacted history—at least at first—Indian athletes gave spectators a timeless (if fuzzy) sense of Edenic nature sometime before the Fall, when natural men walked the earth. Football commentators such as Walter Camp and Caspar Whitney spoke of Indians as "born tacklers" with a "natural knack" for the game. As with Charles Albert Bender, physical power and mental equilibrium were the primary racial gifts that Indians brought to the stadium.

Balance and stoicism were especially important, for they mark one point at which Indian struggles against expectation sometimes reversed themselves, where supposed deficiencies (in civilization, racial character, finesse, training, etc.) gave way to the counterexpectation of Indian superability. [Almost mystically balanced and stoic, Indian athletes seemed to ride the jumbled tide of modernity with calmness and equanimity, giving life to the intuitive notion that the most current and the most primitive could be one and the same.] Anxious whites could learn from Indians, for their primitivism was nothing less than a species of supermodernism. Such notions as these deemphasized and devalued the traditional rhetoric of assimilation by encoding the difference of the pre- or antimodern, primitive physicality of Native men as more compelling than any similarity could be. Viewing Indian bodies displayed on the diamond, on the gridiron, on the hardwood, or in the ring, spectators and commentators naturalized the meanings that they had imagined for Indian difference, placed them in the specific historical moment of modernity, injected them with value, and then used their own rhetoric to spice the stew of melting-pot America as it was blended in athletic performance.

At the same time as they evoked primitivist difference, however, such performances also affirmed assimilation, social evolution, successful Christianization, and evolving forms of ongoing domination. The United States could readily assimilate Indian difference—where better than a baseball park or football stadium?—and fans could understand viscerally how such assimilation would strengthen a multicultural, transnational

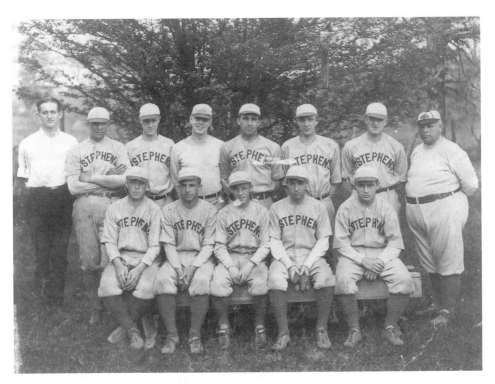

FIGURE 22. *St. Stephen's College Baseball Team, ca. 1923.*
Vine Deloria Sr. (top row, second from left). (Courtesy Vine Deloria Jr.)

America. Bard College's official history, for example, pointedly notes my grandfather's difference (a "full-blooded Sioux Indian") while incorporating him as the school's "greatest athletic hero" (see figure 22).

An expectation of assimilation, however, did not translate to a belief in equality. When commentators like Camp and Whitney thought about Indian social evolution rather than natural Native athleticism and balance, they saw insufficiency. Any manifestation of Indian ability was the product of good, scientific (read *white*) coaching (Camp). Indian insufficiency stemmed from the lack of (white) football knowledge and finesse (Whitney).[26] Even the ideal of sportsmanship—which the Carlisle founder Richard Henry Pratt insisted on using to prove that Indians were becoming like whites—could be read as an acceptance of conquest. According to Oriard, the Carlisle athlete "represented his race as a model sportsman, but more: an honorable, uncomplaining and wholly reconciled loser in a fair fight, the overt stake a football game but the implicit one a continent."[27]

Balance proved key to other clashes of expectation as well. If athletes in general were emblems of postfrontier masculinity around whom a group of students, alumni, and admirers might imagine an emotional community, my grandfather and other Indian athletes proved to be even more complex, evocative symbols for white spectators. Read in terms of the nearly white Ivies, for example, football spoke primarily to the intersection of masculinity and class. Injecting Indian men into the mix immediately called up different expectations, with gender taking its meanings as powerfully from ideas about race and sexuality as from ideas about class. As the historian John Bloom has pointed out: "Indian school superintendents often portrayed Native American men as untrustworthy, irresponsible, lazy, and sexually free . . . in a word, unmanly."[28]

Richard Henry Pratt embraced football, in part, because it gave him a rhetoric that explained how Indian youths might become manly—in the ways that Harvard and Yale spectators understood the term. Becoming manly meant, in many ways, becoming white. Indian players could beat white men, Pratt told his teams, not because they were Indian, but because they were becoming more like white people. Likewise, manliness resulted from a new asexuality. Pratt claimed not to mind adversity in the form of bad calls or unsportsmanlike play from opponents. These things allowed him to enjoin his players to be "bigger" men than their rivals— a declaration of masculinity underpinned completely by a sexuality that Native players were presumably no longer free to practice. Bigness, for Pratt, was not about physical equipment or manliness so much as it was about race, class, and propriety; it was defined through good manners, sportsmanship, grace, and a confident humility—in short, balance and stoicism.[29]

Football evoked additional visions of masculinity as well, visions in which manliness might be defined in opposition to womanliness or as a development out of an immature boyishness. Indeed, sports were often invoked as the training grounds that would make men out of boys, and it is probably not coincidental that Carlisle players were often referred to as *boys* despite the fact that those playing against the big schools were more truly described as *men*. Likewise, though Indian boarding schools and American colleges both had women's teams, the overwhelming public discussion surrounding Indian sports turned on masculinity and the simultaneous development of men from boys, whiteness from Indianness, class character from depravity.[30]

This economy of race, gender, sexuality, class, and modernity reve
how precisely expectations are formulated at specific moments in hist
At the same moments that Indian teams were being celebrated (albeit in
complex ways), African American and Latino athletes were subject to almost total segregation. Jack Johnson's 1910 victory over Jim Jeffries might
have cracked the door open for African American boxers, but instead it
was met with riots and legal repression that drove Johnson out of the
country. Team sports was another issue, and, until the creation of the National Negro League in 1920, Black and Latino players hoping to get in
the game sometimes tried to pass, not as white, but as Indian. And why
not? For a short while, being Indian had, in addition to its usual constraints, a few curious advantages.

LIFE WITHIN EXPECTATION

Though my grandfather was the only Indian at St. Stephen's, he was
one of many Native men who took advantage of the window of opportunity opened by the converging forces of primitivist nostalgia and competitive college and pro sports. When considering Indian athletes, it is
easy to slide into the heroic mode, focusing on Jim Thorpe and perhaps
a few other outstanding individuals—"Chief" Bender, the Hopi Olympic
medalist Louis Tewanima, or William "Lone Star" Dietz, who led football
teams at Purdue and Louisiana Tech as well as the Boston Redskins of the
NFL. But gridirons and dugouts all across America were peppered with
Indian athletes and coaches.

As we've seen, many of these careers—as well as those of Indian actors, musicians, and other cultural producers—were launched at the
Carlisle Indian School, created to teach Indian youths the basics required
for assimilation into white American culture. With a minimal academic
curriculum, the school emphasized manual skills, such as tinsmithing
and harness making for boys and "domestic arts" for girls. In 1893, however, Carlisle began fielding a football team that, like St. Stephen's, rapidly became competitive. Ironically, this extracurricular activity con-
tributed as much to the integrating of Indian and American culture as the
rudimentary book learning and obsolete manual-labor training on which
the school prided itself.[31]

Like St. Stephen's football, Carlisle football was meant to win friends
and influence people. "Nothing we have ever done," remarked Richard
Henry Pratt, "has so much awakened the attention of the country to the

possibilities of the Indian." As David Adams, a historian of boarding schools, has pointed out, football—a physical contest over space—literally took on the language of the now-concluded Indian Wars. Indeed, hundreds of stories—in both metropolitan dailies and the Carlisle papers themselves—used the violent rhetoric of warfare, scalping, and last stands. This language of violence was marked by a continual call to history ("the half-wild men, whose ancestors made things pleasant for us in the olden times with tomahawk and scalping knife") and to racial difference and social development ("Race was matched against race. And the race with a civilization and history won the day"). For Indian players, Adams suggests, football offered one of the few opportunities for a (literally) level playing field. They saw games, suggested the longtime Carlisle coach Glenn "Pop" Warner, not in terms of school pride, but rather in terms of a history in which the odds had always been stacked against Native people.[32]

Like Plenty Horses, a number of Carlisle students who returned to the reservation "went back to the blanket," while others became leaders of progressive factions within tribes. Carlisle's best athletes, however, rarely returned to the reservation (or at least not immediately). They tended to continue playing sports, bouncing among colleges, professional leagues, and minor-league and semipro teams. Bemis Pierce—the first Indian all-American—went on to play for the Akron Pros and the Oorang Indians and to coach at the University of Buffalo and the Sherman Indian School. Joseph Guyon, an Anishinaabe from White Earth, Minnesota, played football at Carlisle in 1911 and 1912. Five years later, as something of a ringer at Georgia Tech, he was named an all-American tackle in 1917 and running back in 1918. Going on to play professional football with the Canton Bulldogs, the Kansas City Cowboys, and the New York Giants, Guyon was inducted into the National Professional Football Hall of Fame in 1966. The Stockbridge-Munsee Jimmy Johnson, a 1903 all-American at Carlisle, played for the next two years at Northwestern. Gustavus Welsh played pro football for the Canton Bulldogs and later went on to coach the team at Washington State. Frank Mt. Pleasant joined Thorpe and Tewanima on U.S. Olympic squads. There were many other Carlisle players who never made it into the professional leagues but still enjoyed careers in sports at the semipro and minor-league levels or as coaches and scouts.[33]

Though, despite their deficient education, a number of Carlisle students went on to a number of professions that implied a thorough degree of assimilation, athletes were different. Modern American society valued them all the more for *not* becoming white, for continuing to embody a primitivist virtue that still looked like racial difference. Many Indian men refused the distinction between assimilation and difference, however, and they used "primitive" sports to acquire an assimilatory education more advanced than that offered by the Indian boarding school. Harold S. Jones—a Santee Sioux who, unlike my grandfather, did eventually become the Episcopal bishop of South Dakota—played semipro baseball to finance his undergraduate education. Louis Bruce Sr., a Mohawk, played with the Philadelphia Athletics and the New York Yankees prior to careers in dentistry and the ministry. His son, Louis Bruce Jr., who would later become Commissioner of Indian Affairs, attended Syracuse University on scholarship as a pole-vaulter. The Oklahoma Choctaw Ted Key attended Murray State Junior College for two years on a football scholarship, then played a year of professional football to fund his final year at Central State University. Jimmy Johnson had no trouble gaining admission to Northwestern's dental school after he announced his intention to continue playing football. Ed Rogers traded Carlisle for the University of Minnesota, where he earned a degree in law, a profession that he practiced for sixty-two years.[34]

When Carlisle closed in 1918, its preeminent place in Indian sports fell to the Haskell Institute, an Indian boarding school in Lawrence, Kansas. Basically a high school, Haskell was stocked with a full complement of Indian athletes, some of whom had already played for four years at Carlisle. Haskell was successful enough in the mid-1920s to build a 10,500-seat football stadium, which was, in its glory years, usually packed for games with Tulsa, Bucknell, Michigan State, and Wichita, among other schools. Like Carlisle, Haskell continued to funnel Indians onto college, professional, and Olympic teams in track, basketball, football, baseball, wrestling, and boxing. Other Indian schools—especially Sherman in Riverside, California—ran similarly successful programs.[35]

Sports—and Indian athletes—had special meanings for white American spectators. Indians often found athletic competition equally significant, but for very different reasons. In the early days of the Carlisle Indian School, government recruiters had to coerce and, sometimes, even kidnap students. Some students, however, like Luther Standing Bear, who enrolled in 1879, did so voluntarily, with a traditional sense of mission: "I was thinking of my father and how he had many times said to me, 'Son, be brave! Die on the battlefield if necessary away from home.' This chance to go East would prove that I was brave."[36] By the early twentieth century, however, such psyching up was no longer necessary, as Native boys at Carlisle, Haskell, Sherman, and a variety of other schools seized the opportunities offered by boarding school sports.

Carlisle, where Indian talent from around the country was first concentrated, acquired something of an Indian national team by default. Between 1907 and 1914, during "Pop" Warner's second coaching stint at the school, the football team went 73-22-5, playing such powerhouses as Yale, Harvard, Army, Navy, Alabama, and Notre Dame. When Carlisle beat Harvard in 1907, Indian newspapers around the country celebrated the victory as a second Little Bighorn. The Arrow, Carlisle's own newspaper, laid claim to elite status, boastfully proclaiming: "Indians Scalp Harvard—the 'Big Four' now the 'Big Five.'"[37]

Later, Haskell's teams would serve as a rallying point for an inter-Indian fan base, and Native sporting heroes such as John Levi and Mayes McLain would become household names in many parts of Indian country. As John Bloom points out, the building of the Haskell stadium required a massive national fund-raising campaign among Indian people, and over seventy tribal representatives gathered for the 1926 homecoming, powwow, and stadium opening.[38]

This inter-Indian athletic culture that grew up around schools like Carlisle and Haskell, and around individuals like my grandfather, flowed back and forth between numerous reservations where American sports had become an increasingly integral part of community life. Native people who did not make the journey to Carlisle, Haskell, or the other schools often enjoyed equivalent athletic experiences closer to home. In 1913, for example, Indian Office Inspector S. A. M. Young observed that Pine Ridge, South Dakota, people "have baseball games with other reservation teams and with teams from the adjacent towns," and he included in his report photographs of baseball diamonds and basketball hoops at the Oglala Boarding School. During the same years when my grandfather was playing for St. Stephen's, Cleveland "Moot" Nelson discovered sports at another Pine Ridge institution, Holy Rosary Mission School. Nelson, whose uncle had played a short stint with the Chicago White Sox, later moved to St. Francis Catholic Indian School on the neighboring Rosebud Reservation because he wanted to play on its well-known basketball team. Though a small reservation high school, St. Francis sent its Scarlet Warriors to the National Catholic Tournament eight years in a row during the 1930s. On the reservation, everyone turned out for their games.[39]

Many St. Francis basketball players went on to play with the Sioux Travelers, an exhibition club that toured the country, occasionally matching up with the Harlem Globetrotters.[40] Indian promoters such as William Conquering Bear sponsored other, less well-known but equally well-traveled exhibition teams. Conquering Bear also put together local organizations like the Wakpamni Lakers, which included men's baseball and basketball, women's softball, and boys' Little League teams.[41] While Harvard and Yale supporters were drawing a sense of community and identity from watching "The Game," the entire Rosebud community (as, indeed, were the Sioux people as a whole) was doing the same, gathering in gyms to watch the Travelers, the Lakers, or the local high school team.

Similar scenes played out across Indian country. By the 1920s, for example, Lumbee students attending segregated Indian high schools in Robeson and adjoining counties in North Carolina were able to play basketball (men's and women's), football, and baseball in an eight-school (later six, and still later four) Indian conference. Barred from competing in either white or black schools, they created a strong sense of local community through basketball competition. Rather than mourning the restrictions placed on them, Lumbees focused, according to the former player Ken Maynor, on their own competitions: "We would fill the gym to the rafters at the college. It was a big celebration playing our rivals, something to look forward to. I'd compare it to our Lumbee homecoming on the Fourth of July."[42]

When talented players were able to move outside local communities and into college and professional leagues, they inevitably confronted the complexities characteristic of intercultural performance. Like the Globetrotters, who fused athletic exhibition with a familiar minstrelsy tradition, Indian athletes were often expected to reflect white cultural understandings of Indianness back to their predominantly white audiences. Perhaps no team better illustrates this kind of self-conscious cultural work than the Oorang Indians, who played a full NFL schedule in 1922 and 1923, the same years my grandfather was throwing passes against the Connecticut Aggies. The team, owned by an eccentric dog breeder who used it primarily to advertise his canine products, consisted almost entirely of Carlisle and Haskell graduates.[43] Jim Thorpe, Joe Guyon, and other alums joined a smattering of Indian men recruited from other schools or straight off the reservation. With no hometown, the Indians—like the Globetrotters—played only away games and proved to be an enormous draw. When the team arrived in a town, the players would don blankets and headdresses and wander around the train or bus station, performing a hackneyed "naive Indian in the big city" act for spectators far less worldly than the players themselves. At halftime, the team would lead the stylish "Oorang Airedales" around the field and perform Indian dances as well as staging knife- and tomahawk-throwing contests, bear-wrestling exhibitions, and World War I "Indian-combat" reenactments. Football was showcased as only one brief act of a theatrical production in which primitive Indian difference was dramatized on the field for the consumption of non-Indian audiences.

The players, of course, interpreted the game and the halftime show quite differently: both were part of the long tradition of Indians playing Indians, a tradition with a certain bicultural sophistication and an array of meanings clustered around labor, adventure, and conviviality. Many of the players saw exhibition football in the same light as a touring Wild West show—a chance to make some money, see the world, and have some fun. "White people thought we were all wild men," recalled the quarterback Leon Boutwell, "even though almost all of us had been to college and were generally more civilized than they were. It was a dandy excuse to raise hell and get away with it."[44]

Other Indians joined barnstorming exhibition baseball teams, such as the John Olson Cherokee Indian Base Ball Club. Each March, John Olson scouted Indian players, assembling a touring novelty club that ranged across the midwest from Nebraska to Michigan. Olson hauled around a twelve-thousand-foot-long, twelve-foot-high fence, a thousand-person grandstand, a complete set of lights, and a ten-piece Indian band. The Cherokees weren't all Cherokees; often they were Michigan Ojibwes, Odawas, or Potawatomis. Sometimes, Olson's wife, Maud, stepped in as a pitcher, just for fun. In 1913, the agent for the Kickapoo school reported: "A number of strong young Indians who have left school spend the summer season traveling with some baseball team; but never have any money when they return home at the close of the ball season."[45]

Athletics meant different things to Indians and non-Indians, but there were also significant points of overlap. Indian mimicry of Indianness back at white audiences made it clear that there was both a shared sense of expectation and a critical Indian intelligence at work. Indian and white athletes likely had similar goals in seeking out professional careers—pleasure, experience, money. Indian and non-Indian players alike used sports in order to open doors, whether they be to travel or education. And, if critics, organizers, and spectators applied different meanings to athletes, drawn around the lines of class, gender, race, and sexuality, it was also the case that sporting audiences—from reservations, to Indians across the country, to well-heeled Ivy League alumni—found commonality and community in spectatorship. Sports served as a meeting place for transformation and persistence; for distinct, even mutually exclusive Indian and white interpretations; and for shared understandings. The fluidity of this meeting ground allowed whites to bracket racial discrimination (even as they practiced it), Indians to move more confidently in non-Indian society, and a modern bicultural athletic world to come into being.

That world, however, could not sustain itself through the rapid changes occurring for both Indians and non-Indians in American society. Indians had been able to move within certain white expectations in the first half of the century, but, in the second half, that changed. How do we make sense of that transformation? Expectation, federal policy, economics, and social relations all meshed in ways that help explain the shift. The antimodern appreciation of racial difference proved central to the entire structure of cross-cultural athletics, and both appreciation and difference lost much of their compelling power during the Great Depression and the Second World War. After the war, a new push to terminate tribes and force Indians to become white and modern helped close the primitivist windows of opportunity that had opened during the first half of the century. My grandfather's protests against the federal policy that would have dissolved reservations and destroyed tribal political identity represent his attempt to defend the validity of the particular form of intercultural world in which he grew up. Termination rejected racial difference and sought, instead, political, economic, and cultural assimilation and homogeneity—and this at a time when white institutions were retrenching against African American integration efforts. My grandfather's fight with the terminationists of the Episcopal Church revealed, paradoxically, how much the intercultural relations based on athletics had relied on the *separatism* that underlay antimodern primitivism. By the late 1940s, Native people, who had little desire to eradicate their distinctiveness, would again find themselves viewed as recalcitrant and backward rather than pure and primitive.

At the same time, the athletic programs in many Indian schools found themselves in institutional trouble, and it became suddenly apparent just how important boarding schools had been to the whole pursuit. As John Bloom relates, the Carlisle coach "Pop" Warner had apparently been paying his Indian players for years, gambling on the team, and selling tickets out of his hotel room and pocketing the cash. When it broke, the resulting scandal played into even larger accounting problems at the school, and, in 1914, both Warner and Richard Henry Pratt's replacement, Moses Friedman, were fired. The damage was done, however. Carlisle had long justified its sports programs as venues for teaching virtue; now it seemed that they were sinkholes of corruption, with young Indian people exposed to alcohol, recruiting scandals, player favoritism, and a generally bad class of associates. The school moved away from big-time sports, and, in 1918, Carlisle was closed down for good.[46]

Haskell picked up the baton and thrived through most of the 1920s, with its $250,000 stadium opening in 1926. Though the school was ranked fourth in the 1927 Associated Press football poll, its fall was abrupt. Colleges began dropping an uncompetitive Haskell from their schedules by the mid-1930s; the school stopped playing at the collegiate level in 1939. As Bloom points out, national shifts in Indian education policy pointed schools away from big-time athletics and toward more broadly participatory intramural programs. At the same moment, Indian people trying to escape racism in their local school systems began to avail themselves of a Haskell education, thereby lowering the age of the average Haskell student. By the early 1930s, Haskell was being prohibited from enrolling students over twenty-one years of age, which effectively prevented its teams—now younger and smaller—from being able to compete even with small colleges.[47] Other, cheaper sports—particularly boxing—began to replace football.

At the same time, the organizational structure of sports changed as well, as professional clubs increasingly looked like corporate business ventures and colleges more like preprofessional assembly lines. Even as Indian people were becoming increasingly alienated from big-time sports and the institutions that had supported them were no longer affording the same opportunities, African American athletes began a successful effort to integrate professional and collegiate sports in the years surrounding World War II. At that same moment, Indian political thought began turning away from the integrationist models that had undergirded cross-cultural athletics and toward a renewed emphasis on autonomy and distinctiveness. College coaches now had a new, and much larger, pool of untapped talent on which to draw. If Indian players failed to fit comfortably within the system, well, there were plenty of other players out there.

Eventually, modernist disorientation and the mass culture of celebrity began to catch up with Native people themselves. In the pure days of 1912, for example, they say that everyone back at Hopi knew runners with better wind and faster legs than the Olympic medalist Louis Tewanima. Sports—within the white arena—represented a complex mix of mimetic performance, metaphoric revenge, cultural acceptance, pan-tribal unity, financial windfall, and educational opportunity, but it was not the stuff of life and death. After winning silver medals in the five- and ten-thousand-meter races in the 1912 Olympics, Tewanima returned to Hopi, lost a few races, gave his medals away, and settled down as a farmer and an Antelope Society priest, with no significant sense of epochal breaks between those experiences.[48]

For postwar Indian athletes, that sense of everydayness began to fall by the wayside; athletic stars were honored and celebrated. Many Indian communities responded by drawing webs of kinship and unity ever tighter, trying to keep sports stars humble even as they were making them local celebrities. It grew increasingly difficult for Indian players to leave the nurturing pond of the reservation. Those players who made the jump found that university programs and minor-league farm systems now moved along different trajectories than the local, tribal, and intertribal leagues available to them.[49] In other words, the entire cultural, social, and economic system that had supported Indian athletes in the early twentieth century had been transformed in ways that almost completely shut them out.

"I AM OF THE BODY"

My grandfather's grandfather, Saswe, had had a vision in which he committed several generations of his family to serve as mediators between Lakota and non-Lakota people. Saswe had been a "medal chief," an interpreter, a go-between. His son, Tipi Sapa, had bridged the gap between Christian mission and Native spirituality. When my grandfather graduated from St. Stephen's, however, he clashed with my great-grandfather over the nature and meaning of that familial obligation in the new, intertwined Indian-white world in which they found themselves. My grandfather, reenvisioning the commitment with twentieth-century eyes, desperately wanted to become a professional football player and coach; looking back toward the late nineteenth century, his father wanted, with equal desperation, for him to enter the ministry. It was, as they say, no contest. A few days after my grandfather was ordained a deacon, his father died. On receiving his degree from General Theological Seminary, the Episcopal Church's flagship institution, my grandfather traded New

York for a series of backcountry South Dakota chapels on the Pine Ridge and Rosebud Reservations.

What must it have been like for him, watching each year pass, and seeing his dreams of playing and coaching become more distant? Torn between his own desires and his deep loyalty to church and family, he turned his lack of playing time into something of a penance. If he could not compete at the same level, he would compete nonetheless. He played first base on the Martin town team, fielding complaints from parishioners who did not think it right for a man of the cloth to slide into second base with his spikes up. He coached the Bennett County High School football team and put together a baseball program for Indian kids, bringing his athletic experience back to South Dakota. Though he was reluctant to have his life play out that way, my grandfather used his love of sports to integrate himself personally, socially, and spiritually into his community.[50]

Sports became a critical part of the expectations haunting American culture during the early twentieth century—and no less critical to an unexpectedly modern inter-Indian cultural system. The same fifty-five-yard pass could carry multiple meanings for both Indians and non-Indians; some were shared, some were not. Likewise, my grandfather's turning at the end of his life to his athletic past meant so much more than the simple loss or rejection of his other identities. Like the complex mix of motivations, attitudes, and traditions that Indian players brought to the field, my grandfather's sports experience became intertwined with his personal sense of spirituality and his place as an Indian in America. He made those connections in explicitly familial terms, looking back to his father and grandfather, and finding in his physicality, not simply performance or pleasure, but a way of serving, a special gift that informed his intellect, spirituality, and moral sensibility.

"I am not like either of my ancestors; one of the spirit, the other of the mind," he wrote in a get-well letter to the former Indian Commissioner John Collier: "I am of the body. I have a good, strong body. Nevertheless, may the *spirit* of my grandfather, Sasway, guided into me by the *wisdom* of my father, Tipi Sapa, impart to you on this paper, by my *physical strength*, the unseen healing resources of the earth, which rise up from the ground when we need them, by the power of the Great Spirit, and restore you to good health."[51] My grandfather took up Saswe's obligation, devoting his physical gifts to the power of the Great Spirit and the restoration of good health to Lakota and non-Lakota people alike. When life and mind began to depart, however, he came full circle, returning to a memory of pure physicality. All else—intellect, memory, spirituality, culture—had been made manifest through his body.

In this life lived through the body, my grandfather was not unlike Jim Thorpe, the great icon of Indian athleticism. As a great icon, however, Thorpe stands alone, as an anomaly, the only Indian that anyone not Native can seem to remember when it comes to American sports. As such, the memory of Jim Thorpe's body carries with it a whole host of expectations about Indian primitivism and modernist balance, ability and inability, history, education, physicality, and character. My grandfather's life was not like Thorpe's, for his athleticism—like that of so many hundreds of Indian men and women—was not anomalous. It was simply unexpected. And it was unexpected, not simply because he had a short career and a long memory built around football, but because he was—like so many Indian men and women at the time—thoroughly creative in crafting an Indian life in the twentieth-century United States. And that is something that should not be unexpected at all.

technology

Geronimo's Cadillac is a historical event. It is a song, an image, a story, a car. It is an idea—or, rather, a cluster of ideas—evocatively represented by Walter Ferguson's 1904 photograph of Geronimo and three companions sitting in an automobile (see figure 23). A short ride in Geronimo's Cadillac can take us through an exploration of the unexpected juxtaposition of Indians and cars. We might start by splitting the person apart from the vehicle. If you had to pick a single person to stand for *Indianness*, you could do worse than Geronimo, the iconic Apache leader who stands in American popular memory for resistant warriors everywhere and the defeated prisoners we imagine they became. (He should also stand for all the Indian cultural actors too easily forgotten and for audiences of indigenous people who might find nothing unexpected about Geronimo's ride in a car.) Likewise, if you had to pick a single car to stand for a world of automobiles, you could do worse than the Cadillac. Its array of rich meanings encompasses, not only technical excellence and social aspiration, but also class and race critique and crossing. It meant something when Elvis Presley bought a fleet of Caddies, for example, and it mattered that one of them was pink. Cars make one visible, asserting publicly that driver and riders are certain kinds of people; it would be hard to top the Cadillac in that regard.

To imagine Geronimo riding in a Cadillac, then, is to put two different symbolic systems in dialogue with one another. Indians, we can assert confidently, have been central symbolic elements in American culture for a very long time. Nature and nation, violence and colonial conquest, race and race crossing, nostalgia and guilt—images of Indians have been used to make sense of these things and many more besides. As we have seen, such images have both endangered and imprisoned Indian people and have presented opportunities—in Wild West shows, films,

FIGURE 23. Geronimo at the Wheel. *Photograph by Walter Ferguson (1904).*
(*National Archives, 75-1C-1.*)

and athletics, for example—to continue waging old struggles on new kinds of cultural terrain. This is not news.

Nor is it news that, in the explosion of mass cultural production that characterized the twentieth century, the automobile has been among our most evocative symbols. Mobility, speed, power, progress: these things matter, and Americans of every race, class, gender, and origin have found ways to express them in automotive terms. Cars serve a utilitarian function of course—and, thus, access to automobility matters critically to those outside the few urban transportation systems in the United States. As important as the moving of people from point A to point B, however, is the fact that automobiles express a driver's sense of self and of the nature of his or her power. The tough guy who needs a military-style sport-utility vehicle, the customized cars emerging out of youth and ethnic cultures, advertisers' gendered invocations of truck-driving manliness and soccer-mom vanliness, the identities, adventures, and nostalgia we invest in the idea of the open road—all these are part and parcel of a culture imaginatively built around automobility.

Things get weird, however, when the symbolic systems built on cars and Indians intersect. Even as today's highways teem with Jeep Cherokees, Pontiac Azteks, Dodge Dakotas, and other "Indian cars," there still remains, for many Americans, something disorienting about Geronimo—and his real and metaphoric descendants—cruising around in Cadillacs. On the one hand, there is a palpable disconnection between the high-tech automotive world and the primitivism that so often clings to the figure of the Indian. At the same time, however, those very distinctions are constantly being squashed back together. Take, for example, the Jeep Cherokee.[1] Jeep and Cherokee overflow in a partnered representation of nature—the latter as its human essence, the former as the ironic escape route that gets you away from the city and back to the natural world. The imagined separation of Indians and cars, and the mixing together of meanings, gets even more estranging when you try to juggle the symbolic ambiguities while at the same time admitting that flesh-and-blood Indian people may own, drive, and like cars. How might one think about the uncertainties conjured up, for instance, when the non-Indian world turns to imagine a Cherokee in a Cherokee—or a Geronimo in a Cadillac?

What kinds of expectations cohered among white Americans when their enthusiasm for automotive technological advance intersected with their twentieth-century perceptions of Indians, newly visible in movies, music, and sporting events? How did Indian people deal with the possibilities inherent in the automobile? And how did their actions appear in relation to the expectations being built around the unexpected meeting of technology and Indianness? In the earlier essays in this book, I pursued similar questions, focusing first on the ideology of violence and pacification, then on the dynamics of Indian performance and opportunity. Here, I turn more explicitly to expectations emerging from ideas of social evolution and racial difference, particularly as they engaged the issue of technological modernity. At the same time, I reverse the geography of expectation, shifting from discussions that place Indian people in urban, national, and international spaces to consider instead the ways in which Indian people engaged modernity in relation to reservations, thought to be premodern in their isolation. Over the course of the twentieth century, automotive Indians may not have appeared in American culture as often as warlike Indians did in Hollywood film, but they have lived behind the wheel in all kinds of powerful ways. It is worth pursuing a few of these in some detail.

EXPECTATIONS

"Getting civilized in a rush!" exulted a 1904 article in *The Indian's Friend*, a publication of the National Indian Association (NIA), a non-Indian missionary organization: "While settlers were pouring into Bonesteel, South Dakota in anticipation of the opening of the Rosebud reservation, no one's entry created such a sensation as that of Two John, a full blood Sioux, who, with his wife, dashed into town riding in a new $2000 automobile which he had recently purchased in Omaha."[2]

If *The Indian's Friend* represents one strand of the early-twentieth-century perspective—excitement over Two John and his car—the Oklahoma poet Paul Eldridge took a different and darker view in his 1936 poem "Gray Roadster":

I wonder what ditch in northeastern Oklahoma
You will presently adorn, slim gray roadster.
Will the slim young Osage who steers you
Snuff you out some flaring night
When the cars roar deep-throated
Down the Bartlesville road?
Or will he destroy you by day
In a flowering plum thicket,

Intoxicating in its sweet perfume?
(There are plum trees at every curve of the road in his country.)
Is your steel more sturdy
Are your fibers more felted
Than those of the eight Nashes and the Paige
Who have preceded you in the hands of the indefatigable
        destroyer . . .
The slim young Osage?[3]

Texas country-folk singer Michael Murphey likely did not know about Two John and his 1904 model automobile but looked back to the same time, to stories he had heard about Geronimo. Living under house arrest at Fort Sill, Oklahoma, Geronimo had apparently once driven a Cadillac around the grounds. Perhaps Murphey had seen Ferguson's picture showing Geronimo in a top hat seated behind the wheel of a car. Or maybe he'd heard about how, in 1905, Geronimo had ridden in an automobile as it chased a poor bison around a rodeo ring in a Wild West spectacle labeled "The Last Buffalo Hunt."[4] Looking, with a sense of irony and mild outrage, from the vantage point of 1972, Murphey wrote a song, "Geronimo's Cadillac," that suggests the extent to which the lives led by Geronimo, Two John, or slim young Osages would be understood as curiosities of the past, framed by expectations that left little room to imagine Indian people taking the wheel:

Sergeant, sergeant don't you feel, there's something wrong with
        your automobile?
Governor, Governor, don't you think it's strange, to see an
        automobile on the Indian range?

Jesus tells me and I believe it's true; the red man is in the sunset too
Ripped off his land, won't give it back; and they sent Geronimo a
        Cadillac.[5]

Consider, finally, a Native critique of automotive expectation, a scene in the Spokane writer Sherman Alexie's 1998 film Smoke Signals: a wide shot of a bleak but beautiful western reservation. Two Native women roll up in an "ndn car," battered and worn and capable of being driven only in reverse. Arms crooked over the seat, bodies turned back, eyes fixed on the rear window as they drive, the women converse easily with the film's male protagonists, who sit in the rear.[6] Alexie is offering viewers a reservation sight gag, to be sure, but his reverse-motion Indian car makes viewers think about what is and what is not natural at the crossroads where Automobile Avenue meets Indian Street. As the car rolls against the grain, its movement draws our attention to the idea of Indian *backwardness* and to the familiar expectation of *forward* motion, a white American ideal that connects technological advance with social progress. Placing an Indian at the wheel, the film asks its viewers to consider the ways in which Native people have been perceived to fit—or to be excluded from—a story of social-technological improvement. And so the car moves forward . . . backward.

Michael Murphey's question—isn't it strange to see an automobile "on the Indian range," being driven by an Indian person?—framed a key expectation that emerged in the early-twentieth-century meeting of Indians, Anglos, and automobiles. The ironic unnaturalness to which Murphey gestured made sense, one suspects, to Paul Eldridge and his readers in the 1930s and to the Christian missionaries of the NIA in 1904. It is the same strangeness that fuels Sherman Alexie's car, a technology possessed but—in the non-Indian imagination—not really controlled or understood by its Native drivers. That strangeness developed historically, in ways that we can trace through these texts, among others.

There are, of course, important social and economic reasons that might help us account for the unexpectedness that Murphey, the NIA, Eldridge, Alexie, and others have sensed in the idea of an Indian driving a Nash, a Paige, a Ford, or a Cadillac. In 1904, it was rare enough to see an automobile anywhere on American roads, let alone on roads in the American west, where most Native people seemed to reside. How much rarer, then, to see an Indian at the wheel?[7] After all, most Native people lacked the material resources that let one acquire an automobile. It was easy to imagine impoverished and primitive Indians along the roadside or beside the tracks, watching as white modernity passed them by (see figure 24). Two John's sensational entry into Bonesteel quite naturally impressed onlookers as a bizarre anomaly rather than an everyday commonplace. And Eldridge's slim young Osage wrecked his expensive cars within an entire social context that was thought to be anomalous: Indians with oil money.

But there is more to it than that. The sense of estrangement has persisted over the entire life of the automotive century itself, from 1904 through the present. Even as social and economic constraints have eased, the pairing of Indians and automobiles has continued to tweak non-Native anxieties about progress and its costs. Symbolic systems surrounding Indians

FIGURE 24. *Los Angeles Limited, ca. 1900. The blanketed Indian can only watch, immobile and downhearted, as white progress and mobility pass him by on their way to the future. (Library of Congress LC-USZC 4 3811.)*

(nature, violence, primitivism, authenticity, indigeneity) and automobiles (speed, technological advance, independence, identity, progress) continue to evoke powerful points of both intersection and divergence. If the estrangement can be tracked back in time, it can also be broadened beyond the question of cars. Indeed, automotive unexpectedness is part of a long tradition that has tended to separate Indian people from the contemporary world and from a recognition of the possibility of Indian autonomy in that world.[8]

Technology has been a key signifier in that tradition, which has been nurtured since the dawn of Western colonialism and which, of course, reaches far beyond Native America. Every moment of contact in which Europeans sought to impress the natives by firing a gun, demonstrating a watch, predicting an eclipse, or introducing mirrors and steel set expectations about the backwardness of indigenous people and their seemingly genetic inability to understand and use technology. Those European expectations emerged from (and then reproduced) representations of untutored primitives looking on in astonishment at the wonders of the West.[9]

Within any expectation, of course, there is ample room for confusion and contradiction—*unevenness*, to borrow the literary critic Mary Poovey's word. Ideologies develop, mature, and decay historically, and they do so in tension with other ideological formations. In the case of Indian violence, as we have seen, one can trace rough trajectories of expectation, as well as moments of rhetorical overlap, around *outbreak* and *pacification*. Expectations bleed together in any single utterance; it is the mingling that often proves most compelling. Such is the case with the ideas that non-Indians held about automobiles and Indians, which have been more uneven and multiple than a bare-bones colonial vision of indigenous technological backwardness.[10]

Here's one expectation. The NIA missionaries believed in evolution and social development, and they placed Indian people on the familiar progressive trajectory of social Darwinism. Indians, they thought, could and would leave behind their supposed lives as hunters and primitive farmers and evolve into modern people fully capable of using white technology—they just hadn't done so yet. With help, however, Indian people's social development might be accelerated. This evolutionary view underpinned various assimilation programs, which sought to advance and then incorporate Indians, not only into American political and social systems, but also into modernity, American culture, and perhaps even whiteness itself. This transition from radical difference to unremarkable similarity was, in fact, the stated goal of most of the Indian policies of the later nineteenth century.[11]

The NIA and other missionary organizations tended to see the adoption of anything from non-Indian culture as a step forward on this developmental trajectory, and technology proved an evocative indicator. The automobile joined telephones, sewing machines, domestic appliances, and other high-technology items as celebrated markers of Indian progress on the road to civilization. The year following the report of Two John's new car, for example, a missionary survey of South Dakota's Rosebud and Cheyenne River reservations proudly claimed to have located 28 pianos, 60 organs (signifying the presence of missionary chapels), an astonishing 320 telephones, and 18 automobiles.[12] At least two Rosebud men, Black Cloud and Billy Two Drinks, had acquired automobiles in order to conduct business. Black Cloud spent the summer of 1904 hauling prospective settlers around the newly opened portion of the South Dakota reservation, while Two Drinks planned to set up a regular stage line through Tripp and Gregory Counties and to underbid horse and wagon teamsters for hauling contracts.[13] Indians launching capitalist enterprises and helping non-Indians settle former reservation lands—this was the sort of anecdotal evidence of social progress that gave missionaries shivers of delight and confirmed the hope that evolutionary development was taking place right before their eyes. The embrace of technology by Two John, Two Drinks, and Black Cloud seemed to prove it.

But, if the very idea of Indian cars signified progress to some, to others it evoked a wholly different set of expectations, one frequently announced in terms of "mindless squandering." In a society that had often claimed to link progress, not only with technology, but also with thrift, automobile purchase (for Indians, at least) was irrational waste. Buying a car inverted, in current terms, the selling of Manhattan Island for twenty-four dollars in beads and trinkets—a little tragic, a little humorous, and all too revealing about an essential Indian inability. Unlike those who saw car purchases as evidence of techno-progress, then, critics of the "squandering school" thought that autos demonstrated the utter impossibility of Indian progress. For them, Indian use of technology revealed, as Paul Eldridge so eloquently suggested, that Indian difference was not evolving into modern sameness but was, instead, racial, essential, and unchanging. Eight Nashes, a Paige, a roadster—Eldridge's slim young Osage would destroy car after car after car after car. Such was his birthright. Indians, claimed even nastier critics, couldn't even *see* cars as progressive technology. Rather, they had always been attracted to "bright and shiny trinkets," of which automobiles were simply the latest fashion. Native people were supposed to be incapable of planning for the future or anticipating the consequences of their actions. They were, in a familiar metaphor, "like children"—or worse. "The Indian who purchases a flivver," observed Indian Office Inspector W. J. Endecott, "is held to be a spendthrift or of unsound mind or of dishonest habit."[14]

These rather different expectations—social development as opposed to essential racial difference, progress as opposed to squandering—emerged from the same root, the idea that technology marked a key difference between the West and the globe's indigenous peoples. Not surprisingly, the expectations collided frequently, often within the same utterance. Even as the NIA commentators celebrated evolutionary development and assimilation, for example, they also noted with a nasty chagrin: "Indians have a passion for machines painted in bright colors. Often when they have received $2000 or more for allotted lands the Indians will go to Omaha or Sioux City, see a striking automobile and spend their entire fortune on one like it."[15] Such apparent contradictions within the NIA report suggested the prevalence of powerful assumptions shared by evolutionists and antisquanderers alike. Both expectations—that automobiles signified Indian progress and that they demonstrated its impossibility—insistently proclaimed Indian people to be distant from contemporary technology in both space and time. Whether racially marked or evolutionarily backward, their rural reservations far from the modernity of the cities, Indians (many non-Indians assumed) could not comprehend, much less appreciate, invention, innovation, or technological advance.

Indian country was always to be seen as an anachronistic space. Depending on how one told the story, Billy Two Drinks might be making progress (though perpetually behind whites, with his progressive inclinations always anomalous in relation to the inclinations of Indians as a whole). Or his squandering might demonstrate the problem that racial inability posed for Native social development (and, thus, Two Drinks seemed representative of Indians in general). Such were the key dynamics that structured non-Indian expectations. No white person could fail to have a *general* opinion—a cultural expectation—about Indian people in cars, and no white observer could look at a single automotive Indian person without activating that opinion. As a result, Indian people behind the wheel almost always proved an estranging sight, even for those who thought it worth celebrating.

Imagining Indians as technological primitives empowered an equal and opposite reaction—a celebration of the mechanical advances of a distinct white modernity. Unlike Geronimo, a white American driver of 1904 was pushing the envelope of history. Nor were such self-understandings confined to a story of social evolution, with whites always at the advanced edge of history and Indians and others destined to trail behind. Technological mastery also proved a racial endowment, a further measure of white superiority. And it was, of course, a gendered notion as well. Seeing technology in masculine terms suggested that Indian men—often feminized historically (and, more recently, in the terms of pacification)—were doubly or trebly unsuited to the automobile. Indian women, caught up the mingled terms of race and gender, might be imagined outside the automobile even more easily.[16]

Indian women and men, one should note, were hardly alone in bringing up the imagined rear. Similar expectations grew up around other social groups as well. How odd, some thought, to see the sons and daughters of slaves driving cars! Wasn't it somehow inappropriate for a Mexican or an Asian immigrant to step behind the wheel? As the historian Virginia Scharff has shown, similar assumptions were equally applicable to white women, at least until they emerged as a market force in the century's second decade.[17] Mobility served as a form of empowerment, and it made Indians, African Americans, Latinos, Asians, workers, and all manner of women just a little more threatening. Automobility seemed an undeserved benefit that those lower down on the social ladder had no right to exercise. One can sense in Paul Eldridge's poem, for example, a certain resentment. It is not simply that Indians did not understand cars; even if they had, they would not have *deserved* them.

Non-Indian observers may have claimed that they wished Native people to join them in modernity as soon as possible, but the reality behind the rhetoric was somewhat different. More often, white observers like Eldridge remained hamstrung by notions of proper evolutionary development as something tied to sequence—hunter, then herder, farmer, mercantilist, industrialist, and so on. The expectation was that Indians would make all the regular stops on the trail up from savagery, skipping none. In the early twentieth century, that meant animal-powered agriculture, the supposed next stop. According to Agent C. H. Asbury: "We must insist upon the Indian making his living upon his land even though he may sometimes go a little hungry or have to lay up his automobile for a while for want of gasoline." Leapfrogging over several stages directly into a world of cars and gas seemed like cheating nature and was not to be tolerated.[18]

The cultural labor necessary to set and reinforce such expectations was surely not mobilized simply to account for Two John, Geronimo, and a few slim young Osages—which suggests that Indian people of the early twentieth century may have engaged automobility beyond the expectations of white American observers. Were there other Indian people driving around in forbidden automobiles? What did Indian automobility look like? And from where did it come?

WINDOW OF OPPORTUNITY

In 1972, Michael Murphey had been struck by the freakishness, the irony, even the tragedy of Geronimo sitting in a car. Geronimo was supposed to be defeated but dignified. In a car, he looked incongruous, like something of a joke. It is possible that he was ordered to sit in the car for Ferguson's photograph, a colonial subject bowing to a command performance. But Geronimo was probably better acquainted with automobiles than most of his non-Indian neighbors. He had conducted a relatively lucrative business in personal appearances and autograph signings at several expositions, events that often displayed the latest in American technological progress.[19] He had been in Omaha for the 1898 Trans-Mississippi and International Exposition. In Buffalo, at the 1901 Pan-American Exposition, he had seen the well-lit Electric Tower, 375 feet tall, not to mention airships and, of course, automobiles. More cars were on hand when he went to work at the 1904 Louisiana Purchase Exposition in Saint Louis. And, along with Quanah Parker, American Horse, Hollow Horn Bear, and others, he had ridden—on horseback—in Theodore Roosevelt's 1905 inaugural parade, which featured one of America's first presidential motorcades.[20] Like the performers who accompanied Buffalo Bill Cody, Geronimo had, in fact, traveled widely and seen American technological innovations firsthand. He'd been painted and photographed countless times. So, when Oklahoma's Miller Brothers 101 Ranch decided to sponsor a "Last Buffalo Hunt" as entertainment for a group of visiting newspaper editors, he apparently had few qualms about riding in the car that chased a bison around the rodeo ring.[21] Nor, we can easily imagine, was he quite so taken aback by the prospect of driving a Cadillac around Fort Sill or of sitting in the front seat to have his photograph taken.

Two John's story would seem to be somewhat different, and, perhaps, more typical, than Geronimo's. After all, Two John did not simply hop into an available car; he took the initiative to purchase one. Such was the case with Black Cloud and Billy Two Drinks, with María Martínez at San Ildefonso pueblo (she invested earnings from "craft performance" at the 1915 San Diego World's Fair in a car), with Marsie Harjo in Oklahoma, with John Bluebird (who got his through a crooked reservation teacher), with Charles Walking Bull (who traded borrowed Indian-issue cattle for his), with William White (who used his as an employee at the Crow reservation school), and with unknown first purchasers on reservations or in towns across the country. What enabled these people to evade the substantial social and economic restraints and use automobiles to imagine and create a new world on their own terms?[22]

For Indians and non-Indians alike, the early twentieth century marked a crucial period of technological transition. From a transportation economy centered around the horse—an individual mode of transport, but one with clear limits of distance and speed—and the train—quick and efficient, but annoyingly communal and constrained by its tracks—the United States began turning to the automobile, a new technology that met the requirements of both efficient travel and individual autonomy.[23] We can almost date the exact moment the car began its ascendancy in American culture: an 1895 Thanksgiving Day race in Chicago. In the following year, American cars were first sold commercially. The expositions in Omaha and Buffalo displayed them, not only to Geronimo, but also to mass audiences of potential consumers. And, in 1903, three cross-country "reliability runs" forced Americans to consider seriously a technological future ruled by automobiles rather than by horses or trains.[24]

Over the next few years, as upper-class markets became saturated, auto companies began to lower prices to attract middle-class buyers. In 1908, accompanied by the progressive rhetoric of social reform, individualism, and the victory of egalitarian America over monopoly capital, Ford Motors introduced the Model T. By 1916, using mass production techniques, Ford was able to offer the Model T for as little as $345.[25] As many owners upgraded or replaced their automobiles, cheap secondhand cars fueled the first used-car market in the United States, forcing manufacturers of new cars to become even more competitive. In the 1910s, as car prices dropped, automobile commerce spread from cities to rural agricultural regions, including the south and the trans-Mississippi west. After 1920, a postwar recession would make prices rise and force many makers out of business. The preceding fifteen years, however, from about 1905 through 1920, offered a window of opportunity for buyers on limited incomes, with prices remaining competitive and relatively low. Even after 1920, Americans of all economic classes continued to desire and to acquire automobiles.

In 1911, rural Americans owned eighty-five thousand autos. By 1920, that number had soared to over two million, and, by 1930, it was approaching ten million.[26] In 1930s North Dakota, for instance, you would find one car for every 3.7 persons—a significantly higher rate than in other places in the country.[27] And South Dakota saw its number of licensed drivers jump from fourteen thousand in 1913 to over sixty-seven thousand four years later. At the same time, the state's auto dealerships— three hundred in 1913—more than tripled in number. With large open spaces, lower population densities, and uneven retail and wholesale landscapes, rural areas proved well adapted to the automobile. The rural spaces of Indian country proved no exception. "What is needed here and needed badly," Inspector W. W. McConihe wrote of the Rosebud reservation in 1910, "is a good automobile. With a machine you could do in one day that which now takes a week to do. The roads around here are admirably adapted for automobiles and with the stupendous amount of traveling that is absolutely required of an agent if he is to do any real good here, a machine is almost indispensable. I believe the returns would be more than fourfold the cost of the machine in the first year."[28]

An economic window of opportunity and a clear realization of the usefulness of automobiles happened to coincide with sporadic infusions of cash on many reservations in the form of payments from claims cases, land and cattle sales, leasing, allotment sales, and Wild West income. On the Sisseton reservation, for instance, sales of inheritance lands during the first decade of the twentieth century alienated nearly twenty thousand acres and brought over $271,000 into the reservation economy.[29] At Devil's Lake, Dakota people received regular per capita payments from 1904 through 1914, the proceeds from a tribal land sale. A 1924 claims settlement put $130 in the pockets of each Santee Sioux tribal member.[30] And, between 1914 and 1918, agents on many reservations allowed the sale of both tribal and individual cattle herds in order to take advantage of wartime demand and high prices.[31] At Rosebud, Inspector Charles Davis noted in a 1909 report the infusion of over $2 million in land sales money, amounting to $700 per capita "with more yet to come." "In my judgement," Davis wrote, "it will be advisable to pay a large portion of these funds to the Indians in cash."[32]

By far the most regular source of cash on many reservations came from the sale of individual allotments. Put into place by the Dawes General Allotment Act of 1887, the allotment policy sought to divide Indian land held in common and to force Native people to occupy individual homesteads. Allotment sought to impose forcibly a change in social evolutionary status, from hunter-gatherer (the default position for Indians in American popular thought) to sedentary farmer (or, at worst, semisedentary rancher). From there, Indians would have, in theory, only a few short steps up the ladder to modern industrial capitalism.[33] Originally, the federal government was to hold the title to an individual's allotment in trust for twenty-five years in order to protect the Indian landholder. Changes and amendments to the policy, however, rendered this provision stunningly ineffective.

In 1913, Indian Commissioner Cato Sells dispatched "competency commissions," which issued patents to Indians judged competent regardless of the wishes (or the competency) of the individuals concerned. Often, status was determined by the individual's blood quantum, with a white ancestor taken as evidence of competency. Being judged competent meant that one could sell land. Patents often passed quickly through Indian hands, resulting in the substantial land loss that characterizes the period and the policy. As a standard part of their annual report back to Washington, reservation agents across the country detailed the assignment of fee patents and the resulting flow of money. As early as 1910, for example, the agent to the Kiowas was reporting that 90 percent of patented land had been sold, with half the proceeds "squandered." Judith Boughter's analysis of the Omaha competency commissions reveals a similarly depressing pattern of "forced patents, mortgages, and quick sales." So too does Janet McDonnell's detailed accounting of land loss under the Dawes Act, which shrank Indian landholdings from 138 million acres in 1887 to 52 million at the time of its repeal in 1934.[34]

Allotment, fee patents, and land sales played out in similar ways on many reservations. The exchanges came at the short- and long-term expense of Indian people. Often, Native people never saw money to which they were entitled, and reservation agents, farmers, storekeepers, and ranchers worked innumerable cold-blooded scams to acquire Indian land and capital on the cheap. In many cases, Indian people sold land against their will while government agents watched. People refused their fee patents only to find that they had been issued, mortgaged, and sold, frequently without their knowledge. Nor did it stop there. On western reservations, the mass sale of Indian cattle herds put an end to a short-lived

economy, sheltered in part by reservation boundaries and agent oversig
that had made sense to many Native people and functioned as well as
reservation economy ever has. The herds sold off, individual parcels or
Indian land were immediately leased to white ranchers, who claimed
them as their own. In many cases, then, even when Native people held
onto their land, the federal government removed it from Indian control.

The story of early-twentieth-century land loss is without doubt one of
the vilest episodes in the long history of American colonialism—rendered
even more so by the professed belief of at least some Indian reformers
that they had done the right thing. We should not hesitate to mark it, not
simply as classically tragic (though it was all that), but as a tragedy
marked by a cold viciousness—and by the pain, damage, and distrust left
in its wake. Indeed, the linked terms *tragedy* and *squandering* provided
cover for those who contemplated the transactions. The rueful comments
of one agent on his issuance of fee patents were shared by many: "At least
80 percent have sold their lands and at least 70 percent have squandered
the proceeds of the sale and have nothing to show for it." It proved eas-
ier to think of sold allotments as squandered than as swindled, for that
placed responsibility on Indian people rather than those who cheated
them. So too does the sympathetic notion of tragedy efface the fact of vi-
cious greed. At the same time we mark this history, however, it is also reasonable to ask a different question, to think more deeply about what Indian people did with the paltry cash that came their way through land
sales, leasing, and per capita payments.[35]

As in the case of Two John, squandered money often went to automobile dealers. At Yankton, the agent noted: "The Indians found it hard to resist the temptation to own a car when they saw their neighbors riding in
one." On the Crow reservation, 80 percent of the proceeds from allotment
sales went for "cars and other luxuries." Another agent observed that,
when the patents were delivered, Indians were dogged by "land buyers,
auto agents and fakes of all kinds." At Cheyenne River, the agent lamented
that almost every Indian who received a patent bought a car if the money
was sufficient. The Round Valley, California, agent reported: "Many of the
Indians who received patents in fee sold their lands or mortgaged them—
bought automobiles and spent their money." And, at Klamath, Agent C.
H. Asbury noted "a number of instances where automobiles have been
taken in exchange for the land . . . whoever gets a second-hand automobile, unless he has a legitimate need for it in his business is cheated."
Crow allottee Frank Shane, according to the local agent, "had a very good

Overland [car], but a dealer got ahold of him, rang up the bank to know if his check was good for $1300, and when advised that it was, Frank came into possession of a Studebaker seven-passenger car and gave his Overland away." In one bit of agency lore, an Indian judged competent was said to have argued against receiving citizenship and a patent, insisting that he didn't know how to drive a car. And, of course, the homesteaders at Bonesteel, South Dakota, most of whom arrived by train or wagon, admitted to being "amazed to see Sioux Indians whirl into town in family automobiles, squaw in front seat and redskinned youngsters in the rear."[36]

There is no reason to believe that Indian people saw anything valid in the dismissive words of agents and bureaucrats, who insisted that capital—in the form of land or cash disbursements—should be reinvested into individual farms or ranches or perhaps small local stores.[37] As many non-Indian homesteaders in the west would demonstrate, it took far more capital than that possessed by Indian people to succeed at most twentieth-century farming or ranching, particularly on the plains. And, by expanding the distance one could travel in a day, the car itself would, by the late 1920s, spell an end to the small stores that once dotted western reservations and surrounding homesteader areas.[38] Given the disinclination of many tribes to farm, the abundant examples of non-Indian farm and ranch failure, and the uncertain future offered by government policymakers, buying a car seemed wasteful only to white Americans. For Native societies, automobile purchase and travel may have been a more sensible way to make a meaningful life than to take a horse-drawn plow to the soil.

And so many Indian people bought cars. In truth, automobile purchase often fit smoothly into a different logic—long-lived Indian traditions built around the utilization of the most useful technologies that non-Indians had to offer. Just as many plains people had eagerly adopted the horse, transforming their societies in the process, so too did Black Cloud, Billy Two Drinks, and other cultural experimenters of the early twentieth century explore the useful potential of the automobile. At the founding of the Rosebud and Pine Ridge reservations, for example, the leaders Red Cloud and Spotted Tail had insisted on negotiating freight-hauling contracts for reservation goods and government annuities, and freighting had become a small, culturally resonant industry on those reservations. It made good sense for Billy Two Drinks to consider moving from teams to automobiles, not only in terms of a capitalist service market, but also in terms of the cultural transformations and persistences that allowed horse nomads to become cowboys and freight drivers in the first place. Would Black Cloud or Two Drinks have seen their automobiles as capital investments? Hard to know. It would not be out of line, however, to suggest that their purchases made sense within the social and cultural frameworks in which they lived.

The *auto* and the *mobility* that made up the word *automobile* pointed exactly to the ways in which mobility helped Indian people preserve and reimagine their own *autonomy* in the face of the reservation system. Reservations, we know, functioned as administrative spaces, meant to contain Indian people, fixing them in place through multiple forms of supervision. Despite the assault on Native land bases, many Indian reservations, particularly in the west, remained landscapes characterized by great distances. Automotive mobility helped Indian people evade supervision and take possession of the landscape, helping make reservations into distinctly tribal spaces. Indeed, one might read in the antipathy toward Indian automobility a slight whiff of the nervousness surrounding outbreak and independence. Even as the Crow agent lamented that the "only tangible evidence" of 1910 allottee William White's land sale was an automobile, for example, he also grudgingly admitted that White was gainfully employed as an engineer at the Crow school and seemed to be doing fine. And, even as agents and reformers complained about the lack of progress among Indian actors, Miller Brothers 101 Ranch show performers James Pulliam, Howard and Alexander Bad Bear, Ralph Red Bear, and Charles Wounded pooled their 1929 salaries, bought a new Ford Model A in Pontiac, Michigan, and drove it home to Pine Ridge. Such long-distance travel—and especially such travel between reservations—allowed Native people to imagine an even broader vision of Indian country, one that transcended individual tribes and places and helped create new expressions of the pan-Indian and the intertribal. It is no coincidence that the rise of an intertribal powwow circuit began at the same moment as Indian people were acquiring and using automobiles.[39]

The ways in which automobiles entered Native languages provide some evidence of Indian views of the new technology. Many words reproduced the same meaning carried by the English word *automobile*. In Lakota, *iyéhikiyake* means "it runs by itself." In Pawnee, *ariisit rawari* means the same thing—"goes about by itself." These words are likely independent descriptions, though they may perhaps represent more literal translations of the word *automobile*. Others, however, center on different descriptive characteristics. In Blackfeet, the car is a "skunk wagon." The Pawnee *kiriir aawis tarusta* means "smoking anus" or "smoke from the anus dragging." Still other words refer to the process of starting or driving a car. In Lakota, *naphópela* describes the sound of a motor being cranked: "it bursts or pops rapidly." The word for wheel—*hugmíya*—means a "round leg." The Blackfeet word for *driving* makes a direct correlation between handling a team and handling a car: the verb for *to drive* is the same as that for *to yell at*, reflecting the practice of yelling at a team of horses in order to start them moving. Finally, some languages may have tried to reproduce the sound of the English word itself. The Kiowas refer to a *caw* and an *aul-mobil*, clearly English derivatives. In Arikara, *kataroopi'Iš* has no clear meaning. The linguist Douglas Parks suggests that it may simply be a pronunciation of *automobile*. These words show Native people working to describe and incorporate automobiles within existing cultural frameworks, even to the point of turning *automobile* itself into a thoroughly Indianized word.[40]

Indian people were hardly immune to the automobile's potential for sheer fun. As a boy, my grandfather, Vine Deloria Sr., was commissioned by the owner of one of the first cars at Standing Rock to drive several prominent men around the reservation. They toured back roads and off-road, along ridge tops and down the hills to the Missouri River. Laughing, the men would jump out to push the car when it became stuck. My grandfather remembered it as an early reservation joyride. Later in life, as a minister, he conducted summer services at the top of Eagle Nest Butte, near Wanblee, South Dakota. Though these must have been very beautiful, his favorite memories were not of spiritual splendor, but of the challenge of getting his car up to the top. The butte's steep slope constantly threatened to overturn the car, which, like Sherman Alexie's car, had to be driven backward in order to take advantage of the lower gear ratio of reverse. My grandmother refused to join him in the car, but he always had someone willing to come along for the ride.[41]

Automobiles must have seemed particularly useful for the ways they opened up the new while continuing to serve older cultural ideals. The car offered transportation for the frequent visits and gatherings so often part of Native life. On the plains, cars easily served as mobile housing, reprising the older functions of both horse and tipi. Indeed, one of the reasons why Native people seemed more inclined to buy cars than motorcycles may well lie in their ability to serve as both transportation and communal living space. My great-aunt Ella Deloria was known to live in her car while traveling the South Dakota reservations during the 1930s and 1940s, and she was hardly alone. Within their cars, Indian families sometimes replicated the social arrangements of the tipi or other lodging, building blanket partitions in order to maintain the avoidance relations necessary to proper kinship behavior. A son-in-law at the wheel might, thus, avoid looking at his mother-in-law, who occupied her own compartment in the back seat. And, where plains people had once decorated and rubbed their horses with sage, they began to place the plant across the front dashboard.

Some Indian mechanics mingled traditional healing techniques with mechanical knowledge. The anthropologist Jaime de Angulo's accounts of fieldwork in northern California in the 1920s recall a seemingly aimless caravan of seven or eight Model Ts being driven by Pit River Achumawi people in circles through the brush. When, after days of wandering, one of the cars broke down, de Angulo—mechanically clueless himself, one should note—found himself confronting his expectations, which were both troubled and confirmed: "I was watching these Stone Age men unscrew and rescrew and take things apart or out of the engine and spread them on a piece of canvas on the ground . . . but the amazing thing to me was their argumentation. It was perfectly logical. '. . . can't be the ignition, look, I get a spark . . . I tell you, it's in the transmission . . . Now pull that lever.'" Even as de Angulo was surprised by the Pit River people's command of the rationality of the automobile, however, he also reported a simultaneous and alternative explanation: "Finally the engine, or whatever was wrong, was repaired. Then I overheard one young fellow say to another: 'You know why this happened? Because he was sleeping with his woman while she was menstruating! That against the rules.'"[42]

Consider the seamless integration of the worlds of the Tlingit photographer, merchant, and trapper George Johnson, who bought a 1928 Chevrolet with beaver skins and had it delivered by paddle wheeler to the Canadian north. Johnson painted the car white and chained the tires, the better to use it for winter hunting on the frozen, ninety-mile-long Teslin Lake. Without access to gasoline, he used naphtha. Lacking antifreeze, he drained the water from his radiator whenever he finished driving and kept a bucket of water on the fire ready to use whenever he spotted game from a lakeside watchtower. He built a three-mile-long road (now part of the Alaska Highway) and, in the summer, charged one dollar per ride in the car, which he had dubbed the "Teslin Taxi."[43]

Rather than succumb to the powerful temptation to imagine Indian automobility as anomalous, we might do better to see it in Indian terms—

as a cross-cultural dynamic that ignored, not only racial categories, but also those that would separate out modernity from the Indian primitive so closely linked to it. Automobiles, in this sense, can be seen to stand for a broader history of Native use of technology. Indeed, cars made up only one prominent branch in a family tree of such engagements, which have ranged from horses and guns to cameras and computers. At the turn of the twentieth century, for instance, Native women often invested in sewing machines, which sped up, not only the manufacture of clothes, but also that of goods for craft markets. Domestic items, such as stoves and, later, iceboxes, evinced, not simply technological desires, but differences in the priorities of Indian men and women (see figures 25–28).[44]

As Native people lived lives that refused the white expectation that they would have an inferior engagement with technology, they have also sought to represent such lives, portraying the ways in which Indian people have created distinctly Native spaces that are themselves modern. That dynamic is nicely captured by Blood artist Gerald Tailfeathers (see figure 29). Painted in 1956, his image Blood Camps refuses any distinction between the contemporary and some other kind of Indian world. Yoked horse and prim automobile, fine tipi and solid-wall tent—all coexist within the frame in a balance that refuses to favor either the old ways or the coming of the new. Tailfeathers rejects, not only the dichotomies built around modern and primitive, but also the developmental trajectory that would separate and sequence nomadic, agricultural, and modern. At the center of the image sits the car, touching both tipi and tent, mediating between the two, linking them together through both color and form.

Cars help center a variety of Native writings. John Joseph Mathews's Sundown (1934) concludes with an auto-powered binge, the car serving as an inadequate means of expressing the trauma of the mixed-blood protagonist's engagement with modernity: "The great car sped ahead and he was filled with a delightful madness. He passed the car ahead of him so fast that the driver almost lost control; almost drove his car into the ditch." After slamming over cattle guards, through clusters of birds, and, finally, off the road, Mathews's Chal realizes: "It was not fast enough dashing through the night at terrific speed. He felt that he had to express himself in some bodily action." So he pulls over for a painfully "tribal" song and dance. In Leslie Marmon Silko's Ceremony, the protagonist, Tayo, turns to the body as well, walking and running to the book's final climax, while cars and trucks serve as the mediums of witchery and death.

FIGURE 25. Native Americans and the Singer Picture Puzzle, 1906, Singer Sewing Machine Co. Though for some viewers the image might achieve a balance between humor and exoticism, for others it carried powerful messages about the durability and reach of the Singer. The beauty of the clothing and the horse gear testifies, not only to the power of the sewing machine and its ease and utility, but also to the desire for authentic Indian goods, for Native craft production had already entered the American primitivist marketplace. (Museum of the American West collection, Autry National Center.)

FIGURE 26. Inside an Indian Tipi, Crow, 1906. Photograph by T. A. Morris. A less idealized, more realistic picture of the interior of a Crow home. A family poses for a portrait—all except the figure contemplating the sewing machine, which sits at the center of the image. The home is awash with cloth and sewing, from the wall coverings on the frame, to the blankets covering the floor, to the everyday dresses and clothes on the people, to the beadwork hanging in the background. (Library of Congress, LOT 12775.)

FIGURE 27. *The New Home, Seattle, 1904. Photograph by Walter P. Miller. Even when home meant a lean-to on the beach and a family's belongings were few, the sewing machine might, nonetheless, occupy a prominent spot in the domestic space. (Library of Congress, LOT 12922.)*

FIGURE 28. New Clothes I. By Arthur Amiotte (1996). Amiotte's explanatory ledger entry helps clarify the relations between sewing machines and Indian users: "When we were young and went to school in the east we dressed like those white girls. When we came home and dressed up we wore our Lakota dresses. We learned how to sew those white woman clothes for everyday wear." (Courtesy Arthur Amiotte.)

Ray A. Young Bear's *Black Eagle Child* tracks a less bleak weave of adventures, many centered on a faded red-and-white 1956 Ford that comes to life in the midst of a tumble of race and gender confusion: "The beastly contraption lifted on hindlegs and analyzed the wind with its nostrils. . . . Falling on all fours, it made the rumbling sounds of an engine and drove away." Sherman Alexie's short story "This Is What It Means to Say Phoenix, Arizona"—the frame for *Smoke Signals*—also uses cars to con-

FIGURE 29. Blood Camps. *By Gerald Tailfeathers (1956).*
(Collection of Glenbow Museum, Calgary, Alberta.)

nect old and new, recounting a short anecdote about Indian boys who
wanted to be modern warriors after enemy horses: "The two Indian boys
stole a car and drove it to the city. They parked the stolen car in front of
the police station and then hitchhiked back home to the reservation.
When they got back, all their friends cheered and their parents' eyes
shone with pride." The film *Powwow Highway* made similarly explicit connections between horses and cars, with junkyards dissolving into nineteenth-century herds and street scenes morphing into old-time horse-
mounted warriors. Both road films and buddy films, *Powwow Highway*
and *Smoke Signals* used cars to lay claim to the essential continuity of Native cultures within a shared history.[45]

The Lakota artist Arthur Amiotte's *New Horse Power, 1913* offers a rich
meditation on the relation between Indians, horses, automobiles, and
culture (see figure 30). Amiotte recognizes an Indian affection for automobility. His touring car is populated by smiling ledger-book figures. At
the same time, he pays equal heed to the assimilatory potentials of the automobile, defining the car with an American flag in the upper-left-hand
corner, and placing it with an Indian in a suit in the lower-left-hand corner. Cars and horses are placed in direct competition in a small image
bearing the title *Autocar Runabout*, and horses and horse-drawn wagons
are prominent in the collage. The bold inscription at top center captures

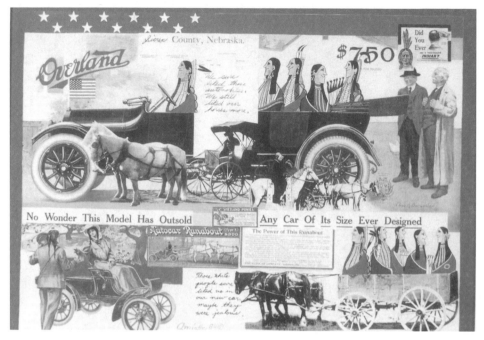

FIGURE 30. New Horse Power, 1913. By Arthur Amiotte (1995).
(Joslyn Art Museum, Omaha, Nebraska.)

the ambivalence of a historical moment in which change might be embraced but not desired or welcomed: "We sure liked these automobiles. We still liked our horses more." Note the syntax: it is not, "We liked our horses *still more*," as in a comparison between horses and cars. Rather, Amiotte insists on historical continuity between horses and automobiles. The judgment, "We *still liked* our horses more," reflects the retention of older ways of thinking and being in the face of the embrace of the new. Below, one finds an additional inscription: "Those white people sure liked our car . . . or maybe they were jealous." Amiotte's inscription takes us back to Black Cloud and Billy Two Drinks. We can imagine them sitting in their cars as the train pulled in to the station, ready to taxi newly arrived white homesteaders—utterly without their own transportation—on a survey of the parcels of land available on the newly opened reservation.[46]

THE WHITE MAN'S (INDIAN) CAR

Native artists like Mathews, Young Bear, and Amiotte have tended to offer thickly multiple visions of Indian automobility. While some non-Indian representations (e.g., Dan Cushman's novel *Stay Away Joe* or

William Saroyan's short story "Locomotive 38, the Ojibway")[47] reflect similarly rich visions, many other texts and images linked symbolic Indians and cars together in ways that spoke primarily to white American anxieties about technology and modernity. Automobility, it turns out, wasn't always a celebration of white social-technical prowess. Antagonism between horse-powered farmers and early motorists, for example, could be angrily expressed and slow to dissipate. Ministers railed against the automobile as a threat to a churchgoing and moral lifestyle. As late as the 1930s, American critics lamented the impending disappearance of the nation's horse culture and pointed an accusing finger at the automobile.[48]

One of the more significant and worrisome changes under way involved the accelerating shift from an ethic of production to one of consumption.[49] While missionaries and government workers sought to impose thrift on Native people, they might have done better to take a closer look at automobile-inspired squandering among non-Indians. In 1910, automobile dealers first began selling on credit, and many Americans eagerly embarked on the reckless margin buying that would characterize many forms of consumer finance during the 1920s. Other non-Indian Americans emptied savings accounts in order to purchase cars. And not just a few sober farmers mortgaged their land and homes for a set of wheels.[50] The number of cars on the road quintupled between 1920 and 1930, thanks in large part to an American mania for automobility that displaced older notions of fiscal responsibility. As Paul and Helen Lynd noted in their famous study of "Middletown," Depression-struck Americans were willing to part with everything—clothes, plumbing, even food—in order to hang on to the car.[51]

Even as non-Indian Americans rushed to embrace the convenience of automotive technology, then, many worried about what that embrace really meant. Cars themselves appeared simultaneously as symbols of the promise of the future and symbols of the ways in which progress wreaked havoc on cherished communities and ways of life. They evoked a difficult problem—the inextricability of the car's potential and its threat—and they hinted at a solution (or at least a diversion) in the form of a reassuring, nostalgic past. Automobile adventuring seemed to offer a pleasurable and safe reprise of the classic frontier journey of self-discovery, sans threatening Indians or nature. Cars—and automobile marketing—began to evoke the individualist freedom of the western frontier, its passing so widely lamented at the turn of the twentieth century. The automobile, it was suggested, offered a compensatory freedom—that of the untrammeled road (the physical road and the idea of the road both literally under construction at the time). Hitting the road, the open road, and the familiar clusters of ideas we've come to expect in road novels and films—all have endured as particularly automotive expressions of a kind of nostalgic, self-actualizing freedom in the twentieth century.

Consider one of the more beautiful and famous advertisements of the early motoring era, the Jordan Motor Company's Somewhere West of Laramie (see figure 31). Unlike images showing horse and car in conflict, this image by the artist Fred Cole makes them partners, with the romance between horse-mounted cowboy and Jordan-driving cowgirl standing as a metaphor for the marriage of nostalgic frontier and automotive contemporaneity. The woman's long scarf whips up in the wind, flashing the same touch of red on the cowboy's neck bandana in the same breeze, while a shared dust cloud blends them together.[52] At the same time as the image suggests a partnership that links the centuries, however, it also reveals other meanings being negotiated around automobility, most particularly in terms of changes in the gender and class of cars. The advertisement renders the car feminine, a common move among westerners inclined to see autos as effeminate when compared to a supposedly masculine horse culture. At the same time, however, the text insists on redefining a tough new sense of modern western femininity—at least for an upper-class white rancher's daughter. A "broncho-busting, steer-roping" woman, she knows "what [he's] talking about" (even if the rest of us are not entirely clear about it). Here in the contemporary west, the advertisement suggests, cars are not necessarily feminized in relation to horses (note how the car and the sassy pony are jumbled together in the text).

Nor are they masculine, at least not in the familiar terms of technology, rationalism, and progress. There is a kind of blurry quality to the character of the automobile in the west, one that complicated the expectations surrounding Indian drivers. Seen as technologically masculine, cars hardly fit the imagined profile of emasculated, pacified Indian men. Seen as fashionably feminine, they excluded both Indian women (on class and race grounds) and Indian men (who were also familiar Hollywood embodiments of the west's masculine horse culture). As such ideas collided, Indian men, at least, sometimes found themseles defined—as Jaime de Angulo had once imagined them—as natural "supermechanics." Balanced and stoic as supermodern Indian athletes, the idea of the Native supermechanic carried its own form of natural and technological

Inside the advertisement:

Somewhere West of Laramie

SOMEWHERE west of Laramie there's a broncho-
busting, steer-roping girl who knows what I'm talking
about. She can tell what a sassy pony, that's a cross
between greased lightning and the place where it hits, can
do with eleven hundred pounds of steel and action when
he's going high, wide and handsome.

The truth is—the Jordan Playboy was built for her.

JORDAN

JORDAN MOTOR CAR COMPANY, Inc., Cleveland, Ohio

FIGURE 31. Somewhere West of Laramie.
From *Saturday Evening Post*, July 23, 1923. (Newberry Library.)

masculinity, one mixed as thoroughly as the new white femininity created
in horse-automobile races somewhere west of Laramie.[53]

As numerous scholars have pointed out, manifestations of modernism
and antimodernism in the early twentieth century fed off one another in
similarly blurry ways.[54] Indian athletes and supermechanics—and cars
themselves—might reflect both modernity and nostalgia. The impulse
behind the symbolic vocabulary surrounding Indians tended to focus on

those things lost to the transformation. As exemplars of a natural life thought to be pure and unchanging, Indians were among the most important symbols used to critique the modern. Indians, it seemed, possessed the community spirit lacking in the city, the spiritual center desired by those troubled by secular science, the reality so missing in a world of artifice. On silver screen and musical stage, in the summer camps of Camp Fire Girls and Woodcraft Indians, in football stadiums and retreats like Taos and Santa Fe, Indians evoked a nostalgic past more authentic and often more desirable than the anxious present. By imagining such a past, projecting it onto the bodies of Indian people, and then devising means to appropriate that (now-Indian) past for themselves, white Americans sought reassurance: they might enjoy modernity while somehow escaping its destructive consequences. In Taos, for example, the primitivist Mabel Dodge Luhan did not feel compelled to give up her touring car, but she did acquire an Indian husband, Tony Lujan, to drive it—and, not incidentally, help her work through her angst (Tony, one should note, brought along on their first motoring trip a natural Indian mechanic, Adolfo).[55]

To preserve the power of such an Indian antimodernism, of course, imagined Indians had to be protected from the contamination of the modern. That separation has driven expectations—even as it has proved impossible to sustain. As in the case of the Jeep Cherokee, the distinct symbolic vocabularies swirling around Indians and automobiles often meshed together smoothly. The pairing of antimodern Indianness with the primitive freedom and adventure of the open road, for example, proved almost irresistible. In the late 1910s, tourism boosters explicitly linked Indians, frontier, and automobility in their hype for the "Black Hills–Sioux Trail," a route that midwesterners took through Chicago and across the Rosebud and Pine Ridge reservations on their way to Yellowstone National Park.[56] Touring guides and maps made the same kinds of connections (see figure 32). The famous Route 66 wound through Indian country, with a resulting swarm of faux-dobe motels, gift shops, and roadside attractions. Indeed, this simulated return to a better past via an automotive migration west through Indian country proved a favorite of promoters of tourism in general. The well-known Harvey Indian Tours, for example, used motor coaches to shuttle tourists from the Santa Fe railroad to Pueblo dances, offering a bracing dose of primitivism to the traveler.

Not surprisingly, the metaphoric linkages between Indians and nostalgic automobility easily extended to the physical form of the car itself.

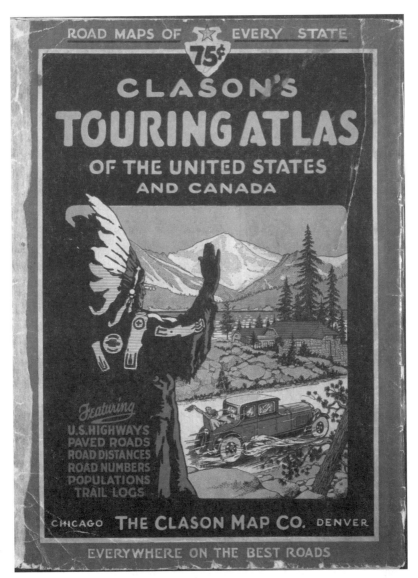

FIGURE 32. Clason's Touring Atlas (1920). (*Newberry Library.*)

In 1916, a group of Oklahoma investors sought to encode Indian meanings in a new automobile, gathering together in Enid to found, appropriately enough, the Geronimo Motor Company. In 1926, the Oakland Automobile Company introduced the first Pontiacs. These vehicles—the ancestors of today's Cherokees, Dakotas, and Azteks—should be seen in the light of the exchanges of meaning among Indianness, antimodern primitivism, the individualism and freedom coded in the open roads of the old west, and the automobile, which allowed one to express these ideas through steel and speed.[57]

DOWN TO THE CROSSROADS

Unlike the drivers of Sherman Alexie's *Smoke Signals* car (heading backward in order to move forward), the white motorist behind the wheel of a Geronimo or a Pontiac automobile on the Black Hills–Sioux Trail would have been driving forward . . . in order to go backward to a simpler time of freedom, autonomy, and purity. Primitivist meanings built around Indianness proved critical to the ways in which drivers imagined a white technological present and future. Yet it was one thing to imagine primitive Indians and quite another to confront Indian people flirting with a modernity from which they had been written out. When Native drivers took the wheel, the world of technology became a landscape of dangerous intersections, with the likelihood of spectacular crashes between the expectations of the white drivers found on Automotive Avenue and the Native drivers who turned in from Indian Street.

Billy Two Drinks, Two John, Black Cloud, the Pitt River mechanics, Geronimo, and others all defined a crucial point of contradiction. Their skill and willingness to embrace automobility revealed that the stories that insisted on racial difference—defined by failure to grasp technology—were fictions. Indian drivers troubled the evolutionary story too, the one in which backward Indians were catching up to the white drivers who occupied the leading edge of technological history. Nor did such drivers allow one to imagine cars in terms of a premodern frontier nostalgia magically devoid of Indians. Equally important, their mobility called into question the very idea of colonial containment, cultural transformation, and eventual subservience to the United States. As Agent C. H. Asbury fulminated: "A long haired blanket Indian who cannot speak a word of English but now makes his living by labor on the land or otherwise is eminently a better man for the community than an educated Indian with white shirt and polished shoes who is riding in an automobile at the expense of his creditors or relatives, and in many cases, we would find the blanket Indian much more disposed to cooperate harmoniously with the authorities than the latter individual who has gotten a perverted sense of his self-importance."[58]

Asbury's sudden affection for the pacified, cooperative blanket Indian reminds one of nothing so much as the murdered Charlie Smith, whom

Sheriff Miller undoubtedly saw as having "a perverted sense of his self-importance." The agent's preferred Indian—primitive, racially and culturally marked, harmless—might also bring us back around to Walter Ferguson's image of Geronimo (see figure 23 above), this time as read through the critique of the Native artist Jimmy Durham. Durham aligns himself with Indian drivers, seeing a social and political engagement beneath the white expectations of Indian backwardness. Geronimo is being represented, to be sure, in a way that reinforces familiar notions concerning Indians and technology. He is anomalous. It is not simply his presence at the wheel that matters, however, but, as Durham has pointed out, also his encirclement by three men bearing the trappings of the nineteenth century—feathers, a pipe bag, long hair. "Archaic Indian past meets modern automotive present," these figures seem to insist. The three are, by white American standards, clearly out of place in the car. Yet, in their company, Geronimo, wearing vest, top hat, and short hair, seems equally out of place. He is suspended, an artifact neither of the Indian past nor of the automotive present. In that suspension, the possibilities of Geronimo's modernity are both evoked (through clothing and hair) and contained (he is still an Indian; in fact, as Geronimo, he is quintessentially Indian). Neither he nor his companions will be able to take the wheel and drive. They sit and, in an instant, after this joking photograph is complete, will quite possibly be rousted from the vehicle. The allure for white audiences of such a representation lies in familiar relations of desire and denial: white reformers hoped that Indians would leap into modernity; at the same time, however, they had difficulty imagining the possibility of an Indian world that included such things as automobiles.

Yet, if Ferguson represented Geronimo photographically, so too did Geronimo present and re-present himself. As Durham has pointed out: "The photo is exactly like earlier photos of Geronimo, when he was obviously at war. If Geronimo had been defeated, he would have stayed on the reservation, dressed 'properly' for America's Indian myths." Geronimo's companions had done exactly that, and their presence in the car makes the case for the impossibility of Indian progress or transformation. The Apache leader—as image, at least—seems to present himself in a more disorienting way. Geronimo, Durham perceptively suggests, was, perhaps, not only the subject of the camera's aggression, but, with his clothes and his tight-lipped stare, also an aggressor every bit its equal.[59] In fact, Geronimo does not look much different here than he does in another, more familiar picture, one in which he grasps another

83726

FIGURE 33. Geronimo (Goyathlay). Photograph by Ben Wittick (1887). This photograph of Geronimo, the earliest known, features the same penetrating stare visible in Ferguson's 1904 image (see figure 23 above), coupled with a similar grasp of—and on—Western technology. (National Archives, American Indian Select List, no. 101.)

FIGURE 34. *White Bull Chief. White Bull Chief stands in front of car and house, holding a key ring and an engine hose in his hands. (Denver Public Library, Western History Department X-31861.)*

kind of Western technology—a gun—and stares with equal hostility (see figure 33). Nor was Geronimo alone in this meeting of Indians, autos, and photography. Consider the images on the following pages (see figures 34–39).

Cherokee author Louis Owens's automotive memories speak well to photos like that of Philip Wildshoe and family (see figure 35 below).

> In photograph after photograph, my mother and father, aunt, uncle, or grandmother, my pudgy baby self, my brothers and sisters and cousins, are sitting on the chrome bumper or shiny fender or hood of a thirty- or forty-something Chevy or Ford or Buick. . . . Adult hands causally touch the chrome and caress the shining hood and shoulders lean confidently into sturdy metal, feet possessively lifted onto the running boards. Only one house holds in my memories of those photographs—the cabin we lived in when I was little in Mississippi—but I remember what seems like scores of sleek, sloping-fendered, chrome-edged cars and an obvious desire to be associated with those vehicles.[60]

Cars and collective family identity. Self-representation. The pride and joy of technology and ownership. When I once asked my father why he favored big, flashy Oldsmobiles, he responded that it had everything to do

FIGURE 35. Philip Wildshoe (Coeur D'Alene) and Family, in His Chalmers Automobile, 1916. In front: Philip Wildshoe, his wife, Eugenia, and baby Eugenia. Middle seat: Sons David (in warbonnet) and Vincent. Rear seat: Daughters Rosie and Anne (child) and unidentified woman. The family proudly posed in their car for an image commissioned and controlled, not by a white photographer, but by an Indian family. (Library of Congress LC-USZ 62 101166.)

FIGURE 36. Inuits in Alaska Driving Car. *Photograph by F. H. Nowell (1905).*
This photograph of Inuit people in an automobile is part of a large collection of images
of everyday domestic and community life taken between 1904 and 1909. (Library of
Congress LOT 12779.)

with growing up in an Indian family in which cars mattered. As a reservation minister, my grandfather administered fourteen backcountry and small-town chapels—two or three every Sunday, several during the week, a few only a couple of times each month. He burned his way through a number of inexpensive cars, and the church's mileage allowance never came close to his expenses. Those cars were the lifeline, nemesis, and opportunity of the family, for, when the car was out of order, so too was my grandfather's ability to serve his communities. Frequently exhausted from his travels and labors, he recruited his wife and children as regular drivers. My grandmother, who wouldn't ride backward up Eagle Nest Butte, had a reputation as a speedster on the back roads. An easterner and a white woman out of context in the rural west, she found a certain freedom in speed, perhaps in imagining herself to be somewhere west of

FIGURE 37. *Spotted Eagle in Car, ca. 1941. In full headdress and convertible, Spotted Eagle and companion sit outside a painted tipi. (Denver Public Library, Western History Department, X-32081.)*

FIGURE 38. *Advertising Image for Toledo Automobiles. Photograph by Edwin Levick (1906). Six Indian men, replete with a mix of regional and cultural gear, perch on a car in a snowy forest.*

FIGURE 39. First Nations People in Automobile. Images such as this—buckskin-clad Indians overflowing a flag-draped car—might have been ironic . . . or commemorative. Many photographers took and marketed Indian photographs for profit. Perhaps this one stuffed a car full of costumed Indians, with the Canadian flag linking nationalism and technological progress together in opposition to an Indian primitive. But it is not so difficult to imagine local leaders posing, like Philip Wildshoe's family or (in the driver's case) like Geronimo, in an early reservation automobile. (Glenbow Archives NA-4069-6.)

Laramie. When my father started buying his own cars, he did so in response to that past, wanting big, fast, reliable, high-status cars in his own driveway.

Non-Indian audiences have had a range of options when it comes to making sense out of such stories and images. They might read disquieting juxtapositions of expectations and Indian lives ironically, like Michael Murphey in his musical treatment of Geronimo's Cadillac. Sometimes, they folded primitivism into the modern context: where Jaime de Angulo marveled at the rationality of Indian mechanics, others came to see something else, untutored natural savants who could understand the essential nature of an automotive problem through a kind of mystical knowledge. Still other people dealt with their uneasiness through the kind of critique—edging into humor—that Paul Eldridge directed at slim young Osages in slim gray roadsters.

Indeed, perhaps no moment in twentieth-century history threatened automotive expectations so visibly as did Eldridge's moment—Oklahoma during the Osage oil boom of the 1910s, 1920s, and 1930s. During the boom, Osage people often received large oil royalties from well leases sited on their allotments—with a resulting campaign of murder and dispossession. Many Osage people used oil royalty money to purchase automobiles and to hire drivers. According to the historian Terry Wilson, it was "commonly believed that in rural Osage County there were more Pierce Arrows than in any other county in the United States." The resulting category confusion—rich, automotive Indians!—caused extreme discomfort, which, not surprisingly, took the form of derisive joking and pointed critiques among non-Indians. Jealous reporters and officials repeatedly criticized the number and quality of Osage automobiles, noting that Osages were rarely content to drive a simple Ford but instead aspired to vehicles inappropriate to their class standing, which was determined as much by race as by actual economic power.[61] And, if the critiques meant to take down uppity and undeserving Indians, they focused quite precisely on the issue of technological ignorance, claimed to result in squandering. Osages were said to abandon brand-new cars when they ran out of gas. George Vaux Jr., an inspector from the Board of Indian Commissioners, observed in 1917: "Automobiles were everywhere filled with them [Indians] and so confirmed has the motor habit become that many of them will not walk two blocks to go from one store to another without hiring a motor for the purpose."[62]

In 1917, the *New York Times* jestingly recounted the story of the Osage oil lessor Wah-pah-sha-sah, who, after depositing a million dollars in a Kansas bank, immediately went shopping for an automobile. His preference, it turns out, was for a hearse: "It had fine curtains on the sides; it had ample squatting room; it, too, cost more than the others." Confronted by the growing crowd that gathered each day to gawk and laugh at the Indian hearse, Wah-pah-sha-sah at last saw the light: "The car with the comfortable squatting facilities was intended only for the dead. He does not quite understand why, but has become resigned."[63] The narrative insistently places Wah-pah-sha-sah in a different world, one where Indians squat rather than drive and lack the ability to perceive or reason across the lines of culture and race. The scant hint that Wah-pah-sha-sah might, for his own reasons, prefer a hearse can never be taken seriously. Indeed, confronted with the normalizing laughter of the white crowd, Wah-pah-sha-sah will make a gesture—unrealizable owing to his essential difference—toward assimilation of his neighbors' attitudes: he will trade the hearse in on a regular touring car. The story essentially recapitulates the ancient techno-colonial tales of steel, gunpowder, and eclipses, with Indian ignorance and inability the ongoing expectations. Even today, there exists a continuing genre of mean-spirited "rich Osage jokes" through which Americans reproduce the unarticulated assumption that there is something inherently unnatural about an Indian in a limousine.[64]

In such situations, we need not be surprised to find that the Indian in the car—estranging and somehow unfair—became the subject of humor and critique (see figure 40).[65] Jokes, songs, poems, postcards, and stories about Geronimo's Cadillac and other occasions of Indian automobility allowed the stories of Indian primitivism and white technological progress to maintain a distinct separation from Indian drivers and, thus, to retain their power as images. Making this choice, of course, meant yet another refusal on the part of Americans to view Indians as real people whose relation to automobiles was similar to their own. Humor allowed listeners and tellers safely to regard Indians in limos and Geronimos in Caddies as anomalies: the meeting of Indians, money, and cars was *not* to be considered the norm.

END OF THE ROAD

This essay has traveled through a genealogy of the expectations surrounding Indians and technology, one characterized by interlocking ideas about Indian development and a racialized inability to advance. Those

FIGURE 40. Pontiac Indian. Photograph by Charles McNally (1934). Pontiac cars always featured a stunning hood ornament, an Indian head with hair streaming back in the wind. Here, McNally has replaced the ornamental Indian with a real one, a humorous living emblem for the automobile. (Library of Congress, LC-USZ62 108393.)

ideas proved valuable when it came to the colonial domination and management of Indian people—but it's worth remembering that American colonialism always requires reassurance. And so, as in other moments of American anxiety, Indians might also be *valued* as primitive exemplars of the virtues lost to progress. That lack of Native social development has been affirmed ("A real Indian in a real car? Certainly not!"), deplored ("Why can't those Indians learn to be like everyone else?"), and celebrated ("Thank heaven there are still traditional people left, pure and untainted by the disaster that is modernity").

We have also steered through a broad series of counterstories found in the material lives of Native people, many of whom completely displaced white expectations by jumping quickly into the techno-modernity represented by automobiles. Those stories continue to run right up to the present: there's a lot of Native cultural vitality wrapped up in cars and trucks. Even as they lived lives that ran counter to white expectations, however, early Indian drivers sometimes reaffirmed those ideologies, crashing, like the slim young Osage, into plum groves and ditches, and, like it or not, appearing as funny curiosities, as anomalies, not ready for automobiles or for contemporary civilization. The annoying irony, of course, lies in the fact that such separations are wholly untenable. When you hear non-Indians talk critically about reservation yards full of rusting cars, for example, you might wonder how they forget about rural white farm and ranch yards, packed equally full of decayed cars that never seem to yield the right parts, or about otherwise critical Indian agents, who, when pressed, sometimes confessed that Indians and non-Indians were experiencing the world together. "The issuing of patents in fee should be advocated by Mr. Henry Ford and others, also by John D. Rockefeller who manufactures gasoline, and some of the tire companies," observed Agent C. H. Asbury, "as a good portion of [Indian] money is apt to find its way to these people, but I do not know that we should criticize the Indian too severely when our white neighbors all about us are hypothecating their life insurance policies and mortgaging their homes for the same purpose."[66]

For me, a powerful and important cultural vitality coheres around the figure of Geronimo in an automobile. It insists on the autonomy of Native individuals, cultures, and societies, and it demands recognition that perhaps your modernity is not distinct from—or better than—mine. Paul Eldridge, on the other hand, sensed the other side of the equation, the one that checks and balances any inclination to wax *too* rapturous about the power and agency of Two John or Geronimo or any of the other occasions of Indian automobility. Eldridge's poem is about death and power and the debris of American colonialism. Appropriately enough, as the poem ends, the clarity of role that seemed initially to exist between Indian destroyer and automotive destroyed is confused and doubled. For Eldridge, the detritus of the history of colonization—signified by alcohol—will produce a second disaster, the destruction of Indian people by their nemesis, a stoic and inevitable modern:

> Will he release you too?
> Leap lightly as a cat from your body
> In the ever-present crisis?
> Or will you kill him? Perish together to the pulsations of a
>   power-house,
> The mutter of a gas-torch,
> The soft blows of a night wind,
> You, wretched and stoical,
> He, twisted and cursing,
> With the fumes of gasoline and whiskey in the soft night air?
> I see menace in the lines of you
> There is a smooth insolence about your beauty
> Equal to his
> There should be written upon your hood the name Nemesis—
> Not Lincoln.
> I wonder what ditch in northeastern Oklahoma
> You will presently adorn, slim gray roadster.

"Gray Roadster" shows exactly how expectations are set—through poems that carry ideas back and forth among photographs of Geronimo, songs about his alleged car, denigrating reports from missionaries and Indian agents, evocative advertising, coy newspaper stories, folkloric legends and jokes. And, while it is tempting to let Eldridge's poetic words mark the end of the road, this book is not simply about the setting of expectations; it is about the kinds of lives Indian people have carved out in relation to those expectations. Those lives have included singing songs about cars—the famous powwow 49 song with its "one-eyed Ford," for example, and, of course, Michael Murphey's "Geronimo's Cadillac," which has been covered brilliantly by Mohican performer Bill Miller. As we pull into the driveway, then, let's take as our soundtrack the Anishinaabe singer Keith Secola's automotive anthem "NDN Kars." His "ndn car" is falling to pieces, for the social, political, legal, economic, and geographic domination of Indian people has left them with second- and thirdhand debris, Indian cars that barely run. But Secola rejects the expectation of death and disappearance laced through the works of Eldridge, Murphey, and others. Even if everything else falls to pieces, his "ndn car" (and his Indian people) will have a modern place and a modern voice—a radio that screams with Native culture—and will have the power to hold it all together:

> My car is dented, the radiator steams.
> One headlight don't work, the radio can scream.
> I got a sticker that says "Indian Power."
> I stuck it on my bumper; that's what holds my car together.

> We're on the circuit of an Indian dream
> We don't get old; we just get younger
> When we're flying down the highway, riding in our Indian car.[67]

THE HILLS ARE ALIVE...
WITH THE SOUND OF INDIAN

music

If I asked you to sing the "sound of Indian," I'll bet you could. The Indian sound, as it crops up in the folklore of non-Indian Americans, has a melancholy, vaguely threatening, minor-key melody and a repetitive pounding drumbeat, accented in a "tom-tom" fashion: "DUM dum dum dum DUM dum dum dum." It takes only a few measures of drumming and a couple of random notes to conjure up the sound and, with it, an array of expectation and imagery: a row of horseback Indians silhouetted against a ridge, to be sure; but also Indians dancing around a campfire or plotting a treacherous attack on the wagons; Indians besieging a burning cabin or preparing a captive to be burned at the stake; a grizzled old soldier glancing up at the sound and muttering to the dark, "The Injuns are up there all right. The hills are alive with 'em."

You encounter the Indian sound more often than you might think. Sports fans find it in the doleful faux Indian chant that accompanies the infamous "tomahawk chop." Film buffs hear it in the countless westerns that remain a staple on cable television. Ironically inverted, it was, of course, used to represent savage English colonists in Disney's animated film *Pocahontas*. Those who prefer syndicated cartoons will find it in the often-repeated 1942 Bugs Bunny classic "Hiawatha's Rabbit Hunt." Generations of children at piano practice have almost always found an Indian-sound piece in their first lesson book.

The tomahawk chop war chant made its way into the Top 40 in 2003. Reaching farther back, baby boomers may recall the long-standing jingle for Hamm's beer: "From the land of sky blue waters, comes the beer refreshing." And, on oldies radio, one can still find the throbbing beat and minor-key melody of Paul Revere and the Raiders' 1971 hit "Indian Reservation" ("Cherokee people! Cherokee tribe! So proud to live! So proud to die!"). In 1968, the Cowsills' "Indian Lake" offered up "Indian bubblegum," concluding with the familiar "woo woo woo woo" hand-over-mouth Indian sound practiced by schoolchildren across the nation. Country-music fans might point to an earlier moment, in the minor cadences and pounding beat of Hank Williams's 1953 "Kaw-Liga." And the list goes on, for, as the sound of Indian has cropped up in popular music, film scores, sporting events, piano pedagogy, and elsewhere, it has come to occupy a quiet little corner of shared cultural memory.[1]

What, exactly, lies in that corner? Music, which often exhibits an uneasy tension between sonic abstraction and the representation of ideas and things, has been a primary way of evoking, not simply sounds, or even images, but complete worlds of expectation concerning Indian people, rich with narratives and symbolic meanings. Indian sounds signify those expectations—primitivism and social evolution, violent conflict, indigenous nationalism, Indian disappearance, the romance of the forbidden exotic, the haunted American landscape, and a host of other anxieties, fears, and expectations. Even when it serves as sonic wallpaper, music retains the power to sock us in the gut or to bring us to tears. It is this emotional power that makes the musical expression of expectation at once insidious and potent.

So where did the sound of Indian come from, and what expectations did it set along the way? How does one track something as elusive as a sound? We can begin to answer that question by looking back to March 1918, to the opening night of the one-act opera *Shanewis: The Robin Woman* at the New York Metropolitan Opera. With music by Charles Wakefield Cadman and lyrics by Nelle Richmond Eberhardt, *Shanewis* was the first opera composed by an American to have performances at the Met in two successive years. It is true that these performances came during World War I, when German opera was banned from the stage, and that, like other American operas before and since, *Shanewis* lacked staying power. It is rarely, if ever, performed today. Nonetheless, it marks an important moment in American musical history—and in the sound of Indian—one well worth revisiting.[2]

The opera tells the story of an Indian girl of musical talent, Shanewis, sponsored by a wealthy southern California clubwoman to leave her Oklahoma reservation and study music in New York. Returning to her benefactor's home after several years, Shanewis sings a piece of idealized "Indian music," a traditional Native melody reworked by a composer trained in European technique. She astonishes a roomful of guests and wins the heart of Lionel, fiancé to Amy, the daughter of Shanewis's patron. Shanewis does not know of Lionel's prior commitment. When he woos her, she hesitates, insisting that he return to her reservation to visit her family. The second part of the opera is set entirely in the Indian country of 1918, at a powwow that admits both tradition and modernity in the form of Ford automobiles, red, white, and blue bunting, lemonade, and ice cream.

As the second act opens, the powwow is winding down, but Shanewis wants to stay for one last dance, giving the composer the opportunity to interject into the opera an unadorned Osage song, sung in a traditional style largely untouched by Cadman's alterations and orchestrations. This musical invocation of the old ways introduces Philip Harjo, a traditional young man who loves Shanewis and who perceptively sees the relation between lovers as a structural metaphor for social relations and history: "I hoped a cruel world would drive you back, into my waiting arms. But while the Red Man waited, the White man stole your love, as he steals all."[3] Harjo offers Shanewis a poisoned arrow, to be used in case of treachery on the part of her white lover. As Lionel gives his reassurances, Amy and her mother enter, and everything falls to pieces in an operatic orgy of love and death. Critics and audiences—at least initially—applauded Shanewis as a particularly American opera.

It seems a bit odd, this claim that one of the first successful modern American operas was an "Indian opera," full of Indian-sounding music, some explicitly traditional, some altered by Cadman's compositional hand.[4] But Shanewis was hardly an anomaly. Beginning with Arthur Nevin's Poia in 1907 (first performed in 1910), one could find in the early twentieth century a mind-boggling series of operatic treatments of Indian life and Indian sounds, including (among an even larger list) Cadman's Daoma (1910), Frederick Converse's The Sacrifice (1911), Victor Herbert's Natoma (1911), Mary Moore Carr's Narcissa (1911), Philip Bliss's The Feast of the Red Corn (1912), William Hanson and Zitkala-Ša's (Gertrude Bonnin) The Sun Dance (1913), Frederick Zech's Wa-Kin-Yon; or, The Passing of the Red Man (1914), Allen Paul Hastings's Last of the Mohicans (1916), Carl Eppert's

Kaintuckee (1917), Henry Hadley's *Azor, Daughter of Montezuma* (1917), Gerald Tonning's *Blue Wing* (1917), Earl Blakeslee's *The Legend of Wiwaste* (1924), Francesco De Leone's *Alglala* (1924), Alberto Bimboni's *Winona* (1926), Charles Sanford Skilton's *Kalopin* (1927), and Bruce Knowlton's *Wakuta* (1928).[5] Many of these operas were obscure, barely produced. The sudden emergence of Indian opera as a proliferating genre, however, spoke to a powerful impulse to place Indian sounds in relation to the performance of literary images and devices, thus helping (along with film) to bundle the visual, aural, and narrative expectations of Indians that would be conjured by tom-tom beats and melancholy minor-key melody lines.

Nor was opera the only form of popular music to engage the Indian sound. Cadman was, in fact, better known as a composer of popular songs. His credits include, among many other pieces, the well-known "From the Land of Sky Blue Waters," which ensured him some measure of fame in early-twentieth-century music circles. His compositions meant to idealize actual Indian music. Cadman refused simply to *imagine* an Indian sound but looked, instead, to Native originals for his sources. Cadman took Indian songs—often Omaha or Osage—and sought to surround their melody lines with harmonies and rhythms that faithfully captured the essence of the original. Those who would idealize Indian music, he thought, could "not lose sight of the original meaning": "A war song should not be treated as a love song, and vice versa."[6] He saw himself engaged in a practice of translation, of accurately representing essential Native meanings in compelling new musical forms. Cadman's gift as an artist, then, was not simply musical—it lay as well in his supposed ability to find and perfect the essential meaning in a Native American song. It should, perhaps, come as no surprise that, in the opera, Shanewis wins the heart of Lionel as she sings one of Cadman's idealized Indian love songs. Who could resist a lovely, civilized Indian chanteuse offering the bewitchingly distilled essence of Indian love music? Cadman used perhaps twenty idealized themes in *Shanewis*, ranging from the Osage powwow song, to existing concert pieces, to newly worked Indian music.

At the same time that he claimed insight into Indian meanings and the ability to re-present them musically, however, Cadman also built his songs around the lyrics of Nelle Richmond Eberhardt, which tended to offer familiar stereotypes—Indian love calls and vanishing noble savages. Consider the overlap of love and death in "Far Off I Hear a Lover's Flute," one of Cadman's well-known *Four Indian Songs*:

Why should I wake and walk tonight when all the lodge is still?
Why should I watch the ghostly road, so high and white and chill?
Why should I hate the crying flute, which happy lovers play?
Ah! Far and white my loved one walks
Along the Spirit Way![7]

Since words tend to center the meaning of songs as much as melody, and since Eberhardt's romantic lyrics usually had *nothing* to do with the original meanings, Cadman's pieces—despite his best musical intentions—usually ended up echoing the originals in melody only.[8] Eberhardt's lyrics worked at cross-purposes with the music, attaching familiar expectations to the idealized melodies that made up early versions of the Indian sound.

Cadman performed his compositions as part of his "Indian Music Talk," a lecture-demonstration that he successfully toured across the country, pressing the case for the importance and richness of his musical translations in chamber concerts and civic halls. He began a typical talk with a series of idealized performances, then turned to a demonstration of original Indian melodies, comparing them with Gregorian chant and Egyptian and other ancient musics, before showing how he had harmonized, framed, and translated them into ideal Indian pieces. Cadman began offering these presentations in 1909 and continued them well into the 1920s.

Nor was Cadman the only musician to make a case for the sound of Indian before a public audience in the years between 1900 and 1920. Between 1903 and 1907, the Indianist composer Arthur Farwell made four trips west, stopping frequently to perform his own Indian talk for large numbers of people. The composer Carlos Troyer had a long-standing Indian-music program, as formalized as Farwell's, that he published in 1915, when he stopped lecturing. Harvey Worthington Loomis gave several lecture-concerts in the first decade of the century. In 1911 and 1912, the photographer Edward S. Curtis toured the United States, his display of images backed by Indian-sound music commissioned from Henry F. B. Gilbert. The popular composer Thurlow Lieurance began offering his musical translations on the chautauqua circuit shortly after 1900, embarking in 1917 on a new show with his wife, Edna Wooley, a singer who claimed to have been raised among Indian people and who dressed in costume to perform his works.[9]

Other composers, including Natalie Curtis, Charles Sanford Skilton, Lily Strickland, Preston Ware Orem, Edward McDowell, Blair Fairchild,

George Templeton Strong, and Amy Beach, published and promoted Indian music ranging from the serious to the popular. The Etude, a popular-music magazine, devoted a 1920 issue to the music of these so-called Indianist composers, and it was able to offer a substantial listing of piano pieces for the consumer, in addition to Indian songs recorded on the Victor label.[10] Tin Pan Alley cranked out Indian songs as well, including "Hiawatha" (1903), "Blue Feather" (1909), "In Tepee Land" (1911), "Wahneka" (1912), "Indi-Ana" (1915), and "I'm an Indian" (1920), to name only a few (see figures 41 and 42).[11]

Why the substantial interest in musical Indianness at this particular moment in time? To begin answering this question, we can track backward—toward Indianist composers themselves and, as important, toward Indian people and the ethnographers who set out to record Native musics in the late nineteenth century. For, if music was intimately involved in the setting and selling of expectations of Indianness, Native American people were involved in recording, contesting, affirming, transforming, controlling, and performing those expectations in critical ways. Those ambitions and necessities were clearly visible in the ethnographic meeting between the versatile Omaha culture worker Francis LaFlesche and the ethnologist Alice Fletcher.

FRANCIS LAFLESCHE AND ALICE FLETCHER: THE ETHNOGRAPHIC INDIAN SOUND

In June 1893, shortly after Two Sticks and his sons committed "murder" and were killed or captured, and even as Indian actors were arriving in Chicago to appear with Buffalo Bill at the Columbian Exposition, Alice Fletcher published her pathbreaking "Study of Omaha Indian Music." Fletcher's report had been ten years in the making and drew on her extensive collaboration with her Omaha informant Francis LaFlesche. Confessing that she had initially found Indian music so much distressing noise ("a screaming downward movement that was gashed and torn by the vehemently beaten drum"), Fletcher had come to understand that it had a logic and order all its own. Omaha music—Fletcher transcribed several hundred Omaha songs as well as those of Dakotas, Otoes, Poncas, Pawnees, and Nez Perces—conveyed heritage, human emotion, and spirituality. "Among the Indians," she wrote, "music envelopes like an atmosphere every religious, tribal, and social ceremony as well as every personal experience."[12]

FIGURE 41. "Red Wing: An Indian Intermezzo" by Kerry Mills (1907). This and other suggestive covers (see, e.g., figure 42) evoked the romance attached to the figure of the Indian princess—fusing familiar cultural expectations to the music inside. (Author's collection.)

FIGURE 42. *"Blue Feather: Intermezzo" by Theodore Morse (1909). (Author's collection.)*

Francis LaFlesche proved a perfect collaborator for Fletcher; he worked with her for the rest of her life. After education in Presbyterian missionary schools, LaFlesche took a job as a clerk in the office of the Commissioner of Indian Affairs in 1881, using his time in Washington to earn a law degree, conferred in 1893. In 1910, he would join the Bureau of American Ethnology, winning distinction as one of the first of a generation of Indian anthropologists. His massive four-volume work on the Osage remains a standard and important work today.

LaFlesche knew both Omaha song and Western musical conventions, and he served as a primary adviser and collaborator for Fletcher and the music theorist John Comfort Fillmore, whom Fletcher had enlisted for his technical expertise. LaFlesche spent a week with Fillmore in Washington, D.C., took him back to the Omaha reservation in Nebraska for another week, and then spent a third week at Fillmore's home. "Without [LaFlesche's] devoted assistance," Fillmore wrote later, "no thorough or complete investigation of the music of his tribe would have been possible. No one else was so thoroughly competent in every way to assist a musician in finding out what needed to be known."[13]

One might wonder who was assisting whom. Francis LaFlesche had already made attempts to record and preserve Omaha music, and his efforts are readily visible in Fletcher's report. In some of the notated songs, for example, Fletcher and Fillmore included an additional "LaFlesche" version. Song 30, "Children's Song for 'Follow My Leader,'" almost certainly comes directly from LaFlesche, and it is likely that many other songs do as well. In an 1894 letter to his sister Susette, LaFlesche included the musical notation (with one minor change) of "Children's Song" found in the report, along with the memory: "We used to form in a single line and march through the village singing this at the tops of our voices, following the leader wherever he went through vacant houses, deserted mud lodges, the tall grass and through mud puddles. Little beaded moccasins would be a sorry sight when we got through. I put it in your album to remind you of the fun we used to have."[14]

Though LaFlesche helped Cadman with Omaha music in 1909, the ethnologist would later employ the composer as his assistant, putting Cadman to work making transcriptions for his Osage research—and would find that Cadman required strict oversight and correction. In 1910, when Cadman and Eberhardt attempted their first Indian opera, *Daoma*, LaFlesche was in the thick of it, constructing the plot scenario on which the piece would be built. And, when, having failed with *Daoma*, the two turned to *Shanewis*, they sent the rough draft to LaFlesche for his comment and correction. Clearly, Francis LaFlesche was more than simply, in Fillmore's words, a "devoted assistant." Enmeshed in the production of expectations, he marks a place of unexpectedness, with a preservationist agenda and musical and ethnographic authority locked quite firmly in place.[15]

MUSICAL PROBLEMS

Alice Fletcher, John Comfort Fillmore, and Francis LaFlesche recorded Indian music using Western notation; in doing so, they transformed it, codifying the music around the established Western concepts of meter, rhythm, and melody. Omaha music confronted the trio with at least two significant problems: first, how to represent the complex multiple rhythms produced by regular drumbeats and melodies that refused to fall evenly on those beats; and, second, how to discover and understand the musical scales that defined Omaha melodies. In the first case, they rose to the challenge; in the second, they did not. Their successes and failures helped produce the sound of Indian that would call up imagery and expectation for most of the twentieth century.

The simplified and stereotypical Indian sound is usually heard in units of four beats, with a strong accent on the first: "DUM dum dum dum, DUM dum dum dum." What the Omahas sang, however, was more complicated.[16] Omaha music often established a drumbeat accompaniment that moved in units of two ("DUM dum, DUM dum"), underpinning a melody that moved in units of three. Try tapping a duplet beat with one hand and a triplet beat with the other—then altering the rhythm and accents of the triplet figure. It's not easy. In order to capture the rhythm, Fletcher, Fillmore, and LaFlesche resorted to notating the melody line in 3/8 time and the drumbeat line in 2/8 time. Each line was then assigned a different tempo: $\downarrow$. = 60 for the 3/8 melody (or "song," as they put it) and $\downarrow$ = 120 for the 2/8 drumbeat. Each *measure* of 3/8 melody (with its three eighth-note subdivisions) would be timed at 60 beats per minute, that is, would take approximately one second of time. Each *beat* of 2/8 drumbeat would be timed at 120 beats per minute, each of the two beats per measure taking approximately half a second of time. Both a measure of the melody line and a measure of the drumbeat line would, then, take about a second's time, but the accents and feel of 3/8 and 2/8, respectively, would be preserved (figure 43).[17]

Fletcher, LaFlesche, and Fillmore's attempt to figure out beat and rhythm helped make the accented drumbeat a central element in the sound of Indian. Variations have included the stereotypical "DUM dum dum dum," in units of four, as well as the tying together of the first two sounds, making a combination: "LONG, short, short; LONG, short, short" (this latter pattern has its own history in Western classical or art music, often functioning as a signifier of primitivism). As musical expectations, these tom-tom beat patterns—some Native, some not, some hybrid—have come to have extramusical meanings. They suggest, not simply Indians, but particular *kinds* of Indian activity, namely, war dances

No. 20. HAE-THU-SKA WA-AN.

FIGURE 43. Hae-thu-ska Wa-an no. 20. From Alice C. Fletcher, with Francis LaFlesche, "A Study of Omaha Indian Music, with a Report on the Structural Peculiarities of the Music, by John Comfort Fillmore" (1893), in Peabody Museum of American Archaeology and Ethnology, Harvard University, Papers 1 (1904): 237-382/1-152.

and other forms of menacing behavior, easily associated with images of Indian violence and savagery.

The *Hae-thu-ska Wa-an* excerpt reproduced in figure 43 above also includes a second familiar Indian device—a "short-long" rhythmic combination that appears in the melody (see, e.g., the first and fourth measures in figure 43). This pattern—so clear in Fletcher's recordings of Omaha music—also has a long history in Western art music as a signifier of exoticism. Musical ideas and meanings mixed together in intricate overlaps. Some (e.g., the "short-long" pattern) existed within the repertoire of Western composers. Others sprung from the imaginations of individual musicmakers such as Cadman. Many—the "short-long" pattern included—existed simultaneously, however, in the Omaha music traditions recorded by Fletcher. An overlap like that suggested an intensification of meaning. The primitivist expectations built on a "short-long" rhythm or a modified tom-tom beat in the classical vocabulary enriched the primitivism of the authentic, which itself rested on the fact that such elements could be found within actual Indian music traditions. Cadman's "From the Land of Sky Blue Waters" offers an excellent example, for it makes the "short-long" figure central to both melody and piano accompaniment, Indianizing the piece in the process.

No matter how authentic the music made them seem, the meanings were, of course, largely Euro-American. Fletcher once pointed out that Indian people traded songs frequently but were always sure to maintain the "copyright"—that is, the recognition of the music's origins.[18] In the overlaps and mixtures with Western music, however, tribal meanings were compromised and transformed in various ways. They were translated by ethnographers seeking to salvage disappearing Indian culture; idealized by those who, like Cadman, thought they could capture Native essences; distorted by older musical renderings of exoticism; and Americanized by those who sought to create artistic expression that was both national and indigenous.[19]

FLETCHER, DVOŘÁK, AND FARWELL:
THE *AMERICAN* INDIAN SOUND

So what were some of the meanings behind the first iterations of the sound of Indian? Alice Fletcher clearly had aims beyond the ethnographic salvage of Indian music. As a young woman, she had expressed an early desire for the creation of a particularly American form of music. Taken with the decidedly avian sounds of nature produced by the flutist Sidney

Lanier, she wrote in 1873: "Your flute gave me that for which I had ceased to hope, true American music, and awakened in my heart a feeling of patriotism that I never knew before."[20] Fletcher's work on Omaha music arrived at a propitious time for the growing number of composers interested in such distinctly American music. The question of musical nationalism, already an issue in Europe, had started to preoccupy Americans as well. What did it mean to have a national music tradition? How could one best present in music the abstraction of national character? Could rhythms, chord progressions, melodic intervals, and tonal textures capture something so elusive?

Such questions crystallized around the three-year visit of the renowned Bohemian nationalist composer Antonín Dvořák, who lived in the United States between 1892 and 1895, composing, teaching, and stirring the musical pot with public prescriptions and pronouncements.[21] Dvořák's main theme, articulated both in his Symphony no. 9 (*From the New World*) and in his writings and interviews, concerned the production of a nationalist fine-art music that would be indigenous to the Americas. The raw material for such aesthetic production, he thought, was vernacular folk music—and he knew too little about American social history to make fine distinctions. "It matters little," he argued blithely, "whether the inspiration for the coming folksongs of America is derived from the negro melodies, the songs of the creoles, the red man's chant, or the plaintive ditties of the homesick German or Norwegian. Undoubtedly the germs for the best of music lie hidden among all the races that are commingled in this great country."[22]

Into this nationalist ferment came Alice Fletcher's 1893 report, which included ninety-two Omaha songs, notated and, in most cases, harmonized simply by John Comfort Fillmore. By transcribing Omaha melodies, Fletcher had consolidated a body of themes and had made them easily accessible to serious nationalist composers. And she knew it. In August 1893, while attending the Columbian Exposition, Fletcher and Fillmore provided a copy of the report to Dvořák in an effort to encourage him to consider Indian songs as possible folk sources for an indigenous art music.[23] Later, Fletcher would encourage Arthur Farwell, Charles Wakefield Cadman, and others to take up the Omaha material in their own compositions. In 1900, she published *Indian Story and Song*, which included, not only musical themes, but also narratives. Fletcher argued that the utility of Indian music to composers would be "greater if the story, or the ceremony which gave rise to the song could be known, so that, in developing the theme, all the movements might be consonant with the circumstances that had inspired the motive."[24]

Nor was Fletcher alone in producing a new public knowledge of Indian music. The German music student Theodore Baker had investigated Native music as early as 1880, and his 1882 dissertation served as primary source material for composers such as Edward McDowell, who used melodies collected by Baker in his *Second (Indian) Suite* (1897). Franz Boas published Eskimo songs in 1888. Jesse Walter Fewkes published Passamaquoddy music in 1890 and joined with Frank Hamilton Cushing to collect the tunes later used by composer Carlos Troyer in his 1893 *Two Zuni Songs.* James Mooney recorded Arapahoe, Kiowa, Caddo, and Comanche songs in 1894. Natalie Curtis would publish, in 1907, *The Indian's Book,* which included melodies collected from Hopi, Cheyenne, Laguna, Wabanaki, and many other Indian peoples. Frederick Burton's Ojibwe work led to his 1909 book *American Primitive Music.* Inspired by Fletcher, Frances Densmore began in 1893 one of the most prolific and productive careers in American ethnomusicology. She published widely on music from around the continent, including compilations of Ojibwe, Sioux, Seminole, Mandan, Ute, and Maidu songs, among many others. All this material became available as grist for the nationalist music mill.[25]

It is not, however, as if this abundance of ethnographic data singlehandedly produced the idea of an Indian sound in the United States. Some melodies were appropriated to Western forms; others were not. And American composers had been building musical representations of Indianness out of their imagination and a repertoire of primitivist musical figures since the late eighteenth century. Some of these, as we have seen, included musical ideas that Fletcher would later show to be simultaneously Native. Others—"long-short-short" beat patterns and the interval of the open fifth in accompaniments, for example—signified Indian only in the context of titles, lyrics, program notes, and performances that *gave* them Indian meaning. By the late nineteenth century, a respectable trove of such Indian representations had, in fact, accumulated in the corpus of American music.[26]

Nonetheless, Fletcher's 1893 report proved transformative, for its presentation of raw musical material—combined with Fletcher's own lobbying and Dvořák's nationalist injunctions—helped structure a small explosion of Indianist composition. Perhaps no American composer embraced Dvořák's admonitions as heartily as Arthur Farwell, who would, in turn, lean heavily on Fletcher's compilations. Farwell came late to music, having studied electrical engineering at the Massachusetts Institute of Technology, but, when he arrived, it was with passion and conviction. American music, he thought, "must have an American flavor": "It must be recognizably American, as Russian music is Russian, or French music, French." To find that flavor, Farwell followed Dvořák in recommending a wide range: "ragtime, Negro songs, Indian songs, Cowboy songs, and, of the utmost importance, new and daring expressions of our own composers, sound-speech previously unheard."[27]

This vision was eclectic, and, to advance it, Farwell founded in 1901 the *Wa-Wan Press*, a periodical publication that took its name from an Omaha word (borrowed from Fletcher) meaning "to sing for someone." During its decade-long existence, *Wa-Wan* published new American music twice quarterly (one issue of vocal songs, the other of piano music). Farwell meant to create a fellowship of young composers and to publish those who were unable to find more established publishers for their notably American works. Although *Wa-Wan* compositions also took up Orientalist practice and appropriated black musics, Indian themes remained prominent, and *Wa-Wan* composers who touched on them at one time or another included Stanley Avery, Natalie Curtis, Henry F. Gilbert, Harvey Worthington Loomis, Carlos Troyer, and, of course, Farwell himself.[28]

In the first volume, Farwell published a collection for piano, *American Indian Melodies*, with tunes borrowed from Fletcher's *Indian Story and Song* and one of her wax cylinder rolls. To Farwell, it was not enough simply to harmonize the melodies; one had to capture the mythic spirit—and, thus, the meaning—of the music. He agreed with Fletcher: "A heightened art-value could be imparted to [pieces] if the composer should consult, not merely [Indian] melodic structure, but the poetic nature of the particular legend or incident of which each song was the outcome."[29] The short pieces, then, are preceded by a long introduction that seeks to re-create the cultural context or story surrounding each melody. Later, Farwell would turn the piano pieces into songs, with lyrics fusing story and music. Both Farwell and Cadman laid claim to an "artistic ethnography," an understanding of the essential meaning of Indian melody that melded ethnographic authenticity with privileged aesthetic vision. In the process, Farwell (in his introductions and lyrics) and Cadman (in the lyrics of Eberhardt) created images and narratives and then assigned them to the semiabstraction of musical sounds.

Farwell's piano pieces suggest the extent to which he and his readers engaged familiar nineteenth-century thematic expectations—warfare, tragedy, love—in terms of Indianness. The majority—four—of the themes deal with warfare ("Approach of the Thunder God," "Song of the Deathless Voice," "Ichibuzzhi," and "Song of the Leader"); three deal with tragic Indian disappearance ("The Song of the Ghost Dance," "The Mother's Vow," "The Song to the Spirit"). The others turn to love ("The Old Man's Love Song") and spirituality ("Inketunga's Thunder Song," "Choral"). Performers of the music were treated to familiar themes that intersected and overlapped with Indian violence and vanishing, the predominant ideological interests of nineteenth-century expectation (with the equally important themes of Indian love and spiritual mystery trailing closely behind).

How did such pieces sound? There is, as Amy Stillman suggests, a substantial distance between Farwell's and Cadman's music and that of other art musics of the period. In their melody, tempo, and accompaniment, the pieces seem one step removed from the American tradition of a composer like Charles Ives, perhaps two steps from the German song tradition explored by Schubert, Schumann, Brahms, and Wolf. The melodies sustain their pitches, moving in unexpected directions and with a certain irregularity that is emphasized by the piano accompaniments. Add the often-melancholy lyrics to the mix, and the songs frequently tend toward the moody, nostalgic, and haunting.[30]

As the first sustained response to the call for musical nationalism, Farwell's turn to Fletcher's quasi-programmatic ethnography suggested the importance of an Indian imaginary, not only to the project of modernity, but to that of national identity as well. Modernist primitivism, with its desire for premodern authenticity, led Farwell to emphasize the importance of land, spirit, heritage, and nature to any understanding of national character. Although black music, particularly jazz, would, by the 1920s, dominate American music (most famously in the works of Gershwin), at the turn of the century the nationalist impulse pushed Farwell and others toward Indianness more often than it did toward African American sounds. Among all the nation's folk exotics, Indians best signified indigeneity and a close historical and spiritual connection to the American landscape.[31]

The ethnographic authenticity of Indianist music proved critical to those touting its national uniqueness. By the time a piece was published, however, composers like Farwell and Cadman had translated other translations. If they were two steps removed from the European art-song tradition, they were equally removed from original Indian performances.[32]

Though they laid claim to authenticity, there was, in truth, no guarantee that anyone was "getting it right." Ethnographers themselves pointed out the difficulties with the very first round of translations: Indian musicians sang loudly, out of doors, to the accompaniment of drumming, with all manner of distractions. It was never entirely clear to many recorders if a singer was willfully using microtones and pitch bending or whether he or she was simply out of tune according to a Western tonal sensibility.[33] Even the confident Fletcher closed her report with a short appendix listing the problems involved in transcription, insisting that she had, in fact, gotten it right, and chalking up to mannerism all the intricacies that were not easily transformed into Western notation. In a paradoxical conclusion, she advised listeners not to listen too closely: "These mannerisms do not form an integral part of the Indian's music; he is unconscious of them. It is easy to be caught in the meshes of these external peculiarities of a strange people, but if one would hear Indian music and understand it, one must ignore, as he does, his manner of singing."[34]

What would it have meant if the ethnologists did get it right, did succeed in capturing accurately the authentic sound of Native America? Would that have changed the nature of the appropriation of Native melody on the part of composers? Would Indian people have preferred to see Native cultures commodified and displayed in their true forms any more than to see themselves represented through the primitivist devices of the imagined Indian?[35] The resulting music could, as we know, never be so clear-cut. Indeed, from the instant it was recorded, through the multiple translations that followed it into print and then into piano music, song, and opera, Native music became part of a mixed-up world of cross-cultural production. Sometimes, these new musical and cultural forms overlapped—in shared rhythmic or melodic figures, for example, that worked to reproduce and harden expectations. At other times, the forms blended together. At still others, they existed in spaces *between* white and Native cultures. Indianist music, for example, never truly convinced those interested in new nationalist or modernist artistic production (too savage!). Likewise, it invariably drifted far from many Indian audiences, who were actively (re)producing musical cultures of their own.[36]

THE PROBLEM OF HARMONY

Even if Alice Fletcher had managed to get it right in recording three of the key elements in Western music—meter, rhythm, and melody—she and John Comfort Fillmore failed in their efforts to understand the structure of Omaha melody. In their efforts to understand, they introduced a radically new concept into Omaha music, that of harmony, which took the transcriptions beyond the recording of overlaps and into the making of new, hybrid musics. *Melody* and *harmony* both refer to pitch, the idea that there is available to composers and performers a set of different tones, usually arranged sequentially from low to high in the form of one of many different kinds of scales. In melody, these tones are played one after another, as a linear procession. When you sing or whistle, you are performing melody. In harmony, the tones are played simultaneously, stacked one atop another to form chords, which are often used to accompany the melody.

Fletcher first tried to make sense of Omaha music by arranging a song's notes sequentially from lowest to highest, in order to form a scale. When she called on Fillmore for assistance, this was his first inclination as well. Fillmore found that, while a number of Omaha songs fit a familiar pentatonic scale (a five-tone scale that omits from the regular major scale the fourth and seventh notes), many did not. Some "scales" kept the fourth and seventh tones, dropping other notes. Others used tones that defied any of the familiar scale forms. Well versed in the ways in which Romantic and impressionist composers brought color to their harmonies by using notes from outside traditional scales, Fillmore reasoned that a more productive analysis might be based on harmony rather than scale. This conclusion seemed to be confirmed by Fletcher's insistence that, when she played melodies back to Omaha people on the piano, they wanted her to add chords.[37]

Omaha music—and Indian musics in general—did not utilize harmony. People sang together in unison. On occasion, with the men singing the melody an octave below the women, harmonic overtones could be created, and the astute listener might pick out additional tones. But these were produced in the sonic relation, not through the assigning of different notes to different singers. In the Western system, however, melody carried with it the implication of harmony. Melodies fit within a harmonic structure, one that began with a "home" or tonic chord, moved off into other chords, and then returned back to the home chord with a reassuring final cadence. Seeking to understand Omaha music, Fillmore and Fletcher asked themselves whether melodies implied particular chords and, with them, harmonic structures. Could Omaha melodies be harmonized in order to understand better the nature of Indian music systems? If so, would such harmonizations produce tonality, that is, a sense of a musical center or home?

Trying to answer these questions, Fillmore harmonized the melodies, relying mostly on basic chords, and sticking primarily with the "happy" sounds of major keys (rather than the "melancholy" sound of minor keys). Fillmore came to believe that his harmonizations were not tied to his own culturally determined ear. Rather, he was simply filling in the natural harmonies implied by the Omaha melodies. Going farther, he posited "a latent harmonic sense which might, unconsciously on their part, be a determining factor in their choice of melody tones." In other words, according to Fillmore, the melodies did imply harmony—indeed, a universally shared harmony—and could, therefore, be understood through standard music systematics. Sending his harmonizations back to Fletcher, he was elated to find that the Omahas approved: "Whatever chords were natural and satisfactory to me were equally so to them, from which it seems proper to draw the conclusion that the sense of harmony is an innate endowment of human nature, that it is the same for the trained musician and for the untrained primitive man, the difference being purely one of development."[38]

Fillmore had stepped right in it, for much of the enterprise of the Indian sound turns on the question of harmony. Along with the tom-tom beat, harmony—particularly those melancholy minor chords or pounding open fifths—serves as perhaps the most powerful signifier of Indianness and primitivism. The addition of harmony, one might argue, transforms the cultural overlaps found in Native meter, rhythm, and melody into the full-blown sound of Indian.[39]

For Fillmore, these harmonies—Eurocentric though they were—represented *latent harmonic sense*.[40] They implied both a natural harmony and a universal human affinity for that harmony. According to Fillmore, even peoples without harmonic expression (e.g., the Omahas) would construct melodies that used *natural harmony* as their necessary underpinning. Fillmore's theory contained within it the key ideas of universalism and developmentalism, ideas that composers and critics would debate as they considered the utility of Indian melody in nationalist art music. Universalism—in the form of a natural harmony common to all humans—suggested the commensurability of Western and non-Western music, opening the door to the borrowing of Indian melodies. It also suggested the basic equality of different human cultural systems and aligned itself with the first tentative glimmerings of cultural relativism being pondered by Franz Boas.[41]

At the same time as he proclaimed universal harmony, however, Fillmore also gestured toward the more actively powerful metaphor of development.[42] Was the difference between Fillmore himself and the Omaha singers simply one of musical training and development? That is, could an *individual* of modest talent—Indian or otherwise—develop his or her sense of *universal* harmony? Or was the difference more profound? Did a social or racial group have to develop *together* in order to close the gap between civilized concertmaster and underdeveloped primitive? If so, what were the dangers that racial essences would overwhelm universal harmonic sensibilities? Fillmore skirted the edge of arguments already taking place in American society (e.g., around automobiles): Were Indian people capable of developing through social evolutionary stages? Or were they racially doomed, unable to compete or change and, therefore, destined for extinction?

Fillmore seemed to suggest that the idea of development might refer to both individuals and societies. But, when one put the idea of harmony itself in developmental terms, social development began to look more important than individual development. The expression of universal harmonic sense, in the context of Western art music, was most often seen as a historical development. Western music had seemingly evolved from the primitive drone harmonies of medieval church music, to a lighter touch using thirds and sixths, to the classic tonal explorations of the baroque, to the gradual elaboration of that system through the classical and Romantic composers. Fillmore certainly understood the contemporary composer Richard Wagner's chromaticisms, which pushed the familiar system of harmony and tonality to its outer edges and suggested further evolution around the corner. In other words, the idea of universal harmony in fact made the very contingent history of Western music the natural foundation for understanding the entire world.

In this intellectual context, it was only too easy to assign peoples who had never had harmony a retrograde spot on a developmental spectrum. Indeed, harmony, melody, and rhythm themselves might reflect different levels of social hierarchy. Addressing in 1918 the troubling rhythmic power of jazz, one critic explained the relation in detail:

There are many mansions in the house of the muses. There is first the great assembly hall of melody—where most of us take our seats at some point in our lives—but a lesser number pass on to inner sanctuaries of harmony, where the melodic sequence . . . has infinitely less interest than the blending of notes into chords so that the combining wave-lengths will give new aesthetic sensations. This inner court of harmony is where nearly all the truly great music is enjoyed. In the house there is, however, another apartment, properly speaking, down in the basement, a kind of servant's hall of rhythm. It is there we hear the hum of Indian dance, the throb of the Oriental tambourines and kettledrums, clatter of the clogs, the click of Slavic heels, the thumpty-tumpty of the negro banjo, and, in fact the native dance of a world.[43]

The house of music suggests the ways in which even a genial developmentalism inevitably tangled with racial difference. If Fillmore gestured toward universalism, a shared harmonic sense, and a process of social evolution, he also forced Indian people and their music into a racial bind, one familiar to theorists of Indian assimilation and disappearance. What happened to those farther back along a developmental path when they encountered people considered more advanced? The options were usually seen to be two: social growth and concomitant assimilation to white society or tragic but inevitable disappearance caused by racial difference that prevented a successful game of catch-up.

RACE, MUSIC, APPROPRIATION, AND DISAPPEARANCE

John Comfort Fillmore's sense of universal harmonic commensurability suggested that Indian music could readily serve as source material for Westerners. As a legitimate form of cultural production, however, Indian music seemed to have little or no future, except as a primitive curiosity, unable to develop on its own terms and, therefore, in danger of dying out. Ethnographers flooded Indian country in the late nineteenth century, recording, among other things, its music, because of a widespread belief in the need to salvage vanishing Native cultures. Alice Fletcher put the idea in a particularly harsh form, one that reminds us of her long career, not only as a salvage ethnologist, but also as an advocate and worker for allotment and assimilation. "The Omahas as a tribe," she said, "have ceased to exist. The young men and women are being educated in English speech, and imbued with English thought; their directive emotion will hereafter take the lines of our artistic forms; therefore, there can be no speculation upon any future development of Omaha Indian music."[44]

Indians, in other words, would be incorporated—as both individuals and a social group—into modern development. Musical expression would follow the same trajectory as social evolution: it would take Western artistic forms. Such incorporation would deny Indian people the possibility of making Indian music (or any other cultural production) on Indian terms—or even in terms of musical hybridity. If Native people were denied the possibility of maintaining old forms or of producing new ones, however, their old forms would not go to waste. Collected and cataloged, they could be easily and profitably taken up by white composers as the ground for new cultural production centered on American nationalism.

Given racialized expectations of Indian barbarism, how seriously could art composers take Indian music? The very act of taking it seriously cut firmly against the grain of expectation and, therefore, allowed rebellious Western composers to challenge their own systems. Perhaps never were the contrasts between expectation and the unexpected so stark as when Indian song was put into dialogue with the elite world of art music. When Dvořák, Farwell, Fletcher, and others began suggesting the possibilities that Native music might have for American composers, they met stiff resistance, most of which sought to reaffirm older expectations. Many critics elaborated on the racism implicit in Fillmore's developmentalist position, suggesting that Indian music was far too backward. Composer and critic Daniel Mason expressed horror that "the crude war dances and chants of the red aborigines of this continent should be in any way representative of so mixed a people" and celebrated the "vaunted intelligence" of "we who have exterminated and displaced them." Others argued, not (only) that the music was crude, but that it was not sufficiently part of the national heritage to be truly American. "The exotic flavor of [Indians'] wild dances," according to critics like John Tasker Howard, was "too far removed from the comprehension of the rest of us to ever become vital to our artistic expression."[45]

THE OTHER SIDE OF THE SOUND OF INDIAN

John Tasker Howard saw Indian people far outside the pale of the lore and traditions that he recognized as belonging to the contemporary United States. His argument was, of course, anathema for composers who insisted that Indian music *best* represented the national consciousness. Howard's criticisms removed Indian people from contemporaneous time, space, and social development. Nor did they square with the complexities of Fillmore's developmentalism, which simultaneously cast

Indians in terms of racial difference, denied them the chance to develop their own musics, and vaguely hinted at their assimilation into musical modernism. While banking on the nationalist allure of the indigenous primitive, many of the Indianist composers were, nonetheless, forced to recognize the utter contemporaneity of Indian people. Alice Fletcher, John Comfort Fillmore, and Charles Wakefield Cadman were called back in line by Francis LaFlesche at one time or another. Cadman, Thurlow Lieurance, Natalie Curtis, Arthur Nevin, and others all had music-collecting relationships with Indian people. They found that their interactions often extended beyond collecting to performance as well. Cadman and Lieurance, in particular, established durable performing relationships with Indian singers, whose unexpected presence on the concert stage surely troubled the sounds of expectation that their music and lyrics carried to critics like Howard.

As Fletcher had pointed out, music enveloped Native life. It proved a natural place for cross-cultural meetings. Indeed, such exchanges had been occurring throughout the nineteenth century. As early as the 1840s, the Narragansett composer Thomas Commuck had engaged Western style and notation. Missionary Christianity introduced pump organs, pianos, and congregational hymn singing across the continent. Responses varied, of course, but many Native peoples established music traditions based on hymns translated into Indian languages.[46]

By the late nineteenth century and the early twentieth, Indian singers were coming to such exchanges from a variety of entry points. Many had already absorbed tribal musical training and repertoire, at least to some extent, when they first systematically encountered Western music. Music, seen in developmentalist terms, made up a critical part of boarding and day school experience for many Indian children. Bands, orchestras, choruses, and music lessons of all types—these were among the signifiers of civilization. Native students often took up instruments easily, and they brought their musical training with them when they left.[47] Zitkala-Ša, the well-known Yankton Dakota writer and activist, for example, learned violin while at boarding school, seems to have studied music in Boston, and collaborated with William Hanson on the 1913 opera *The Sun Dance*.[48]

Some Indian people engaged in vernacular musical exchanges with non-Indian neighbors. Others came from long traditions of cross-cultural performance in Wild West shows, medicine shows, and the like. Still others had musical training sponsored by patrons and sympathizers. Thurlow Lieurance in particular saw himself as a promoter of Indian musicians, who, he observed, "like modern music because it seems a kind of tonic for them and something to taste and use." Lieurance testified to the innate power of Indian voices, insisting on instances in which Crow singers could be heard eight to ten miles distant. He also presumed, however, that Indian performers needed, not only innate talent, but also the training that could be found in contemporary white America, pointing to his own work with several protégés who had gone on to the chautauqua circuit and the concert stage.[49]

Writing in 1920, Lieurance listed a number of Indian concert performers, including the Creek singer Oyapela, the Miami violinist Pejawah, the Haida performer William Reddie ("the foremost Indian cellist"), Paul Chilson, a Pawnee tenor, and Robert Coon, a Lakota sousaphonist in the John Phillip Sousa band. The two major figures of American Indian concert and opera performance in the early twentieth century, the Creek mezzo-soprano Tsianina Redfeather and the Penobscot mezzo-soprano Princess Watawaso, trailed in their wake a number of "Indian princess" vocal performers, including Floating Cloud, Princess Wantura, Princess Pakanli, Angela Gorman Andretti, and Irene Eastman. Before she died in the influenza epidemic of 1918–1919, Eastman (the daughter of the Indian progressive Charles Eastman) was, according to the obituary in the *New York Times*, on her way to a successful career, with her "soprano voice of unusual quality and her songs, based on the melodies of various Indian tribes."[50] Similarly, a group of male Indian singers established a parallel tradition of what might be called "singing chiefs." Perhaps best known were the Iroquois baritone Oskenonton and the Yakama singer Daniel Simmons, familiar to early film viewers as the actor Chief Yowlachi. The Ojibwe tenor Carlisle Kawbawgam worked as a vaudeville performer in Europe until his voice caught the ear of music critics in Berlin and Vienna, who dubbed him "the Red Caruso."[51]

Kawbawgam took his name from the Carlisle Indian School, where, like so many Native performers, he began singing Western music. Other singers, however, had grown up in the business. Lucy Nicola (Princess Watawaso) could look back to a number of Penobscot performers and managers who had gotten up Indian shows and toured them around the east for much of the nineteenth century. Her father, Joseph Nicola, served as Penobscot governor and tribal representative to the Maine legislature and had spent time on the road as a traveling performer and lecturer. In 1897, at the age of fifteen, Lucy Nicola moved to Cambridge, Massachusetts, where she developed her musical skills and honed her performances before white elites. After further musical training in Chicago, she began touring the chautauqua circuit between 1913 and 1918, appearing with Lieurance as Princess Watawaso and bringing his songs to life. Watawaso later made the Indian-talk format her own, performing tribal melodies in buckskin while being certain to mix them with challenging operatic arias. "A voice of singularly lovely quality," noted a *New York Times* critic, "of rare resonance, and of sufficient cultivation to justify the inclusion of one opera air."[52]

Oskenonton performed before a faithful public at all manner of concerts in New York City throughout the 1910s, occasionally taking time out for chautauqua tours. By the 1920s, he had won a larger audience, basing himself in London for most of the decade, and touring Indian songs across Europe. He added California to his circuit in 1927 and 1928, maintained a popular annual Easter concert in New York, and continued to book additional European performances. Like Princess Watawaso, Oskenonton planned concerts that mixed the now-familiar Indian-talk format with his own inclinations, which often included, not simply Indian songs, but concert and operatic pieces that showed off his vocal talents.[53]

It would be hard to overemphasize the importance of the various Indian school programs, which sought to use music to ready Indian children for assimilation. Robert Coon learned the sousaphone while at Carlisle, the school whose polished Indian bands played at every presidential inauguration during the life of the school. The Oneida bandleader Dennison Wheelock led both the Carlisle and the Haskell Institute bands, transforming the latter into the U.S. Indian Band, a fifty-piece ensemble that toured widely. Coon made his leap to Sousa's band—the most important and well-respected of the era—after a stint in Wheelock's Indian band (see figure 44).[54] Wheelock's band, formed first for the Saint Louis exposition in 1904, presented programs well into the 1920s, often featuring the Sioux cornet soloist James Garvie. In the early 1910s, the Indian String Quartet, a group organized at the Chemawa (Oregon) Indian School, toured chautauquas, sometimes performing in tails, other times in full Native regalia ("Sweetest Music of the Masters and Wild Melodies of the Primitive Indian"!).[55] The quartet included the Quapaw violinist Fred Cardin, the Inuit violinist Alex Melovidov, the Flathead violist William Palin, and the Haida cellist William Reddie (see figure 45). Cardin would later join the Kansas City Symphony and serve on the music faculty at the University of Nebraska before joining up with Thurlow Lieurance in another quartet. Later in the 1910s, Cardin and Reddie would

FIGURE 44. *The Carlisle Indian School Band. The band, led by Dennison Wheelock, would later transform into the U.S. Indian Band, playing a full program on the chautauqua circuit. (Records of the Redpath Chautauqua Collection, Special Collections Department, University of Iowa, Iowa City, Iowa.)*

FIGURE 45. The Indian String Quartet in Action. Left to right: Fred Cardin, William Palin, William Reddie, Alex Melovidov. Programs were split between Native garb and formal concert wear. Note the mix of authenticating clothing, Melovidov sticking with Inuit fur while Reddie adopted a plains headdress inappropriate to the Haida's Queen Charlotte Islands. (Records of the Redpath Chautauqua Collection, Special Collections Department, University of Iowa, Iowa City, Iowa.)

combine to form the Indian Art and Music Company, which promised fine music and the Indian atmosphere created by costumes, rugs, curios, and storytelling. Filling the singing princess role was the Cherokee vocalist Sausa Carey, accompanied by the Quapaw pianist Wanita Cardin.[56]

Such artists as these led the way for further generations of Indian performers—the composers Lemuel Childers, Ingram Cleveland, and Jack Kilpatrick, the Creek/Kaw saxophonist Jim Pepper, the Tohono O'odham jazz trombonist Russell Moore, the Chickasaw baritone Albert Stewart, the Chickasaw singer Mary Stone (Ataloa), and the tenor Kiutus Tecumseh, a popular radio performer of the 1930s. Many reservations featured their own bands (see figure 46). The Penobscot Indian band, David Hill's Indian Band, the Nez Perceans—these and many others helped create a culturally rich music controlled primarily by Indian people rather than by white composers.[57]

TSIANINA REDFEATHER AND SHANEWIS

Native performers played with expectations even as those expectations were forming around the sound of Indian. At the same time, however, they did not hesitate to contest expectations and to work to set them differently. The result was often a peculiar pastiche in which racist stereotypes might be simultaneously reinforced and questioned through Indian musical performances. Charles Wakefield Cadman's and Nelle Richmond Eberhardt's *Shanewis* offers a case in point. If Cadman was quite possibly the leading popular composer of the Indianist school, his longstanding partner, the Creek singer Tsianina Redfeather, was quite possibly its leading performer. Born in Indian Territory in 1882 (or possibly 1892), she demonstrated her musical talent early on in both public and Indian schools. Assisted by the patronage of Oklahoma Congresswoman Alice Robertson, Tsianina moved to Colorado to study piano, quickly shifting to voice in the studio of Denver's leading vocal coach, John Wilcox, who introduced her to Cadman early in 1913.[58]

Tsianina shone in her trial performances and began a five-year run of the Indian Music Talk's most successful tours. Cadman's program now opened with Tsianina's singing, and its second-half lectures centered on *her* demonstrations of idealized Indian themes. Her authenticity was the show's most valuable commodity, for now Cadman's idealized melodies seemed to be coming directly from the Indian's mouth. Tsianina's performance struck many critics as utterly and completely Native. "She is aboriginal and charmingly so," wrote a Chicago paper. "Tsianina has the

FIGURE 46. The Nez Perceans. A regionally successful jazz band, the Nez Perceans mixed headdresses and blankets with saxophones, trumpet, banjo, and percussion. (Courtesy McCormack Family Collection.)

fine, strong beauty of the aristocrats of her race," wrote another. "A voice that is haunting, appealing—and more than anything else, Indian." A Colorado Springs paper took the familiar comparison between singers and birds to an extreme suggested by her Indian connection to nature: "All the notes of the nightingale, the meadowlark, the bluebird, the robin, and the dove seemed to be harmoniously blended in her wonderful voice."[59]

Tsianina Redfeather—and singers like Princess Watawaso, Oskenon-ton, and others—crystallized a sense of surprise among white audiences. If Indian music was nothing more than savage screeching and howling, mindless pounding of drums and rattles, then what were Indian mezzo-sopranos and baritones doing on the concert stage, singing Native melodies—much less opera!—to elegant and stylishly modern piano accompaniment? Native performers played with white expectation, holding out familiar signs that proclaimed "Indian" even as they offered more nuanced musical performances. For the Indian Music Talk, for example, Cadman draped the stage with Navajo rugs, Indian baskets, instruments, and, of course, Tsianina Redfeather, outfitted in a white beaded buckskin costume, beaded headband, and even beaded purse. Audiences did not fail to read these signs. At Tsianina's coming-out performance before Denver's musical elite, the audience assumed that she could not speak English, and they put their surprise on display in the postconcert reception, wondering aloud in front of her if she was "real or made up" and commenting "how strange for an Indian to sing so well."[60]

Cadman frequently closed his lecture with "The Moon Drops Low," a song based on an Omaha melody collected by Fletcher. Eberhardt's lyrics sought to set familiar expectations, offering the old sentiment of Indian disappearance:

The moon drops low that once soared high
    As an eagle soars in the morning sky;
And the deep dark lies like a death-web spun
    'Twixt the setting moon and the rising sun.
Our glory sets like the sinking moon;
    The Red Man's race shall be perished soon;
Our feet shall trip where the web is spun,
    For no dawn shall be ours, and no rising sun.[61]

What must it have been like for audiences to hear an Indian woman singing this lament? Did it seem the last gasp of a dying race, with Tsianina an anomaly, a lone survivor of a racial group that had failed to adapt and develop? Almost certainly, some listeners followed that interpretation. The Denver critic Margaret St. Vrain Sanford suggested that Tsianina could "not be compared to other artists": "Because of inheritance, environment and loyalty to her native race, she stands a lonely figure. . . . [S]he is of necessity a unique symbol of all that is best and finest in the fast disappearing race."[62] From the stage, however, Cadman began rejecting his lyricist's invocation of Indian disappearance. A Chicago critic, for example, observed: "When the composer announced that the theme of *The Moon Drops Low* was no longer true because the latest government reports showed that the Indians were increasing, the spontaneous burst of applause was a direct compliment to the singer and her race."[63]

Other observers might choose to see Tsianina as having been fully assimilated and, thus, no longer truly Indian. The performance turned, however, on her authenticity, and so the promotional pamphlets and brochures for the Indian Music Talk took pains to legitimize her in several ways, all necessarily dependent on a racial imaginary. Tsianina, one brochure proclaimed, was not a made-up Indian. Rather, she was "full-blooded" and a Native "aristocrat" (a descendent of Tecumseh, no less). She never wore "the garb of the paleface"; her stage costume was no costume at all but, rather, her everyday wear (see figures 47 and 48).[64]

As with Indian athletes, the key factor complicating Tsianina's racial position was her talent, for it allowed her to refuse to be seen as either a remnant or an object of assimilation. After outlining her racial authenticity, then, the brochure's description shifted abruptly, denying that race mattered in the face of a different brand of uniqueness, musical talent: "Nor does Princess Tsianina claim public recognition on the strength of racial difference. She has a beautiful voice, guided by an artistic intelligence and trained to expressive ends. In any environment she is a charming singer."[65] Other critics followed this lead, mixing together racialized signs of authenticity ("this free-limbed Indian girl, with the body of a wind-swayed sapling and the grace of a wild doe") with precise assessments of her musical skill ("effortless tone production, perfect breathing, smooth velvety legato and easily sustained power").[66]

In effect, Cadman and Tsianina had created a fail-safe performance. Some might admire her vocal talents while dismissing her racial identity; others might appreciate her Native color while doubting her voice; many would praise both. In the juxtaposition between primitivism—figured as a racial expression of universal musical sense—and the modern—figured

FIGURE 47. Tsianina Redfeather. *The promotional image at left suggests the elements necessary to the presentation of oneself as an Indian princess—new and nicely tanned buckskin, with bead and shell decorations and copious fringe, braids, headband, arrowhead necklace, and moccasins. In later images, such as the one presented in figure 48 at right, Tsianina would adopt a different look, combining headband and necklace with skirts, blouses, and a beautiful woven blanket jacket. (Denver Public Library, Western History Department, X-33262.)*

FIGURE 48. Tsianina Redfeather. *(Denver Public Library, Western History Department, X-33263.)*

as individual training and development that went beyond race—there was surely something for almost everyone. Equally important, Cadman and Tsianina crafted a space in which Tsianina could find cross-cultural breathing room. In some situations, she might emphasize her Indianness, in others her talent. Most interesting, however, were those moments in which she laid claim to both at once.

Perhaps the best example of this claim came with *Shanewis*, which was marketed as having been based on Tsianina's life. Though Cadman and others have played down her role, a close reading of the plot suggests the active hand of Tsianina, who, in one accounting, is said to have suggested to Cadman: "When you write the opera, you might use my transition from the tepee to the drawing room. Surely the people would understand that, and you could 'idealize,' as you say."[67] There is, of course, the parallel in premise and characters: Indian girl with talent placed in difficult cultural situation by patron who allows her to leave Indian community in order to receive musical training. While the love plot is manufactured, even it may, in fact, be touched by Tsianina's life.[68] Her memoir, *Where Trails Have Led Me*, includes, for example, a short section in which her first wooing comes from a young man making arguments similar to those made by the character Philip Harjo. He wonders why she wishes to go further into the white man's world, points out whites' lack of kindness, recalls to her mind their thefts and cheats, asks her to come with him to the Indian world, and, when she demurs, promises to be there if ever she needs him.[69]

While Tsianina would appear as Shanewis in later performances in Denver and Los Angeles, her stage fright seems to have kept her from appearing at the Met.[70] Nonetheless, she made sure to appear conspicuously in the aisles during intermission at the Met opening. In full Indian ensemble, she was naturally mistaken for the soprano lead, blurring the relation between frontstage performance and backstage authenticity in a way that would have done Buffalo Bill Cody proud. Her challenge to the experience of the opera audience suggests that she wanted to make sure that the story was read, not as fiction, but as something that spoke to real, contemporary Indian people, herself in particular. Equally telling, however, is the way in which the plot inverts the vanishing Native–Indian love call conventions that usually made up Nelle Richmond Eberhardt's bread and butter.

And, here, we can at last return to the opera's climax, with the entry of Shanewis's patron and her jilted daughter, Amy. Amy's final plea to her supposed fiancé, Lionel, begins on the personal note of a woman scorned but quickly turns to the larger structural question of racial difference and race crossing: "I plead for you and for the unity of blood. Each race is noble when the line is clear. But mingled bloods defile each other. It is the law. Neither of you should allow infatuation to blind your vision of the right." Shocked at the news of Lionel's commitment to Amy, Shanewis rejects him. Like Amy, however, her rejection too is premised on larger issues. Insisting on a racial difference set in motion by the history of colonialism, she laments that his intimate betrayal is of a piece with the relation between white and Indian societies: "For half a thousand years your race has cheated mine with sweet words and noble sentiments." Philip Harjo then rushes from the nearby woods, shooting the poisoned arrow into Lionel's heart. "In death," sings Shanewis to the fading Lionel, "thou art mine."[71]

Audiences were undoubtedly familiar with the idea of two women—one Indian, the other white—vying for the affection of a white man. It was, as we have seen, a staple of the early film narrative. The classic Indian love plot, however, *never* asked that the white man die—not for love, and certainly not for a treachery that was both personal and historical. Usually, it was the Indian woman who either had to die or had to take herself away so that the white lovers could have a future (after betraying her people for the love of the white man, naturally). Here, Lionel dies still loving Shanewis. His betrayal is multilayered—a betrayal of Shanewis and of Indian people in general, of Amy, and (as framed by the latter) of the purity of the white race.

Yet the opera's central struggle is not among the main characters but between two supporting ones—Harjo and Amy. Both reject the idea of a cross-race romance, one on the eugenic grounds of race purity and superiority, the other arguing that a history of white betrayal will lead to more betrayal and to a cultural loss. The unholy alliance between the opposites, Amy and Philip Harjo, is counterpoised to the relationship between Lionel and Shanewis. For the lead characters, love offers the possibility of racial and historical redemption. Lionel will come to *her* people, and he will do so with the open mind of the modern primitivist. Of *course* it is the universalizing lilt of Indian song that gives their love a potentially transcendent power over race. It is critical, then, that it is not Amy's racialist argument that undoes the lovers but Harjo's historical one. Shanewis and Lionel prepare to part, reluctantly. Lionel moves to Amy but never adopts her racialist position; indeed, he is still pledging his love to Shanewis when the fatal arrow strikes, and he dies, not in Amy's arms, but in those of Shanewis, who reclaims him at the moment of death.

The act of parting is fully controlled, not by white racial fear, but by Indian history, given form in Shanewis's parting lament. The wayward fiancé's death is not sacrifice, but Indian vengeance; Lionel dies for the sins of the colonial past. Philip Harjo, ambiguously savage, stands at opera's end as the Native critic who understands the folly of allowing the ideological figure *white man–Indian woman* to remake itself yet again. This liaison, he seems to say, is the expectation that has driven our history. It means, not simply innocent romance, but white triumph and Indian dispossession, made visible through the capture of future generations via the bodies of Indian women.

Harjo's awareness that the personal is, in this case, also the political prevents him from seeing that Shanewis has problematized, not only expectations built on race, but also those built on gender. He sees her as an Indian in modernity who might be drawn back to the tribal. He fails to see her as someone who might inhabit modernity equally powerfully as a woman. As Shanewis rejects Lionel as the betrayer of herself and her history, then, she also rejects Harjo as someone who would use tradition to control her as an Indian woman. In the end, Shanewis affirms a richly layered identity: She is Indian, as demonstrated in her rejection of Lionel. She is modern, as witnessed by her refusal to wield the poison arrow herself. She is a woman, both Indian and modern, as demonstrated in her refusal to be used by either man. And she is independent, for, in returning Lionel to Amy, she declares herself freed of her debt to her patron. While it may seem that the play ends in tragic love-death, in fact it ends with a new affirmation of Shanewis, who is left in possession of identity, moral standing, and, in a sense, love.

One might take Shanewis as a brief for Tsianina's subsequent career, which was marked by durable independence (and an unsuccessful romance). Tsianina served as a traveling entertainer for American troops in Europe during the First World War. Her adventures included the torpedoing of her ship and meetings with Lillie Langtry and various minor royals. Arriving with letters of introduction, she courted Lord Northcliffe, a newspaper publisher who immediately developed a series of sympathetic articles on American Indians, and Sir Thomas Lipton, who introduced her to London society and had chocolates delivered to her room daily. She followed the front lines to Paris, across France, and into Germany, where she noted the depth of German knowledge concerning Indians. Returning home, she became actively involved in the Santa Fe Fiesta, appearing there for nine straight years. She undertook several Indian Music Talk tours with Cadman before his death in 1946, and she sang the lead in performances of *Shanewis* in Denver in 1924 and at the Hollywood Bowl in 1926 (at that performance, she was joined by the Yakama baritone Yowlache, singing a prelude, and Oskenonton, who sang the role of Philip Harjo).[72]

Tsianina realized, over the course of her early career, that her performances offered her a political and educational platform. At the 1916 Pan-American California Exposition, for example, Cadman repeatedly deferred to her in speaking to public audiences. "This was shocking to me at first," she recalled, "but the inner voice said 'This is your opportunity to tell the truth about the Indian race.'"[73] She adopted a sort of generic pan-Indian position from which to critique American policy and culture. In doing so, she sought to put social considerations back into any discussion that would focus solely on *her* as an example of individual development. In 1921, at the Santa Fe Fiesta, for example, she refused to stand alone as an individual but insisted on drawing attention to Indian people as a social group. Coming back onstage for an encore, she decided to turn her back on the (predominantly white) grandstand and sing for the Indian people gathered in the plaza behind the stage. "Indian Day" at the fiesta had been full of music—traditional songs and dances, an Indian school chorus, a pair of small girls singing a duet—but observers agreed that Tsianina's back-to-her-audience performance was the highlight. "A more dramatic picture could not be imagined," commented Dorothy McAllister. "There was no mistaking the fact that the Indian princess was giving her best to her people, and that she was unconsciously receiving inspiration from them."[74] Tsianina made it clear that it was not simply Indian melodies that mattered but also Indian people.

Nor was she tied to Cadman. In 1924, for example, she appeared, alone, in the descriptions of available chautauqua acts. In 1927, she undertook a series of concerts with the Iroquois baritone Oskenonton. In 1928, she traveled and sang as a fund-raiser for the Republican Party. Health problems led to her retirement from active performing during the 1930s, but she remained active socially and politically for the rest of her life. She continued to serve on the board of the Santa Fe Fiesta, devoted much of her energy to Christian Science, and, as John Troutman points out, played a significant role in establishing the Foundation for American Indian Education, an organization created to send Indian students to colleges in Albuquerque and Phoenix.[75]

FROM MAJOR TO MINOR

Cadman and Tsianina, Lieurance and Watawaso, Oskenonton and Yowlachie, Cardin and Reddie, and all the many other Indian and Indianist musicians scattered across the country point toward a powerful reworking of familiar expectations. They crossed back and forth between Indian melody and Western harmony, generating an Indian sound built on expectations and ethnographies, constructed for art-music listeners and popular audiences. Old primitivist themes mingled in their work with Native rhythmic and melodic ideas, the latter made available through a flurry of musical ethnography.

Many of the elements of the Indian sound that we hear today at baseball games and in Disney movies originated in the decades between 1890 and 1930—the founding years and the boom years for the sound of Indian. Those same years, however, saw the development of new Indian musical forms—most notably the beginnings of the powwow tradition, itself rooted in older musics but now infused with a significant amount of intertribal exchange.[76] They also saw the development of a cadre of Indian performers—Indian vocal princesses and baritones, ethnographic informants, and hundreds of local bands and performers—expressions of Indian–non-Indian musical crossing. Many of these performers were able successfully to question the older formulas of expectation. At the same time, however, the Indianness that brought them in front of favorably disposed audiences also constricted the possibilities that they might have to effect change.

Perhaps the most important thing that the composers and performers of Indianist music did was to attach concrete and specific images to sounds. When Arthur Farwell included detailed descriptions of the stories surrounding the melodies that he appropriated, he was not simply educating American listeners to emotional and cultural contexts for his music. He was also linking the sound of Indian to imagery, be it that of the love song sung in the early morning or the war party preparing to attack. The fact that these two particular images preoccupied many, if not most, Indian-sound compositions helped create the perceptual frames through which non-Indians imagined Indian people when they heard the sound of a tom-tom beat or a descending minor-third "short-long" pattern in a melody.

Likewise, when Tsianina, Watawaso, Falling Water, Irene Eastman, Sausa Carey, Ataloa, and others appeared onstage in nearly identical costumes, surrounded by the props of Indian primitivism, they connected Indian sounds together with mental images, giving those sounds meaning. Consider, for example, a promotional poster for Princess Watawaso, which evokes any number of expectations and images (see figure 49). Familiar signs of Indianness are jumbled together. A birch-bark canoe mingles with plains tipis, Pueblo pottery, the words *Princess Watawaso* built out of rustic wood, and, in case we are in doubt, a prominent identification of the singer as "full blooded." The image is divided vertically in two, and these Indian objects sit, nearly enclosed, amid a dark forest of seemingly dead trees. A small path shows Watawaso emerging from this Indian landscape, a place with a certain lingering cultural vitality, perhaps, but also a place of death and quiescence. Figured as every bit as "in between" as Tsianina Redfeather, Watawaso is placed exactly in the middle of this landscape, on the beach between water and woods. Ahead lies un-

PRINCESS
WATAWASO
A Full Blooded Penobscot Indian Mezzo Soprano
SONGS LEGENDS DANCES

THE PRINCESS USES THE WEBER DUO-ART PIANO.

FIGURE 49. *Princess Watawaso Flyer. From Tsianina to Watawaso and across the board, the Indian princess dress code remained the same. (Records of the Redpath Chautauqua Collection, Special Collections Department, University of Iowa, Iowa City, Iowa.)*

known—but apparently not Indian—land, characterized by the waiting canoe, which promises to take her to that new place.[77]

Indianist music tended, as the musicologist Michael Pisani points out, to offer more sympathetic portrayals of vanishing Indians than did most literary representations.[78] And, indeed, listening now to the music of Cadman, Farwell, and others, one is struck by the plaintive appeal of those settings. Even as the Indianists created a sonic melancholia distinct from that of other American and European composers, many followed John Comfort Fillmore in relying frequently on major keys and chords, saving the minor accompaniment (or that of open fifths) only for the most rollicking war dance songs. If many of the key elements of our contemporary imagining of the Indian sound were in place by 1920, they had, nonetheless, not yet tilted so heavily toward pounding war themes and minor cadences.

And so we must suggest one last critical transition. In the midst of the flurry of Indian-sound music being produced in the early twentieth century, film producers like James Young Deer and Thomas Ince established the production efficiencies and Indian plot thematics that drove so many of the early silent films. The silents offered only bare-bones textual narration, relying instead on their imagery to tell stories. Musical accompaniment helped advance the stories from placard to placard, and organists and pianists sat below the screen, pounding out music designed to work with the films' images to set mood, signify character, and enhance action. Music provided critical clues to audiences, signaling them to feel suspense, hate the bad guy, celebrate the hero, and fall in love with the heroine. As we have seen, by the 1920s film had become a repository for many of the images of violence and savagery found in nineteenth-century dime novel literature and anti-Indian propaganda. As films grew less sympathetic toward Indian characters, so too did the accompanying music.

In 1913, John Zemecnik, a composer who had studied under Dvořák, put together a collection of music to be played for silent films. Included in his array were the sounds of ethnicity ("Oriental," Chinese, Mexican), work (cowboy, sailor), events (battle, church, festival, storms), and emotion (death, mystery, struggle, duels, and plaintiveness). Included also was, of course, the Indian sound—with pounding tom-tom beats on the interval of the open fifth and a minor-key melody—and a four-part battle sequence, with plenty of the bugle-call imagery so characteristic of film cavalry charges. Zemecnik had little of the sympathy, artistic aspirations, or nationalist agenda of the Indianist composers, and his collection reflects the consolidation of a number of stereotypical expectations into simple sonic shorthands. Zemecnik's was only one of the many collections available, and most theaters had their own libraries of various musical accompaniments. As silents became talkies in the early 1930s, music remained central to films, aural cues to the impending conflicts to be found on western ridges silhouetted with saddled warriors. Such westerns as *In*

Old Arizona (Fox, 1929; the first sound western), *The Big Trail* (Fox, 1930), *Cimarron* (RKO, 1931), and the Eddie Cantor spoof *Whoopie!* (United Artists, 1930) all had Indian-music soundtracks warning viewers that Indians were "up there in them hills," plotting attacks or preparing to fall in love with whites.[79]

By the time the tom-tom beats and minor-key Indian melodies announced that Apaches were about to attack John Wayne in the genre-founding film *Stagecoach* (United Artists, 1939), Indian music had been both displaced from the nationalist tradition (by the move toward jazz and blues found in Gershwin and others) and embraced as a popular marker of Indian difference. Indeed, as Kathryn Kalinak suggests, *Stagecoach* made an argument about national character by quoting a tremendous range of (Anglo) folk songs, while the musical codes attached to the sound of Indian "reinforce cultural stereotypes about Otherness and establish Native Americans as wild, powerful, primitive, and exotic."[80] The gradual move from sympathetic Indian primitivisms to savage imagery—and the simultaneous move toward the different racial codings found in jazz and blues—shifted Indian performers like Tsianina, Watawaso, and others from cultural centers to cultural margins.

From opera and art music, to popular song and piano studies, to silent film accompaniment, to film background music, Indian sounds had become part of a broad, shared cultural sensibility. By midcentury, the sound of Indian had become so familiar it was like sonic wallpaper, only dimly heard as anything other than completely natural. Even as it solidified expectations, however, Indian-sound music no longer afforded Indian people the opportunity to take to the stage and complicate the sounds through their unexpected presence, words, and performances. Like the athletes who were pushed from the arenas by new economic structures, new desires, and new tastes, Native performers were likewise displaced by similar cultural shifts. Indian people kept making music, of course, but the Indianists and the Native performers who had accompanied them fell into obscurity.

If their histories disappeared, however, the expectations that they created did not. The sound of Indian continues to lurk along the ridge tops and in the deserts of our cultural memory, ready to mobilize its powers of evocation with a few accented beats, a couple of pounding chords, or a snippet of melody. It moves us to act, in cultural terms. Like the ideological chuckle that greets the unexpected image of Red Cloud Woman in a beauty parlor, many Americans almost unconsciously find themselves chopping right arms up and down in fascist unison in response to the tomahawk chop war chant. These are the ways—through the images and sounds of popular culture—that expectations work their way into lives and actions and, from those seemingly innocuous actions, into other, more damaging, forms of racism and oppression.[81]

conclusion

MY HEADACHE

As I have been working on this book, my preadolescent son has come to understand that he can define himself through the music he listens to, that even the crassest pop hit can wield emotional power, and that you can always find something to make your parents crazy. We go back and forth with one another: he loves beats and grooves; I long for melody. He likes hip-hop wordplay; I find his favorite lyrics pointless at best, in need of parental censorship at worst. He likes Top 40 stations; I encourage him to check out college radio alternatives. He teases me with indecipherable kidspeak; I toss faux-intellectual observations back at him, stuff like, "A form has reached its most pathetic stage of decadence when it can *only* be self-referential." He is sometimes thrown for a moment, but then tosses down the card that wins every time, the slyly delivered question: "Dad, did your parents like your music?"

This autumn of 2003, as he has decided to blast his boom box throughout the house, there's been a song that plays over and over again: "Shake Ya Tailfeather," by P. Diddy, Nelly, and Murphy Lee, which uses the "tomahawk chop" war chant as melodic wallpaper for its chorus.[1] I avoid this song, but the war chant melody has this awful way of soaking down into you, repeating over and over as a soundtrack for your life. One day in November, I snap just a bit, and there's an extra edge in my voice as I yell at him, "Turn that song off!" He is slow to act, however, and I find myself pleading, almost begging him to spare me. He knows something is up, and he's a little worried: "I'm sorry, Dad. Do you have a headache?"

"Yes," I snarl. "It's a five-hundred-year-old headache, and it's called disrespect, injustice, and oppression." He is confused, and I suppose I am unsubtle. The song seems pretty harmless to him—as it does to a lot of people, I suppose. The war chant is just a little fragment of culture, picked up and remixed. But, as I've suggested in this book, it is far from harmless. It sets and reinforces expectations. Those expectations occur in little fragments and in sweeping narratives throughout American and, indeed, global culture. War chants and Indian-named automobiles make their way into our souls, and they lay the groundwork for day-to-day social interactions. They underpin the many ways non-Indian Americans blithely ignore the requests, opinions, and assertions of Native people. ("The tomahawk chop and the mascot are meant to honor you. We *don't care* if you don't feel honored.")

Such cultural expectations and social relations exist in dialogue with economic, political, and legal structures. The same unarticulated expectations that surround the war chant (not honor and courage, let's admit, but Indian violence, transmuted to sports) help explain the seeming naturalness of Indian poverty and the active hostility to the very idea of Indian wealth or modernity. They help explain the indignant opposition to indigenous people's efforts to move from the political margins by contributing to political campaigns or the efforts to roll back the legal rights embedded in treaties, including those to hunt and fish. Expectations, in short, exist in relation to concrete actions.

Once upon a time, at the turn of the twentieth century, changes in the expectations and actions of white Americans helped establish a moment of paradox and opportunity. On the one hand, it was for many, if not most, Native people the lowest of historical low points. Old economies proved unsustainable on land bases shrunken and transformed by American colonialism; new economies were barely possible under its tight management. Social and cultural institutions and practices wavered under stifling reservation surveillance. The threat of violence hung in the air, and the forced reeducation of the next generation of Indian children threatened an abrupt end to cultures and languages. Devastating legal decisions, political helplessness, grinding poverty, white racist antipathy—all these things combined to place Native people in a truly desperate state. Tribal peoples all have their own histories and memories of these times as well as the memories of a full century's worth of recovery work, undertaken while facing continuing challenges to rights and autonomy. The American national story of that desperation is told differently, however, for it easily draws from the old expectation that Indian people either assimilate or die out. Indeed, in American history texts today, the Indian people living between 1890 and 1934 often simply vanish from the master narrative.

On the other hand, expectations, actions, anxieties, and new social conditions also combined to open up a window of possibility. It seemed

as if Indians and non-Indians might be able to challenge the old script—
and maybe even write a new one. A range of people—singers, drivers, actors, athletes, and writers—began drafting such scripts. Thus, Tsianina—
"a free-limbed Indian girl, with the body of a wind-swayed sapling and
the grace of a wild doe"—could thrill audiences with her "effortless tone
production, perfect breathing, smooth velvety legato and easily sustained
power." And, with his sharp natural reflexes and effortless mental equilibrium, "Chief" Bender might "lash the white man to the Post." James
Young Deer and Princess Red Wing could create films in which white
people blessed mixed-race marriages, which were then rejected by Indian
people who carved out a future for themselves, in part by laying waste to
white civilization!

It soon became clear, however, that such people had largely failed to
capture and sustain a sympathetic non-Indian audience. The window of
opportunity through which they peered did not slam shut, exactly, but it
surely swung back toward the sill, and, by the late twentieth century,
many of their efforts had been forgotten outside of Indian country. Those
efforts, I have suggested, are worth our continued reflection, for they
speak from the past to the world of the twenty-first century. This book has
tried to build such a reflection by thinking through four questions. First,
how might we understand the shifting histories of non-Indian expectations? Second, how might we think of the unexpected nature of Indian
lives lived in dialogue with such expectations? Third, how might we sit-
uate Native people in relation to the particular historical moment of the
late-nineteenth- and early-twentieth-century United States? And, finally,
how might we explain the changes among both Indian and non-Indian
people that seemed to nudge shut that window of opportunity?

OCTOBER 1911: A COHORT
CONFRONTS EXPECTATION

On October 12, 1911—Columbus Day—a group of "Indian progressives" gathered in Columbus, Ohio, to found a reform group, the Society
of American Indians (SAI). The SAI is today recognized as perhaps the
first modern intertribal political organization. In its *Quarterly Journal* and
annual conferences, the group debated and proposed reforms in Indian
policy ranging from education, to the role of the Indian Office, to Wild
West performance (to which it was generally hostile), to the question of
peyote use. Its members were largely boarding school or university educated, and they tended to work as ministers (Sherman Coolidge, John

FIGURE 50. *Chief Bender Baseball Card, American Tobacco Co., ca. 1911.*
(Library of Congress LOT 13163-18, no. 329.)
FIGURE 51. *Chief Meyers Baseball Card, American Tobacco Co., 1911.*
(Library of Congress LOT 13163-25, no. 68.)

Eastman), Indian Office employees (Charles Dagenett), teachers (Angel DeCora Dietz, Emma Johnson, Henry Roe Cloud, and Elizabeth Bender Roe Cloud), museum and anthropological workers (Arthur C. Parker, J. N. B. Hewitt), physicians and lawyers (Carlos Montezuma, Charles Eastman, Thomas Sloan), and cultural producers (Zitkala-Ša, John Oskison, and Henry Standing Bear). The SAI sought to weld together a coherent Indian political response to the issues that affected individuals, tribes, and Indians as a whole.[2]

On October 14, even as the SAI political meeting was still in session, the Philadelphia Athletics' pitcher Charles Albert Bender (figure 50) took the mound against the New York Giants in the 1911 World Series. Though Bender would win two decisive victories in the series—and though he gave up only five hits—he lost this first game when the Giants' catcher John "Chief" Meyers (figure 51)—who batted .300 for the series—scored the winning run. (A week later, after the dust had cleared, the Essanay Film Company—an Indian on its logo—released a film of the contest, undoubtedly the most indigenous World Series ever, though it was not figured as such at the moment. Essanay was busy producing westerns that fall and would, two years later, provide the technical expertise for Buffalo Bill Cody's 1913 *Indian Wars* film.)[3]

In 1911, three Indian operas hit the stage—Frederick Converse's *The Sacrifice*, Victor Herbert's *Natoma*, and Mary Moore Carr's *Narcissa*—quite possibly inspiring the Indian writer and activist Zitkala-Ša, who collaborated two years later with William Hanson on the Indian opera *The Sun Dance*. Only a year before, in 1910, Charles Wakefield Cadman had sought the help of Francis LaFlesche on his first operatic effort, *Daoma*. In the fall of 1911, Cadman was likely on the road, touring the Indian Music Talk he had been giving since 1909. His future partner, Tsianina Redfeather, studied piano. Two years later, in 1913, she would move to Denver and begin performing with Cadman, imparting Indian authenticity to his idealized treatments of Indian melodies.

In the California autumn of 1911, James Young Deer and Princess Red Wing were busy setting up the West Coast branch of Pathé Frères. We can imagine them musing on the plot structures of romantic racialism and preparing to make the critical 1912 films *The Prospector and the Indian*, *The Squawman's Revenge*, and *Red Eagle the Lawyer*. Redwing's career was heating up, and she starred, in those years, in *Little Dove's Romance* (1911), *A Redskin's Appeal* (1912), *The Unwilling Bride* (1912), *The Penalty Paid* (1912), and quite likely several others (her filmography is incomplete). In 1911, the Selig Studio's *Curse of the Redman* was mobilizing Indian critics. Even as Bender and Myers were facing off in New York and Philadelphia, John Standing Horse was writing to *Moving Picture World*, calling Indian pictures "a joke" and noting the presence of a substantial number of Indian actors in New York City. Louis Tewanima and Jim Thorpe were training for the 1912 Olympics, where Tewanima would win two silver medals and Thorpe would take the gold in both the pentathlon and the decathlon. In 1913, Indian Commissioner Cato Sells instituted the competency commissions, which swept across the country granting the fee patents through which a number of Indian people exchanged land for automobiles. The first car on the Rosebud reservation, according to photographer-observer John Anderson, arrived in 1911. Luther Standing Bear, William Eagleshirt, William Darkcloud, and Thomas Ince all came to California in that same year.

I have tried in this book to take practices commonly marked as anomalous—sports, automobility, film and musical performance—transform them into legitimate categories, and then populate those categories with

Indian people. In some cases, the people occupying these categories formed intellectual, political, or cultural communities of a sort—the SAI, for example, or the groups of Pine Ridge Wild West actors that traveled together. In most cases, however, it makes more sense to see them as disparate individuals or groups acting largely in parallel, overlapping on occasion. In this sense, one hesitates to name them a movement, for they had no shared leadership or guiding ideology. Nonetheless, I think they had a kind of coherence, built around indigenous cultural production within a wider world. In moments like October 1911 we can see, if not a community or a movement, then a recognizable *cohort* of Indian people engaged in a congruent activity: the making and remaking of a spectrum of expectations.[4] The musicians, actors, athletes, and drivers who populate this book reflect only a portion of that group. Other authors have offered thorough treatments, for example, of the Penobscot dancer and actress Molly Spotted Elk, the Tallchief sisters and other members of the Oklahoma ballerina tradition, the artists, potters, and weavers of Santa Fe and Oklahoma, the peyote believers who created the Native American Church, the twentieth century's Indian cowboy and rodeo circuits, Christian Indian ministers and lay leaders, and Indian progressives such as Charles Eastman, Arthur C. Parker, Susan LaFlesche Picotte, Zitkala-Ša, and others.[5]

Many of these people—with various degrees of awareness, intent, and purpose—recognized that, even as the military conflicts of the nineteenth century were concluded, new grounds for struggle were being opened up to Indian people. Those struggles would often take place on the terrain of culture—who controls it? who defines it? who transforms it? At the turn of the century, white Americans already had a head start in this struggle, with reservation surveillance, boarding schools, allotment, missionization, and other overt efforts at the transformation of Indian people already well under way. Those efforts did not fail to shape the lives and experiences of Native Americans. Indeed, a number of the Indian people I've located in unexpected places did not, in fact, live as part of tribal communities. Tsianina Redfeather and Luther Standing Bear stayed mostly in California. James Young Deer's tribal connection is sketchy at best. Francis LaFlesche, a troubling figure for his people back in Nebraska, made his headquarters in Washington, D.C. Charles Albert Bender worked in the Philadelphia Athletics organization for most of his career. Other athletic figures took coaching jobs around the country. Many, and especially the so-called Indian progressives, believed in assimilation—at least for some portion of their careers—and they used it as the base on which reform efforts might be built. They too tended to locate themselves in urban areas and to travel in cycles between home and away.

But to read this cohort strictly in terms of assimilation is to mistake the rhetoric used in *planning* white cultural domination for the actual encounter, which proved far more complicated—even among those who adopted the idea of assimilation itself. In that encounter, new generations of Indian people—some with prereservation memories, others raised in reservation contexts, still others brought to culture in cities or on the road—figured ways to move within the institutions that did, in fact, constrain, dominate, and transform them. Likewise, they often learned to move within the rhetoric—of assimilation, for instance—that structured expectations. These people were diverse, with differing views on race, blood, culture, progress, assimilation, and disappearance, all of which changed over time.

Products of a cultural encounter laced with colonial intent, these people were at the same time producers—of images and ideas ripe for white consumption. Even as they tried to fend off attacks on Indian cultures, a number also used white anxieties to launch their own attacks—constrained, we must always admit—on white American culture itself. And, though many others did not see themselves explicitly challenging the colonial order, such cultural producers never acted in a world devoid of political import. If the Indian buyer of an automobile did not necessarily see his or her act in political terms, the challenge to white expectation was at once social, cultural, and political in its effects. So too was that of the Indian athlete who tricked Harvard or "scalped" Yale or the singing Indian princess who insisted in making an opera speak to her own place in the modern world.

Such culture wars took concrete shape around struggles over representation. Intentionally and unintentionally, collectively and individually, this Indian cohort inevitably confronted prevailing expectations. And, indeed, I've tried to follow in these people's path, telling a history that wishes to smash apart the expectations that continue to linger in far too many American hearts and souls. Those expectations have concerned, among other things, Native technological incapacity, natural proclivities toward violence and warfare, a lack of social development, distance from both popular and aesthetic culture, and an inability to engage a modern capitalist market economy. Even as this book has questioned the origins and naturalness of such expectations, it has also tried to question them by telling histories of Indian unexpectedness, stories suggesting that things have *not* always been the way they have seemed. Indeed, these histories have been named anomalies and buried, in part, precisely because they have failed to accord with familiar and powerful expectations.

Similar expectations continue to be mobilized today to structure and constrain the social, political, and economic lives of Indian people. They literally remake racial—and racist—understandings of who and what Native people should be. When Makah whalers adopt modern harpoon guns, those older expectations kick in—real Indians must remain in a pretechnological state. When Indian people enter the military, expectations bubble beneath the surface—natural warriors, maybe they should walk point and take the first bullet. Expectations underlie the objections when Native people pursue gaming enterprises (Indians should not have money), seek to develop wind-power farms (Indian environmentalism should be spiritual, not technological), make the rosters of professional sports teams (Indians cannot compete in such structured settings), craft careers as actors or writers, play blues, or mix jazz and powwow music together. All too often, these expectations tend to assume a status quo defined around *failure*, the result of some innate limitation on the part of Indian people. Success is written off as an anomaly, a bizarre little episode that calls up a chuckle.[6]

THE HISTORICAL MOMENT

This book argues that some Indian people—more than we've been led to believe—leapt quickly into modernity and not necessarily because they adopted political and legal tools from whites or because they were acculturated into the educational, political, and economic order of twentieth-century America.[7] They leapt, I think, because it became painfully clear that they were not distinct from the history that was even then being made. Whether they liked it or not, other people were building a world around, on top of, and through Native American people. That world took as its material base the accumulation of capital ripped from indigenous lands, resources, and labor over the course of centuries. At the turn of the century, that process of accumulation was in full force, with the Dawes General Allotment Act and its modifications enabling the transfer of millions of acres from Indian hands to white. The oil resources under Indian lands would, in a very few years, produce even more capital for American corporations while fueling (quite literally) the automotive transportation that would support twentieth-century industrialization.

Likewise, the imaginative superstructure that helped define modern American senses of self relied heavily on long histories of nationalism and primitivism figured around Indianness. The real significance in the shift from *surround* to *outbreak* to *pacification*, it turns out, was not just the bridge it built from nineteenth-century vanishing ideology to twentieth-century (anti)modern primitivism. Nor was it the (failed) attempt to incorporate Indians into the civic structure of American colonialism. Assume—and I think we can—that the nation-to-nation distinction recognized in the Plenty Horses case was also seen as a distinction between modern and not-modern. The final moment of conquest, pacification, and incorporation of Indian people, then, might also be seen to represent one of the many critical instants in which the United States became aware of its own modernity. Pacification served as a marker for the new epoch, and it was figured constantly in the most popular entertainment of the era—Cody's Wild West, which managed for its audiences the tensions between frontier and postfrontier. For those in modern urban strongholds, Indians quickly became objects of nostalgic desire as they reflected both an earlier, virile time of colonization and an authenticity that modernity seemed to deny.

Young Deer, Red Wing, Tsianina, Standing Bear, and athletes and performers of all kinds engaged in representational acts in which primitivism and modernity were juxtaposed and revealed to be false categories. At the same time, however, a critical part of representational struggle also involved the real actions of real contemporary people—actions that often challenged the performances found at arenas, stages, and stadiums. Lives lived around liberating travel and cosmopolitan sophistication mattered. So did engagement with technology—not just cars, but sewing machines, merry-go-rounds, telephones, and film cameras. All these things pointed to the ways in which Indian people created modernity in dialogue with others. Indian space was *not* only reservation space, and reservation space was anachronistic *only* in white expectation. Reservations marked the last possibility of social, cultural, and political homelands for Indian people; of course, Native people have marked them *Indian* in as many ways as possible. But it is also the case that the entire world of the modern belonged—and belongs—to Indian people, as much as it does to anyone else.

THE WINDOW CLOSES

The members of this Native cohort were not the first Indian people to engage American popular culture, to be sure. They were the first to do so, however, in its particularly modern forms, at the very moment when those forms were developing, and in terms of the white ideological anxieties surrounding the beginnings and ends of American eras. In effect, the cohort offered a foundational narrative for a kind of cultural politics that would be constantly rediscovered and renewed by Indian people throughout the twentieth century. Lest anyone mistake these assertions as simply uncritical celebration, however, I want to return finally to the window of opportunity—both its constraints and the fact of its closing.[8]

It becomes apparent in hindsight that many of these pioneering efforts in cultural politics failed, even on their own terms. As Indian people tried to maintain the most positive representations of their historical moment—often based on romantic primitivism—they found themselves both escaping familiar expectations and reinforcing them. Nor were they able truly to seize the mechanisms of cultural production. Tsianina Redfeather built a brief for her own modernity into a white composer's opera—which fell into obscurity. The Oorang Indians created the football halftime show and showcased intertribal athletic talent—for two years. Luther Standing Bear thought he had convinced Thomas Ince to make real Indian films—and never heard from him again. Young Deer and Red Wing successfully reworked classic melodramatic plot forms—only to be reined in by the Pathé studio and then brushed to the margins of the film world at the moment it began to gather substantial cultural power.

The failures of Redfeather, Young Deer, Standing Bear, and others were real, and they were not simply the product of Indian failure. That is, they cannot be seen simply in the economic terms of competition—as an inability to offer Indian selves and products capable of succeeding in a marketplace of culture and consumption. The failures were the products (at least in part) of transformations in economic structures and institutions. In sports, that meant the advent of an industrial model in professional and collegiate athletics. In Hollywood, it meant the rise of a studio system in which whiteness became the color of versatility and audience response the way of measuring just how much authenticity was absolutely necessary. In that sense, it is worth noting the ways in which race, gender, class, and sexuality serve as channels through which some people achieve economic and social power over others.

But there is more to the closing of the window of opportunity than this. Why, for example, did the Indianist movement in American art music give way to white appropriations of the blues notes and syncopated rhythms of African American expression? After all, you could find blues notes and complex syncopation in Indian musics as well. I want to suggest that the failures of Indian representational politics might also be seen in relation to the development of *other* forms of indigenous creativity, specifically, the modern development of the idea of Indian political nationhood—in other words, sovereignty. I am not going to trace the complex origins of this idea here; others have done so quite thoroughly. Suffice it to say that, while arguments for Native sovereignty are largely based on nineteenth-century legal decisions, they have been a key twentieth-century phenomenon, gaining momentum and institutional status over the course of the century.[9] As an argument for nothing less than political autonomy, sovereignty has always lived, in the American context, in tension with the powerful idea of *inclusion.*

For much of the nineteenth century, of course, a rhetoric of conquest and insufficiency was paired with one of inclusion. Indians could assimilate. Indians would mingle their blood. Indians could make their way up the evolutionary ladder into whiteness. The new expectation of Indian pacification, too, suggested the inevitability of inclusion—in the legal structures of civil society, at least (and, indeed, a number of pieces of legislation worked similarly inclusive magic on Indians, concluding with the 1924 Citizenship Act). Don't mistake the word for the altruism it often carries today. *Inclusion* was largely a colonial ideal that had everything to do with proper management of people rather than their equality, and it took particular shape around programs that aimed to assimilate Indians while still assuming them to be inferior peoples.[10]

At the turn of the century, this sensibility of inclusion ran straight into a new idea. Now, inclusion could be seen, not only in the terms of assimilation, but also in those of antimodern romantic primitivism. The collision of these ideas allowed Indian people an early and privileged point of entry into modernist performance—a window of opportunity. And so, even as the Indian progressives of the SAI performed assimilation, other Native people began playing with the primitive. The former sought a political voice, the latter access to the formative spaces of twentieth-century mass and popular culture. These goals were not unconnected, for the lines between performances of primitivism and assimilation blurred as often as did those between politics and culture. When inclusion met antimodern primitivism, putting on a headdress created a little bit of room to maneuver—for athletes on the field, singers on the concert stage, actors in the film studio, and progressives in lobbying and publishing.

Attuned to the ethos of tricksters, Indian people shapeshifted from suits to headresses to buckskins and back as suited their needs.

Even as it allowed inclusion, however, primitivism also required an assertion of Indian difference—and that assertion had attached to it a not-so-secret political memory/dream. In the twentieth century, the memory of independence helped give birth to the dream that began to take shape under the name *sovereignty*. Welding together cultural, political, and legal distinctiveness and autonomy, modern Native-centered assertions of sovereignty were, in fact, the creations of Indian people within, and in dialogue with, the broad cultural contexts of the twentieth century. Nor were Indian people the only ones with dreams for the future. One might also suggest that the modern discourse of civil rights and integration was being created by African Americans and Latino Americans at the very same moment and out of similar contexts.[11]

The differences are instructive. Forged in a cruel history of diaspora and slavery that brutally mingled together a wide range of African peoples, African Americans had no collective land base and no continuous, viable memory of political autonomy. Many Indian peoples possessed a diasporic history as well, but their migrations often allowed them to retain memories—fragile at worst, vigorous at best—of discrete social identities. And, even as Indian removals took land away, they frequently substituted new territories, allowing the maintenance of land bases even in moments of dispossession. At the same time, the social fluidity characteristic of Native societies in the first periods of colonial disruption gave way in the nineteenth century to more rigid social and political identities: treaties codified tribal units, and the federal government began identifying and tracking tribal members associated with discrete territories. Black, Latino, and Asian Americans created all manner of social and political organizations, to be sure, but their populations were far more individualized, without the opportunity to work within tribal social structures that linked together land, identity, legal rights, and government visibility.

For African Americans, and for many Latino and Asian peoples as well, the ideal of inclusion offered the best available path to justice, equality, and a better life. The sons and daughters of slaves—enmeshed for generations in American society—sought to include themselves in the ideals of American freedom, equality, and opportunity. The legal tools at the disposal of different peoples—the Fourteenth and Fifteenth Amendments for black Americans; the Treaty of Guadalupe Hidalgo for some Mexican Americans; the Jones Act for some Puerto Ricans, the Fourteenth

Amendment for others—pointed them in different ways toward inclusion and incorporation.[12] Uplift, citizenship, integration, civil rights, statehood—these were among the distinct demands and admonitions that emerged out of these particular histories. The tools available to Indian people were very different: treaties might frequently look toward future Indian assimilation, but their legal logic rested on Indian people possessing a distinct national status, in the words of John Marshall, as "domestic dependent nations."[13]

Inclusion offered Indian people a cultural—and, thus, political—platform. The model of interaction and rights being developed in some early-twentieth-century African American political thought had a cachet for many Indian progressives, but it never offered justice in terms that made sense to most tribal peoples. Indeed, for many Native people, the most productive avenues to justice seemed to point to sovereignty, treaties, and nation-to-nation political relations rather than to inclusion and the demand for civil rights within American society. Despite devastating decisions such as *Lone Wolf v. Hitchcock*—which recognized Congress's plenary power over indigenous people—many saw in dreams of the future the fragmented political identities of the past and the treaties that, according to the U.S. Constitution, were to be the "supreme law of the land."[14]

In the early twentieth century, then, Indian people—who both clung to and looked toward autonomy and separation—participated in the making of an inclusive American cultural modernity. At the same time, other Americans of color—including those who sought inclusion and equality—served as complicated essences of exclusion, the subjects of Jim Crow segregation, lynching, and legal and political restriction. Their political dream of justice *within* an American political framework came to structure much of twentieth-century culture, which had opened with the metaphor of the melting pot and closed with the inclusive rhetoric of multiculturalism.

By midcentury, these trajectories had crossed paths, and they did so in the meetings of culture and politics. In the early decades of the twentieth century, Indian people opened a small window of opportunity in which they might be valued and included in American culture. It should come as no surprise that black and Latino athletes sometimes passed as Indians or that dark-skinned black tricksters like Buffalo Child Long Lance and Two Moons Meridas should claim redness rather than whiteness as their entrée into American culture and society.[15] Native ideals and practices of sovereignty pointed in a different direction, however, and inclusion—whether couched as assimilation, antimodern primitivism, or just lived life—began to seem less compelling. The allure of Indian inclusion faded, not simply for Indians, but also for non-Indians, and developmental rhetoric gave up ground to older expectations of racial difference.

With the 1934 Indian Reorganization Act (IRA), Indian people achieved a small measure of political autonomy, which they continued to build, in fits and starts, throughout the century. By the 1960s, it had become clear that distinct political status rested, in large part, on distinct cultural and social status, and Indian people sought to reclaim, consolidate, and patrol, not simply lands and sovereignty, but cultures and languages as well. One bird's-view history of the twentieth century might tell of the ways Indian people reworked a sense of distinctiveness and difference, fighting off the colonizing ways the United States sought to include them, and demanding a very particular kind of inclusion, one based on unique political status.[16]

African, Latino, and Asian Americans, on the other hand, built quite different versions of inclusion brick by brick over the course of the century, fighting for equal rights and opportunities in housing, employment, voting, and education—what we today think of as integration. Each of these peoples had been "integrated"—as forced or low-wage laborers in the economy that helped produce the modern United States. And, if each was framed through a rhetoric of exclusion and segregation, each had also long been part of a shared social fabric, reinforced through cultural exchanges of varying intensity. Minstrel shows, for example, dominated the American popular culture of the nineteenth century and the early twentieth, jumbling black and white traditions and performers together. As Thomas Holt has suggested, the increasing emphasis on consumption continued that jumbling—and in cultural realms such as sport, music, and entertainment. In 1910, for example, the black boxer Jack Johnson appeared as both minstrel dandy and the essence of machine-like urban modernity, while the white challenger, Jim Jeffries, evoked the primitivist possibilities more often associated with people of color. And black Americans quickly perceived the problem of cultural representation, contesting the imagery of *Birth of a Nation* and the stereotypes that powered *Amos 'n' Andy*. These things helped define the cultural politics of modernism, and one might as easily trace their appearance in social and cultural interactions among other groups marked by race.[17]

Demography and the geography of urbanism made a difference. In the decades following the turn of the twentieth century, landless African

Americans migrated to northern cities in significant numbers, establishing large urban clusters of black cultural production. Such clusters made black music and arts far more easily accessible to white neighbors. The composer who might once have trekked to the rural south or the reservation west in search of "authentic" material now found African American cultural expression readily at hand. Available in any city, for example, jazz had been embedded from the start in a context of integration and appropriation. Prepped by decades of musical exchange, jazz entered the modernist vocabulary far more easily than Native American musics, which, as we have seen, posed problems of their own. It should come as no surprise, then, that the black arts renaissance overwhelmed Indianness and quickly came to dominate and to transform American modernism. Black cultural production operated within a history and context of interaction, and it aligned itself with African American social and political desires in ways that Indian people—working against inclusion—could not duplicate.[18]

And so even a shared modern culture remembers Josephine Baker more easily than Molly Spotted Elk or Maria Tallchief. The filmmaker Oscar Micheaux comes to mind before Young Deer and Red Wing, Paul Robison before Yowlatchie, Marian Anderson before Tsianina Redfeather. Jackie Robinson has imprinted on our culture with vastly more force than Chiefs Bender or Meyers. As a trailblazer rather than an anomaly, he carries far more cultural weight than even Jim Thorpe. And, of course, the Harlem Renaissance can be named as a discrete thing, which is more than can be said for the cohort of Indian writers, actors, dancers, and artists also active in the modernist moment. The linkages between forms of cultural production and very different political projects—all aimed at achieving justice—helped produce radically different histories, memories, and expectations. In these and other cases, however, the agency of people of color has to be seen less in the terms of "we had a voice" or "we were there too" and more as an affirmative statement: "We have always participated in the production of modern discourse—and of modernity itself."

When Red Cloud Woman sat down underneath the hair dryer, she was engaged in exactly this kind of production. Was she really getting her hair done? With her braids still tied up tightly, almost certainly not. In fact, the photograph that begins this book is one of a series of three. (Another is reproduced in figure 37 above. That's her in the car, along with Spotted Eagle.) The final photograph in the series shows Red Cloud Woman, Spotted Eagle, and a child at a soda fountain enjoying a sundae (see figure 52).

FIGURE 52. Red Cloud Woman, Spotted Eagle, and Child at Soda Fountain, ca. 1941. (Denver Public Library, Western History Department X-32080.)

They were models, working for an unknown photographer who was, we can assume, letting his or her expectations structure the photographs. Indians in salon; Indians in car; Indians in ice cream store—these things were unexpected, enough to raise a chuckle or two. And perhaps they were not part of the lived lives of Red Cloud Woman and Spotted Eagle (though perhaps they were). Down in my soul, I think I would like it if Red Cloud Woman had simply popped by her regular salon to get a picture with her stylist: "Just dropping by with my photographer friend! No time for a perm today, but maybe a quick manicure, please!"

What matters, however, is Red Cloud Woman's willingness to shape the imagery around which Indian people—and Indian women in particular—were to be seen. I would like it much, much better, in fact, if Red Cloud Woman were to talk to me across the years and say, "I knew that the photographer thought this was funny. But I also knew that, if Indian people piled up lots of these images, they would stop being funny. People might decide to take us seriously as something other than primitives. I claimed for myself the privilege of a middle-class white woman—to pamper my body and to have someone else (a white woman) do the drudge work of cleaning and polishing my fingernails. I wanted to turn the tables in *every* way. It was a trickster moment, when the person performing a trick—the photographer, I mean—and the person being tricked—me, I suppose—become one and the same, and it's not clear who is tricking whom." We will probably never know, of course, what Red Cloud Woman thought she was up to—her personal history of modernity will remain a secret history. But we owe her the courtesy of taking her seriously as a shaper of images, a member of a cohort, a participant in a politics of race and gender representation, an Indian person acting with intent and intelligence in one of many unexpected places.

notes

INTRODUCTION

1. The photograph was first published in *Partial Recall: With Essays on Photographs of Native North Americans*, ed. Lucy Lippard (New York: New Press, 1992), 182.

2. There are legitimate historical questions to be asked about the production of this or any image. When and where was the photograph taken? By whom? Was Red Cloud Woman posed by the photographer in order to appear anomalous? According to the critic Lucy Lippard, the back of the photograph bears the penciled legend "assimilation," which suggests a purpose for the photograph (ibid.). Was it staged to represent assimilation into white American culture, as represented by the beauty parlor? Or was the notation added later, as an explanation? (It turns out that the inscription is a cataloging notation, left by someone at the Denver Public Library—which suggests how the image was to be seen and ordered, if not necessarily taking us directly back to its moment of origin.) Was the image government propaganda? Did it have an intended audience? How might that audience have seen the image? And how did Red Cloud Woman experience the photograph? Was she a paid model? Was she creating her own form of humor? These are all critical historical questions. In the sense that they expect context to "explain away" the anomaly, however, they participate in the same ideological practice.

3. Trevor Purvis and Alan Hunt, "Discourse, Ideology, Discourse, Ideology, Discourse, Ideology . . . ," *British Journal of Sociology* 44 (September 1993): 478. See also Terry Eagleton, *Ideology: An Introduction* (London: Verso, 1991); Louis Althusser, "Ideology and Ideological State Apparatuses," in *Lenin and Philosophy and Other Essays* (London: New Left, 1971), 123–73; and Raymond Williams, "Base and Superstructure in Marxist Theory," in *Problems in Materialism and Culture* (London: Verso), 31–49.

4. Purvis and Hunt, "Discourse, Ideology," 485. Theoretical readers will note my debts here to the more detailed readings offered by Louis Althusser, Raymond Williams, Antonio Gramsci, T. J. Jackson Lears, Stuart Hall, and Michel Foucault, among others.

5. While it may appear that I am mapping my own figuration of *category* and *anomaly* over this historiographic problem, I would argue that *generalization* and *unique case* are, in fact, different analytic forms. Category necessarily imposes a rigid order, with anomaly not only unique but also wrong. General-

ization, a more flexible practice, seeks to find commonality and overlap among multiple cases, each with its own unique character. Where anomaly names the outlier within a more rigid categorical system, uniqueness insists on a diversity of experiences. Category and anomaly, in other words, speak well to ideological formations; generalization and uniqueness speak better to historical contingency.

6. My thanks to Carlo Rotella for suggesting the "first-draft" nature of an essay in relation to a larger historical structure.

VIOLENCE

1. Crossing the fence line meant moving from reservation control into relative mobility and freedom, but that movement was paradoxical. The reservation was meant to enact state control over Indian "savagery." Yet, even as it sought to remake Indian people, the reservation offered something of a safe space for Lakota cultural preservation and resistance. If crossing the fence line meant movement and freedom from control, it also meant encountering the threats of modern America—and threatening that modernity with one's own Indian primitivism. Such movement, then, required a pass from the reservation agent, who demanded to know the purpose of any travel, the route, and the amount of time Indian travelers would step outside the reservation regime. On the useful notion *anachronistic time*, see Anne McClintock, *Imperial Leather: Race, Gender, and Sexuality in the Colonial Contest* (New York: Routledge, 1995), 30, 40–42.

2. On Smith, see "Encounter between Sioux Indians of the Pine Ridge Agency, S. Dak., and a Sheriff's Posse of Wyoming," 58th Cong. 2d sess., S. Doc. 128, p. 25 (hereafter S. Doc. 128). My thanks to Louis Warren (personal communication, August 20, 2003) for sharing information with me on William Brown.

3. Treaty with the Sioux, April 29, 1868, 15 Stats. 635 (1868), art. 11.

4. *Ward v. Racehorse* (163 U.S. 504, 41 L. Ed. 244, 16 S. Ct. 1076) followed an attack on several Bannocks by a quasi-official posse. See also Charles F. Wilkinson and John M. Volkman, "Judicial Review of Indian Treaty Abrogation: As Long as Water Flows, or Grass Grows upon the Earth—How Long a Time Is That?" *California Law Review* 63 (1975): 601–58; and George Cameron Coggins and William Modrcin, "Native American Indians and Federal Wildlife Law," *Stanford Law Review* 31 (1979): 375–408.

5. Ernest Richardson, *The Battle of Lightning Creek* (Pacific Palisades, Calif.: Ernest Richardson, 1956), 11.

6. *Newcastle (Wy.) Daily News*, July 25, 1901, quoted in Richardson, *Lightning Creek*, 10.

7. For conflicts over game and the definition of *hunting* and *subsistence*, see Louis Warren, *The Hunter's Game: Poachers and Conservationists in Twentieth-Century*

America (New Haven, Conn.: Yale University Press, 1997); Karl Jacoby, *Crimes against Nature: Squatters, Poachers, Thieves, and the Hidden History of American Conservation* (Berkeley and Los Angeles: University of California Press, 2001); and Mark David Spence, *Dispossessing the Wilderness: Indian Removal and the Making of the National Parks* (New York: Oxford University Press, 1999).

8. S. Doc. 128, p. 77. For other accounts of the Lightning Creek fight, see Barton R. Voigt, "The Lightning Creek Fight," *Annals of Wyoming* 49 (spring 1977): 5–21; and Lee R. Boyer, "Conflict over Hunting Rights: Lightning Creek, 1903," *South Dakota History* 23 (winter 1993): 301–20. While my account is based primarily on the congressional inquiry, I have benefited greatly from these other interpretations.

9. Ibid., p. 49.

10. Ibid., p. 50.

11. See, e.g., Richard Slotkin, *Regeneration through Violence: The Mythology of the American Frontier, 1600–1860* (Middletown, Conn.: Wesleyan University Press, 1973), and *The Fatal Environment: The Myth of the Frontier in the Age of Industrialization, 1800–1890* (New York: Atheneum, 1985); Richard Maxwell Brown, *No Duty to Retreat: Violence and Values in American History and Society* (New York: Oxford University Press, 1991); Clare V. McKanna Jr., *Homicide, Race, and Justice in the American West, 1880–1920* (Tucson: University of Arizona Press, 1997), esp. 117–54; and David T. Courtwright, *Violent Land: Single Men and Social Disorder from the Frontier to the Inner City* (Cambridge, Mass.: Harvard University Press, 1996), esp. 109–30.

12. For a concise statement and critique of the trope *the defensive conquest of the continent*, see Richard White, "Frederick Jackson Turner and Buffalo Bill," in *The Frontier in American Culture*, ed. James R. Grossman (Berkeley and Los Angeles: University of California Press, 1994), 6–10.

13. Angie Debo (*Geronimo: The Man, His Time, His Place* [Norman: University of Oklahoma Press, 1976], 406–7) notes the lingering fear of outbreak that accompanied Geronimo, a fear so great that, on one occasion when, as an older man, he became lost in the cornfields outside Fort Sill and was late returning home, newspapers immediately warned that he had broken out and was escaping to Arizona.

14. By focusing on the discursive history of Wounded Knee, I by no means intend to displace the reality of the event. But Wounded Knee almost immediately became embedded in discourse—Lakota discourse concerning the treachery of the United States; a broader Indian discourse concerning the same; military discourses of heroism and self-justification; critical discourses that sought, in limited ways, to intervene in armed American colonialism. Underpinning each of these was the question of social difference and the concomitant possibilities of violence, which always returned the discursive to the material.

15. For an account of the historical depth and range of such traditions, see Gregory Evans Dowd, *A Spirited Resistance: The North American Indian Struggle for Unity, 1745–1815* (Baltimore: Johns Hopkins University Press, 1992). My brief account of the Wounded Knee massacre draws on James Mooney, *The Ghost-Dance Religion and the Sioux Outbreak of 1890*, Fourteenth Annual Report, pt. 2 (Washington, D.C.: Bureau of American Ethnology, 1896); Mario Gonzalez and Elizabeth Cook-Lynn, *The Politics of Hallowed Ground: Wounded Knee and the Struggle for Indian Sovereignty* (Urbana: University of Illinois Press, 1999); Conger Beasley, *We Are a People in This World: The Lakota Sioux and the Massacre at Wounded Knee* (Fayetteville: University of Arkansas Press, 1995); William Coleman, *Voices of Wounded Knee* (Lincoln: University of Nebraska Press, 2000); and Richard Jensen, R. Eli Paul, and John E. Carter, *Eyewitness at Wounded Knee* (Lincoln: University of Nebraska Press, 1991).

16. *Black Elk Speaks: Being the Life Story of a Holy Man of the Oglala Sioux as Told through John Neihardt* (1932; Lincoln: University of Nebraska Press, 1979), 230–38; Raymond J. DeMallie, ed., *The Sixth Grandfather: Black Elk's Teachings Given to John G. Neihardt* (Lincoln: University of Nebraska Press, 1984), 256–82.

17. For examples of Ghost Shirts, see Harold Peterson, ed., *I Wear the Morning Star: An Exhibition of American Indian Ghost Dance Objects* (Minneapolis: Minneapolis Institute of Arts, 1976), esp. 52–83.

18. For a compelling treatment of the army's role in the conflict at Wounded Knee—indeed, for a new reading of Wounded Knee—see Jeffrey Ostler, "Conquest and the State: Why the United States Employed Massive Military Force to Suppress the Lakota Ghost Dance," *Pacific Historical Review* 65 (1996): 217–48.

19. Ibid., 217.

20. "The Desperate Chief's Career," *New York Times*, December 16, 1890, 1. For a thorough reading of the different positions and approaches of individual reporters shaping at least the immediate discourse framing Wounded Knee, see George R. Kolbenschlag, *A Whirlwind Passes: Newspaper Correspondents and the Sioux Indian Disturbances of 1890–1891* (Vermillion: University of South Dakota Press, 1990).

21. John Coward, *The Newspaper Indian: Native American Identity in the Press, 1820–90* (Urbana: University of Illinois Press, 1999), 101–2, 159–91; Charles Cressey, *Omaha Bee*, November 22, 1890, 1, quoted in Kolbenschlag, *A Whirlwind Passes*, 36. On Cressey, see Kolbenschlag, *A Whirlwind Passes*, 16. Kolbenschlag also details the ways in which on-site reporters functioned as a press pool, exchanging information, dividing up responsibilities, occasionally writing stories together.

22. On the Tibbleses, see Thomas Tibbles, *Buckskin and Blanket Days: Memoirs of a Friend of the Indians Written in 1905*, ed. Theodora Bates Cogswell (Garden City, N.Y.: Doubleday, 1957); and Kolbenschlag, *A Whirlwind Passes*, 20–21.

23. For Pettigrew, see U.S. Congress, *Report of the Secretary of the Interior, 1890,* 51st Cong., 2d sess., H. Ex. Doc. 1 (Washington, D.C.: U.S. Government Printing Office, 1890), 125, quoted in Kolbenschlag, *A Whirlwind Passes,* 26–27. For Eastman and Dawes, see Kolbenschlag, *A Whirlwind Passes,* 26–27. For Miles, see *Chicago Tribune,* December 3, 1890, 2, and *New York World,* December 3, 1890, 1, both quoted in Kolbenschlag, *A Whirlwind Passes,* 44.

24. Ann Laura Stoler, "Tense and Tender Ties: The Politics of Comparison in North American History and (Post) Colonial Studies," *Journal of American History* 88 (December 2001): 829–65, 854. See also Homi Bhabha, "Of Mimicry and Man," in *The Location of Culture* (London: Routledge, 1994); and McClintock, *Imperial Leather,* 61–69 (a reading of Bhabha and Luce Irigaray). In *Imperial Leather,* McClintock observes that mimicry appears in Bhabha's work as both "self-defeating colonial strategy" and "a form of anti-colonial refusal" (64) and cautions against allowing a formal structure in and of itself—hybridity, e.g., or cross-race ambivalence—to serve as an agent capable of subverting colonial power relations.

25. Ann Laura Stoler, *Race and the Education of Desire: Foucault's "History of Sexuality" and the Colonial Order of Things* (Durham, N.C.: Duke University Press, 1995), and "Tense and Tender Ties."

26. This brief analysis of the colonial importance of categorizing, listing, locating, and other dividing practices as modes of knowledge, control, and generalization is obviously indebted to Michel Foucault. See, e.g., his *Discipline and Punish: The Birth of the Prison,* trans. Alan Sheridan, 2d ed. (New York: Vintage, 1995), 135–230. For a similarly Foucauldian interpretation, see Thomas Biolsi, *Organizing the Lakota: The Political Economy of the New Deal on the Pine Ridge and Rosebud Reservations* (Tucson: University of Arizona Press, 1992), 7–19. For spatial organization, see Emily Greenwald, *Reconfiguring the Reservation: The Nez Perces, Jicarilla Apaches, and the Dawes Act* (Albuquerque: University of New Mexico Press, 2002). And, for a useful meditation on the nature of colonial lists as historical documents, see Frederick Hoxie, *Parading through History: The Making of the Crow Nation in America, 1805–1935* (Cambridge: Cambridge University Press, 1995), 126–30.

27. Frederick Hoxie, "From Prison to Homeland: The Cheyenne River Reservation before World War I," in *The Plains Indians of the Twentieth Century,* ed. Peter Iverson (Norman: University of Oklahoma Press, 1985), 55–75. For a detailed treatment of a tribal community confronting a reservation regime, see Hoxie, *Parading through History,* esp. 126–68.

28. Plenty Horses quoted in Robert Utley, "The Ordeal of Plenty Horses," *American Heritage* 26 (December 1974): 16. See also the broader treatment in Robert Utley, *Last Days of the Sioux Nation* (New Haven, Conn.: Yale University Press, 1963), 252–70. For another treatment of the Plenty Horses case, see William T. Hagan, *The Indian Rights Association: The Herbert Welsh Years, 1882–1904* (Tuc-

son: University of Arizona Press, 1985), 115–26. Hagan and Utley include particularly useful accounts of the Culbertson case, which undoubtedly influenced the outcome of the Plenty Horses case. The Culbertson brothers had, under the guise of wartime confusion, attacked and murdered an Indian family returning from a hunting trip.

29. Here, I'm returning to Homi Bhabha's often-quoted phrase remarking on the ambivalence of colonial discourse, which seeks to produce a "reformed" Other *"that is almost the same, but not quite"* (*The Location of Culture* [London: Routledge, 1994], 86). As much as this was a discursive project, it was, as in the case of boarding schools and reservation surveillance, deeply material as well. See also Stoler, "Tense and Tender Ties," 853–56.

30. In effect, Plenty Horses and reservation people represented two distinct forms of hybridity. To reject Plenty Horses as contaminated elided the hybrid cultural "contamination" of Lakota culture as a whole. For a similar case involving the young Apache Nah-diez-az, also known as the "Carlisle Kid," see McKanna, *Homicide, Race, and Justice,* 140.

31. Utley, "Plenty Horses," 16.

32. Ibid., 84. On Miles's own distaste for the Wounded Knee action, particularly in the context of the Plenty Horses incident, see Virginia Weisel Johnson, *The Unregimented General: A Biography of Nelson A. Miles* (Boston: Houghton Mifflin, 1962), 292–96. Miles's memoirs, *Personal Recollections and Observations of General Nelson A. Miles* (1896; New York: Da Capo, 1969), detail every Indian campaign—except Wounded Knee, which, in a 590-page book, gets no mention whatsoever.

33. For Wounded Knee Medals of Honor, see U.S. Army Center of Military History, www.army.mil/cmh-pg/mohind.htm (accessed February 16, 2004). The army website lists two additional medals given for "Sioux Campaigns" in 1890. For Robinson, see www.dickshovel.com/wagnerB.html (accessed June 21, 2001).

34. For a discussion of the definitions of *war* and their applicability to Indian warfare, see Tom Holm, "Warfare," in *Blackwell Companion to American Indian History,* ed. Philip J. Deloria and Neal Salisbury (Malden, Mass.: Blackwell, 2002), 154–72. For similar concerns regarding the potential for Apache violence, see McKanna, *Homicide, Race, and Justice,* 129–33.

35. Utley, "Plenty Horses," 82–83. For American Horse, see ibid., 85. For Plenty Horses's subsequent life, see ibid., 86.

36. Luther Standing Bear, *My People, the Sioux,* ed. E. A. Brininstool (Boston: Houghton Mifflin, 1928), 160–76, 183–84.

37. For the Two Sticks killings, see Helen H. Blish, *A Pictographic History of the Oglala Sioux,* with drawings by Amos Bad Heart Bull (Lincoln: University of Nebraska Press, 1967), 416–20; and a series of articles from the *Black Hills Daily Times*: "Shedding Blood Again," February 5, 1893, 2; "No More Blood

Shed," February 7, 1893, 1; "Time Alone Tell," February 8, 1893, 1; "Two Sticks' Confession," February 9, 1893, 2; "The Indian Murderers," February 10, 1893, 2; and "Indian Murderers," February 11, 1893, 2.

38. William Brown to Commissioner of Indian Affairs, February 4, 1893, February 5, 1893, National Archives, M-1282, reel 19, Letters Sent by the Pine Ridge Agency, 1875–1914 (all letters from Brown to the commissioner subsequently cited are taken from this collection).

39. "The Indians," *Rocky Mountain News*, February 5, 1893, 1; "The Sioux Trouble," ibid., February 6, 1893, 1.

40. Anne Marie Baker, ed., "A Doorkeeper in the House of God: The Letters of Beatrice A. R. Stocker, Missionary to the Sioux, 1892–1893," *South Dakota History* 22 (spring 1992): 51.

41. "The Indians," *Rocky Mountain News*, February 5, 1893, 2.

42. William Brown to Commissioner, February 5, 1893, p. 3.

43. "Discontent," *Rocky Mountain News*, February 7, 1893, 1.

44. Standing Bear, *My People, the Sioux*, 238.

45. Baker, ed., "Doorkeeper," 51.

46. See, e.g., William E. Huntzicker, "The 'Sioux Outbreak' in the Illustrated Press," *South Dakota History* 20 (winter 1990): 299–320; and Robert G. Hays, *A Race at Bay: New York Times Editorials on "The Indian Problem," 1860–1900* (Carbondale: Southern Illinois University Press, 1997), 168–69, 290–91.

47. William Brown to Commissioner, February 4, 1893, p. 3, and February 5, 1893, p. 2.

48. "The Sioux Trouble," *Rocky Mountain News*, February 6, 1893, 1; "Discontent," ibid., February 7, 1893, 1.

49. Baker, ed., "Doorkeeper," 51–52.

50. For a similar example, see the treatment of transitional and developing Crow leadership in Hoxie, *Parading through History*, 117–22, 150–54, 154–64 (in the context of a local outbreak).

51. For Bear Eagle being fired on, see William Brown to Commissioner, February 4, 1893, p. 1. For Young Man Afraid's intercession, see "The Sioux Trouble," *Rocky Mountain News*, February 6, 1893, 1. For Brown's assertion of Indian condemnation, see William Brown to Commissioner, February 6, 1893, p. 4.

52. Though Foucault, in particular, has seemed bound to a particularly Western tradition, work that emerges from Foucauldian thought—beginning with Edward Said and extending to Greg Dening, Ann Stoler, and others—has offered useful entries into cultural-contact situations. Likewise, a Gramscian or neo-Gramscian apparatus seems to me a useful way into a discussion, not only of the relation of culture to social domination in a cross-cultural context, but also of the particular social formations that made up the shifting hegemony of American society at the turn of the century—

and that then exercised other forms of power on Native Americans and others. Within—but also outside—both these apparatuses, it seems to me, the crucial question—particularly for one concerned with ideology—has to do with the formation of new Indian subjectivities/subjects. For an important exploration of this question, see Frederick Hoxie, "Exploring a Cultural Borderland: Native American Journeys of Discovery in the Early Twentieth Century," *Journal of American History* 79, no. 3 (December 1992): 969–95. For a historiographic provocation, see Stoler, "Tense and Tender Ties."

53. William Brown to Commissioner, February 18, 1893.
54. "A Good Indian," *Black Hills Daily Times*, December 29, 1894, 1.
55. S. Doc. 128, pp. 18, 19. This despite the fact that only two Lakotas were returning the fire of thirteen men.
56. Ibid., p. 25.
57. Despite the sociological differences, there are notable rhetorical parallels here to lynchings in the South, particularly those surrounding "uppity" Indians or African Americans who dared to step from their assigned place into a different category. Understanding and using Anglo law represented a contamination of the categories surrounding whiteness.
58. S. Doc. 128, pp. 7, 9.
59. Ibid., pp. 29, 25.
60. It is worth noting that, in the same year, 1903, the U.S. Supreme Court handed down one of the most devastating legal opinions in Indian history. In *Lone Wolf v. Hitchcock*, 187 U.S. 553 (1903), the Court ruled that Congress had plenary power over Indian peoples, which allowed it to abrogate treaties. Native people were clearly defined as abject subjects of the colonial state, lacking even basic civil or collective rights or protections.
61. In effect, Miller was no longer required to imagine a gender distinction between Indian men and women (which he, of course, did *not* do), for both now fit the category *harmless*. For comparisons of white-on-Indian and Indian-on-white violence in Arizona, see McKanna, *Homicide, Race, and Justice*, 139–54.
62. S. Doc 128, p. 25.

REPRESENTATION

1. For accounts of the Cody films, see Kevin Brownlow, *The War, the West, and the Wilderness* (New York: Knopf, 1979), 224–35; L. G. Moses, *Wild West Shows and the Images of American Indians, 1883–1933* (Albuquerque: University of New Mexico Press, 1996), 229–48; Joy Kasson, *Buffalo Bill's Wild West: Celebrity, Memory, and Popular History* (New York: Hill & Wang, 2000), 255–63; Don Russell, *The Lives and Legends of Buffalo Bill* (Norman: University of Oklahoma Press, 1960), 46, 457–58; and Jacquelyn Kilpatrick, *Celluloid Indians: Native Americans and Film* (Lincoln: University of Nebraska Press, 1999), 19–22.

2. Though Cody had considered filmmaking before, he had entered this particular endeavor in a state of desperation and distress. His Wild West show had been stripped from him through the financial wrangling of the Denver newspapermen Harry Tammen and Frederic Bonfils, who coveted Cody as a circus act. Cody had (with the pair's sponsorship) turned to moviemaking in an effort to recoup his finances and to reconnect with audiences that had drifted away over the course of the Wild West's long run. Though nominally in charge, Cody was, in truth, far from it. Miles was free to pull his troops out of the project, and his cooperation was critical to its success.

3. "Buffalo Bill Picture Shown," *Moving Picture World*, March 14, 1914, 1370. See also Brownlow, *War, West, Wilderness*, 232.

4. See Moses, *Wild West Shows*, 234. For a similar account of Indian menace in the context of film production, with threat transmuted to representation, see "Here's a Real Bad Man: Movie Director Impresses Indians with 'Prop' Revolver," *New York Times*, November 22, 1914, X9.

5. On the camera as cross-cultural violence and Indian photographic innocence, see the critique in James C. Faris, *Navajo and Photography: A Critical History of the Representation of an American People* (Albuquerque: University of New Mexico Press, 1996). On photographic sophistication, see Frank Goodyear III, *Red Cloud: Photographs of a Lakota Chief* (Lincoln: University of Nebraska Press, 2003). And, for a powerful tracing of the history and issues involving Native people and photographic representation, see Martha A. Sandweiss, *Print the Legend: Photography and the American West* (New Haven, Conn.: Yale University Press, 2002), 208–73.

6. Yellow Robe quoted in Moses, *Wild West Shows*, 239. Yellow Robe's critique was delivered at the third annual meeting of the Society of American Indians, where it would have become part of the critical arsenal of a leading group of Indian progressive reformers. As Moses recounts, Yellow Robe's speech would be reprinted in the *Rapid City Times*, where it would inspire other critical attacks on the film. It is worth noting, as well, that Yellow Robe, a vocal critic of sensationalized Indian performances, would later appear in and introduce *The Silent Enemy*, a 1930 film with a near-complete cast of Indian actors that strove for documentary accuracy. Yellow Robe's introduction "points out the usefulness of the film in preserving an authentic image of the old days." Also participating in the film were Molly Spotted Elk and the faux Indian Buffalo Child Long Lance. See *Native Americans on Film and Video*, ed. Elizabeth Weatherford with Emilia Seubert (New York: Museum of the American Indian, 1981), 103; Donald B. Smith, *Long Lance: The True Story of an Imposter* (Lincoln: University of Nebraska Press, 1982), 164–78; and Bunny McBride, *Molly Spotted Elk: A Penobscot in Paris* (Norman: University of Oklahoma Press, 1995), 96–127.

7. Nor, one should note, did twentieth-century film shy away from the educa-

tional rhetoric surrounding the Wild West and *The Indian Wars*. The realism that underpinned the claim to educate would carry forward into a new tradition of documentary filmmaking.

8. Louis Warren's observation on the performance sealing the alliance between the Fifth Cavalry and the Pawnee Scouts is taken from a manuscript-in-progress on Buffalo Bill. (Thanks to Louis Warren [University of California, Davis] for permission to quote from this manuscsript.) On Arikara ceremonies and white spectators, see Louis Warren, "Nishanu's People in American History: Reconsidering the Arikara" (1989, typescript), relying on George F. Will, *Notes on the Arikara Indians and Their Ceremonies*, Old West Series, no. 3 (Denver: John Van Male, 1934), 39–40; and James Howard, "The Arikara Buffalo Society Medicine Bundle," *Plains Anthropologist* 19, no. 66, pt. 1 (November 1974): 248–49. On Laramie, see Henry Morton Stanley, *My Early Travels and Adventures in America and Asia* (1895; London: Duckworth, 2001), 279. On the Pawnee Scouts' performance, see James T. King, "The Republican River Expedition June–July," *Nebraska History* 41 (September 1960): 173. Roger T. Grange ("Fort Robinson, Outpost on the Plains," *Nebraska History* 39 [September 1958]: 217–18) suggests that, in the 1870s, visits to Indian dances were a prominent social activity among the whites at Fort Robinson.

9. For an overview and typology of Native performance, see Jeffrey F. Huntsman, "Native American Theater," in *Ethnic Theatre in the United States*, ed. Maxine Schwartz Seller (Westport, Conn.: Greenwood, 1983), 355–86. For Indian plays and Indian touring, see Don B. Wilmeth, "Noble or Ruthless Savage? The American Indian on Stage and in the Drama," *Journal of American Drama and Theatre* 1, no. 1 (spring 1989): 39–78, and "Tentative Checklist of Indian Plays," *Journal of American Drama and Theatre* 1, no. 2 (fall 1989): 34–54; and Werner Sollors, *Beyond Ethnicity: Consent and Descent in American Culture* (New York: Oxford University Press, 1986). For Native drama, see Burl Donald Grose, "Here Come the Indians: An Historical Study of the Representations of the Native American upon the North American Stage, 1808–1969" (Ph.D. diss., University of Missouri–Columbia, 1979).

10. Among the numerous works dealing with Cody's construction of celebrity through the conflation of representation and action, see Kasson, *Buffalo Bill's Wild West*; Richard Slotkin, *Gunfighter Nation: The Myth of the Frontier in Twentieth-Century America* (1992; Norman: University of Oklahoma Press, 1998), 63–79; and Richard White, "Frederick Jackson Turner and Buffalo Bill," in *The Frontier in American Culture*, ed. James R. Grossman (Berkeley and Los Angeles: University of California Press, 1994), 7–65. For new insights into Cody's place within representational practice, see Louis Warren, "Buffalo Bill Meets Dracula: William F. Cody, Bram Stoker, and the Frontiers of Racial Decay," *American Historical Review* 107, no. 4 (October 2002): 1124–57, and "Cody's Last Stand: Masculine Anxiety, the Custer Myth, and the Fron-

tier of Domesticity in Buffalo Bill's Wild West," *Western Historical Quarterly* 334, no. 1 (spring 2003): 49–70.

11. On the Columbian Exposition, see Robert W. Rydell, *All the World's a Fair: Visions of Empire at American International Expositions, 1876–1916* (Chicago: University of Chicago Press, 1984), 2–8, 38–71; Alan Trachtenberg, *The Incorporation of America: Culture and Society in the Gilded Age* (New York: Hill & Wang, 1982), esp. 208–34; and Curtis Hinsley, "The World as Marketplace: Commodification of the Exotic at the World's Columbian Exposition, Chicago, 1893," in *Exhibiting Cultures: The Poetics and Politics of Museum Display*, ed. Ivan Karp and Steven D. Levine (Washington, D.C.: Smithsonian Institution Press, 1991), 344–65.

12. White, "Turner and Buffalo Bill," 9.

13. See Frederick Jackson Turner, "The Significance of the Frontier in American History," in *The Frontier in American History* (New York: Holt, Rinehart & Winston, 1962); and Kerwin Lee Klein, *Frontier of Historical Imagination: Narrating the European Conquest of Native America, 1890–1990* (Berkeley and Los Angeles: University of California Press, 1997), 13–31 and passim.

14. Theodore Roosevelt, *The Winning of the West* (1885–1894; Lincoln: University of Nebraska Press, 1995). On Cody, Roosevelt, and conquest, see White, "Turner and Buffalo Bill," 27–35; and Slotkin, *Gunfighter Nation*, 29–87.

15. The Wild West reflected only one of the ways Indian people found themselves at these and other expositions. At Chicago, fair officials imported some Native leaders for opening ceremonies; others were recruited for ethnological exhibits in the Anthropology Building and for more commercial enterprises on the Midway. At the Louisiana Purchase Exhibition in 1904, Indian students would be brought as demonstrations of Indian education. See Hinsley, "The World as Marketplace," 346; Rydell, *All the World's a Fair*, 63–64; Moses, *Wild West Shows*, 129–39, 150–67; and Robert Trennert, "Fairs, Expositions, and the Changing Image of Southwestern Indians, 1876–1904," *New Mexico Historical Review* 62 (1987): 127–50.

16. "World's Fair Doings," *Chicago InterOcean*, April 20, 1893, 1, "From Wounded Knee," *Chicago Times*, April 20, 1893, 1.

17. "In Paint and Plumes," *Chicago Herald*, April 20, 1893, 1. The irony here rests, of course, in the fact that Plenty Horses's act of violence came about precisely because he was *not*, in EuroAmerican terms, "wild."

18. Ibid. For a more detailed article on John Burke Low Neck, see "Gild Their Tepees," *Chicago Tribune*, April 20, 1893, 1. Indeed, if anyone among the actors was capable of serving as an icon of both uncontrolled violence and civil containment, it was Plenty Horses. The very same legal judgment that named his act as being outside the law had, paradoxically, worked to reincorporate him into American civil society. That is, he had been forced to acknowledge that American law held the power of life or death over him. Even as it acquitted him, the law made Plenty Horses its subject.

19. "Gild Their Tepees," *Chicago Tribune*, April 20, 1893, 1; "World's Fair Doings," *Chicago InterOcean*, April 20, 1893, 1. Try replacing the identity *Indians* in this sentence with *African Americans*. In the Indian case, whites took comfort in the fact of conquest of a distinct enemy, one that they had been trying to incorporate into the American body politic for almost a century. That incorporative, Jeffersonian language lingered. Black Americans, on the other hand, had been all too incorporated into an American political, social, and cultural situation. The redefinition of that incorporation was very much at stake and miscegenation a key trope through which whites insisted on the utter finality of segregation.

20. Moses, *Wild West Shows*, 65.

21. "Sioux Chiefs Arrive," *Chicago Record*, April 20, 1893, 1; "Noble Redmen in Want," *Chicago Times*, June 27, 1893, 3; "Buffalo Bill's Deserters Found," *Chicago Tribune*, June 16, 1893, 1. On the deserters, see also Moses, *Wild West Shows*, 125–26.

22. On Hampa Nespa, see Moses, *Wild West Shows*, 66–68. On the 1896 Cincinnati Zoological Society summer, see Susan Labry Meyn, "Who's Who: The 1896 Sicangu Sioux Visit to the Cincinnati Zoological Gardens," *Museum Anthropology* 16, no. 2 (1992): 21–26. Photographs of Wild West Indians in Europe can be found in *Buffalo Bill and the Wild West* (Brooklyn: Brooklyn Museum, 1981), 52, 54. For additional treatments of Indian travelers in Europe, see Christian Feest, ed., *Indians and Europe: An Interdisciplinary Collection of Essays* (Aachen: Edition Herodot, Rader Verlag, 1987). Carolyn Foreman (*Indians Abroad, 1493–1938* [Norman: University of Oklahoma Press, 1943]) offers a richly detailed collection of instances of Indian travel, primarily to Europe. For an evocative fictional treatment, see James Welch, *The Heartsong of Charging Elk* (New York: Doubleday, 2000).

23. Moses, *Wild West Shows*, 111.

24. For a compelling treatment of Sitting Bull's Wild West experience, see Kasson, *Buffalo Bill's Wild West*, 171–83.

25. For Black Elk, see Raymond J. DeMallie, ed., *The Sixth Grandfather: Black Elk's Teachings Given to John G. Neihardt* (Lincoln: University of Nebraska Press, 1984), 245. Black Elk later went on to propose and perform in a theatrical pageant in the South Dakota Black Hills. For Standing Bear, see Luther Standing Bear, *My People, the Sioux*, ed. E. A. Brininstool (Boston: Houghton Mifflin, 1928), 124. For Rockboy, see Moses, *Wild West Shows*, 279. These subtleties and variations escaped white reformers, who focused almost completely on the idea that performing a remembered culture and history might lead to its preservation. Perhaps they were right. If nothing else, however, their opposition to Indians' Wild Westing reflects the reformers' intuitive sense that reservations and schools—rather than travel and performance— were more effective vehicles for leading Indians to assimilation. Cody, of

course, argued differently, and he had a point: if travel liberated Indian people from reservation-based forms of colonial domination (as reformers feared), it also fit into a long tradition of discipline and didacticism.

26. *London Globe*, April 17, 1887, quoted in Alan Gallop, *Buffalo Bill's British Wild West* (Gloucestershire: Sutton, 2001), 56. On Red Shirt's career, see Moses, *Wild West Shows*, 44–53.

27. Gallop, *British Wild West*, 70.

28. Herman J. Viola, *Diplomats in Buckskins: A History of Indian Delegations in Washington City* (Washington, D.C.: Smithsonian Institution Press, 1981).

29. "See Themselves in Battle," *New York Times*, January 22, 1914, 3.

30. For a suggestive treatment of this relation between the filmic, the "pro-filmic," and the real, see Richard deCordova, *Picture Personalities: The Emergence of the Star System in America* (1990; Urbana: University of Illinois Press, 2001), esp. 23–46. For a twentieth-century survey, see Armando José Prats, *Invisible Natives: Myth and Identity in the American Western* (Ithaca, N.Y.: Cornell University Press, 2002).

31. The film no longer exists. For the original scene list, which focused almost completely on Wounded Knee, see Moses, *Wild West Shows*, 231–32. As originally planned, the film was to open with "Indians in their natural condition" and close with "portraits of prominent Indians and of men distinguished in the Indian Wars." Apparently, its final version ended with images of "industrious" postwar Indians. While there is a certain narrative movement within the Wounded Knee section, Cody seems to have compromised the film's overall narrative structure by introducing disconnected framing scenes and sections recounting his own activities at the (less well-known) fights at Summit Springs (1869) and War Bonnet Creek (1876). Though shot in the autumn of 1913, the film was in editing for an extremely long time (for that period, at least) and was not released until the winter of 1914. Thanks to Louis Warren for pointing out Cody's ambivalence about Wounded Knee and the general disfavor for it as a subject.

32. Michael Hilger, *The American Indian in Film* (Metuchen, N.J.: Scarecrow, 1986), 9. See also Michael Hilger, *From Savage to Nobleman: Images of Native Americans in Film* (Lanham, Md.: Scarecrow, 1995).

33. Standing Bear, *My People, the Sioux*, 270–71. Standing Bear suffered two dislocated hips, a broken left leg, a broken left arm, two broken ribs, a broken collarbone, a broken nose, and several severe cuts on his head and face.

34. On Standing Bear, see Richard Ellis, "Luther Standing Bear: 'I Would Raise Him to Be an Indian,'" in *Indian Lives: Essays on Nineteenth- and Twentieth-Century Native American Leaders*, ed. L. G. Moses and Raymond Wilson (Albuquerque: University of New Mexico Press, 1985), 139–58. Henry Standing Bear had previously taken South Dakota Lakotas to New York to perform for the summer at Coney Island. In 1906, after accompanying his band of actors

back to South Dakota when the Hippodrome closed, he then returned east for a summer working at the Jamestown Exposition. For Henry Standing Bear at Coney Island, see "Indians Call on Mayor," *New York Times*, June 3, 1903, 16. For Jamestown, see "Hippodrome Staff Seeks Summer Joys," *New York Times*, May 20, 1907, 9. For the agent's critique of the Standing Bear brothers, see "Report of S. A. M. Young," May 23, 1913, sec. 9, p. 1, NARA (National Archives and Records Administration, Washington, D.C.), RG-75, 12914, box 45, file "Pine Ridge 1900–1913." For other examples of Indian performers' mobility and urbanism, see "Indian Actor Heard Great Spirit Call," *New York Times*, March 10, 1906, 7; "Indians Do Well in City," *New York Times*, December 15, 1912, X8; Will Rogers, *The Autobiography of Will Rogers*, ed. Donald Day (Boston: Houghton Mifflin, 1926); McBride, *Molly Spotted Elk*; and Lili Cockerille Livingston, *American Indian Ballerinas* (Norman: University of Oklahoma Press, 1997).

35. Standing Bear, *My People, the Sioux*, 278.

36. Dark Cloud actually appeared in *Birth of a Nation*, playing a general. See Brownlow, *War, West, Wilderness*, 327–44; "A Golden Quiver of Noted Native Americans from the Silent Era," http://www.mdle.com/ClassicFilms /FeaturedStar/star14.htm; and Angela Aleiss, "Native Americans: The Surprising Silents (Race in Contemporary American Cinema: Part 4)," *Cineaste* 21, no. 3 (summer 1995): 34–36.

37. "Riders of the Plains," *Moving Picture World*, November 12, 1910, 1125.

38. *Moving Picture World* quoted in Hilger, *The American Indian in Film*, 24. Hiawatha, particularly when viewed alongside other silent films of the period, does in fact have a very different look, sometimes edging on the documentary in its setting, costumes, and movement. It is easy to see how actors and critics came to focus on "authenticity" as an important critical notion. The film, according to Michael McNally ("Contesting the Real in Song of Hiawatha Pageants" [Carleton College, in progress, typescript]), was an adapatation of a Hiawatha pageant that had come, over the course of the twentieth century, to play an important role in Ojibwe life in Northern Michigan. The actors, in other words, had had plenty of experience and rehearsal. Thanks to Michael McNally for sharing with me his work-in-progress.

39. Ernest Alfred Dench, "The Dangers of Employing Redskins as Movie Actors," (1915), in *The Pretend Indians: Images of Native Americans in the Movies*, ed. Gretchen M. Bataille and Charles L. P. Silet (Ames: Iowa State University Press, 1980), 61–62; Standing Bear, *My People, the Sioux*, 284. Besides *Pretend Indians*, the other classic, if sometimes problematic, treatment of Indians and films is Ralph Friar and Natasha Friar, *The Only Good Indian: The Hollywood Gospel* (New York: Drama Book Specialists, 1972). I have, however, more often profited from Kilpatrick, *Celluloid Indians*; and Beverly R. Singer, *Wiping the War Paint off the Lens: Native American Film and Video* (Minneapolis: University of Minnesota Press, 2001).

40. On Darkfeather, see Buck Rainey, *Sweethearts of the Sage: Biographies and Film-ographies of 258 Actresses Appearing in Western Movies* (Jefferson, N.C.: McFarland, 1992), 17–19; "Golden Quiver of Noted Native Americans"; and Arlene B. Hirschfelder, *The Native American Almanac: A Portrait of Native America Today* (New York: Macmillan USA, 1993), 180–82. For other actors and a differing analysis, see Ward Churchill, Mary Anne Hill, and Norbert S. Hill Jr., "Examination of Stereotyping: An Analytical Survey of Twentieth-Century Indian Entertainers," in Bataille and Silet, eds., *The Pretend Indians*, 35–48.

41. "Indian Actors," *Photoplay*, February 1913, 111.

42. "Ince to Start School," *Moving Picture World*, February 19, 1916, 1111–12. According to Brownlow (*War, West, Wilderness*, 261) and the film historian Angela Aleiss (personal communication, September 24, 2003), Ince had had to sign a care and education agreement with the Indian Office in order to hire Indian actors, an agreement probably similar to the contractual agreements that Cody negotiated.

43. Liza Black, "Looking at Indians: American Indians in Movies, 1941–1960" (Ph.D. diss., University of Washington, 1999). See also Kilpatrick, *Celluloid Indians*, 51–52; and Singer, *Wiping the War Paint*, 20. By *ethnogenesis*, I mean a process that produces a new social group—e.g., Hollywood Indians—that uses markers of cultural difference to define a distinct ethnic identity.

44. For a personal account of early film production, including work with New York Moving Picture/Bison, see Fred J. Balshofer and Arthur C. Miller, *One Reel a Week* (Berkeley: University of California Press, 1967), esp. 14–42.

45. This paragraph relies on Andrew Brodie Smith, "Shooting Cowboys and Indians: Silent Western Films, American Culture, and the Birth of Hollywood" (Ph.D. diss., University of California, Los Angeles, 2000). The book arising from Smith's dissertation—Andrew Brodie Smith, *Shooting Cowboys and Indians: Silent Western Films, American Culture, and the Birth of Hollywood* (Boulder: University Press of Colorado, 2004)—was not yet available as I completed this project. For the Selig experiment and the Miller brothers, see Smith, "Shooting Cowboys and Indians," 79–83. For the essential place of Wild West shows in the 1909 developments in Hollywood, see ibid., 46, 82–83. For the augmentation of chase scenes, see ibid., 83. See also Kilpatrick, *Celluloid Indians*, 12–27.

46. This story has been well told, both in general histories of the film industry and in the stories of specific companies and studios, and it need not be repeated here. For a useful survey, see Eileen Bowser, *The Transformation of Cinema, 1907–1915* (Berkeley and Los Angeles: University of California Press, 1990), esp. 149–77. For a detailed technical analysis of the transitional years 1907–1913, see Charlie Kiel, *Early American Cinema in Transition: Story, Style, and Filmmaking, 1907–1913* (Madison: University of Wisconsin Press, 2001). See also David Robinson, *From Peep Show to Palace: The Birth of Ameri-*

can Film (New York: Columbia University Press, 1996), 113–19; and William K. Everson, *American Silent Film* (New York: Oxford University Press, 1978), 238–41.

47. For a critical brief overview of Ince's career, see Anthony Slide, *Early American Cinema* (Metuchen, N.J.: Scarecrow, 1994), 77–93. On Griffith, see Tom Gunning, *D. W. Griffith and the Origins of American Narrative Film: The Early Years at Biograph* (Urbana: University of Illinois Press, 1991); and Michael Allen, *Family Secrets: The Feature Films of D. W. Griffith* (London: British Film Institute, 1999). For a filmography of Griffith's Biograph films to 1914, see Edward Wagenknecht and Anthony Slide, *The Films of D. W. Griffith* (New York: Crown, 1975), 265–70.

48. For Ince's claim, see Thomas Ince, "The Early Days at Kay Bee," *Photoplay*, March 1919, 42. For Bison's call for more complex scenarios, see "What Bison Wants," *Moving Picture World*, January 13, 1912, 119. For a strained effort to name Indians as "Lo," see D. W. Griffith's 1916 film *The Half Breed*. The protagonist's Indian name, "Sleeping Water," is translated to "L'Eau Dormante," which is then pronounced "Lo Dorman" and, finally, shortened to "Lo."

49. Louis Reeves Harrison, "Custer's Last Fight," *Moving Picture World*, June 15, 1912, 1116–18.

50. Ibid., 1118. Taking advantage of the California hills, Ince used the figure of a watching Sitting Bull ("brainiest of the Sioux") to offer a high camera angle perspective. He cut between Custer's view of approaching Indians, Indian perspectives on a charging Custer, and middle-distance narrative perspectives. The film had at least two versions. In one, "Tom Custer Meets a Soldier's Death" (intertitle card). In a second version, he meets a soldier's death "and an Indian victim's fate when later Rain in the Face wreaks vengeance by cutting out his heart" (intertitle card). A muddled copy incorporating both versions is at the Library of Congress.

51. W. Stephen Bush, "The Overproduction of Western Pictures," *Moving Picture World*, October 21, 1911, 189. On Indian melodrama, see Kilpatrick, *Celluloid Indians*, 33–35. On melodrama in general, see Allen, *Family Secrets*, 1–5, 12–73.

52. Many of these films no longer exist, which occasions a reliance on plot analysis and a dependence on trade journal summaries and reviews. A check of *Moving Picture World* plot synopses against available films suggests that such capsules were generally accurate, particularly for shorter, one-reel films. For Indian romances, see *A Noble Red Man* (Bison, 1911), *The Indian Flute* (Vitagraph, 1911), *Red Eagle* (Vitagraph, 1910), and *The Medicine Woman* (Pathé, 1911).

53. On *Squaw Man*, see Smith, "Shooting Cowboys and Indians," 112–13.

54. Note that, while this displacement of violence from white to Indian makes complete sense, it necessarily entails serious problems in the gender ide-

ologies attached to masculinity. If Jim is to be manly in the western sense, shouldn't he be defending his own honor, following the lead of, say, the Virginian? Because the *heteronormative* cross-race romance necessarily crosses race and gender both, one of these axes will always end up privileged over the other, with all manner of compensatory devices to, in this case, reaffirm Jim's masculinity. In truth, the symmetry built around race exchange would have been better served had both principles been the same gender. Of course, the use of romance as cross-race bond would then necessarily have been homoerotic. Might we locate in the mutual constitution of race/gender and the problems of its apparent asymmetry the origins of the cross-race "buddy film"? On race/gender in general, see Gail Bederman, *Manliness and Civilization: A Cultural History of Gender and Race in the United States, 1880–1917* (Chicago: University of Chicago Press, 1995).

55. See, e.g., *The Indian Squaw's Sacrifice* (Defender, 1910) and *The Sealed Valley* (Metro, 1915), which duplicate the plot exactly.

56. In nineteenth-century writing, e.g., Lydia Maria Child (*Hobomok: A Tale of Early Times* [1824]) and Catharine Maria Sedgwick (*Hope Leslie; or, Early Times in the Massachusetts* [1827]) assertively hinted at female equality by pairing— at least temporarily—white heroines with Indian men. For a reading of the social/cultural contests evident in such plots, see Carolyn Karcher, introduction to *Hobomok and Other Writings on Indians*, by Lydia Maria Child, ed. Carolyn Karcher (New Brunswick, N.J.: Rutgers University Press, 1986), ix–xxxviii; and Christopher Castiglia, *Bound and Determined: Captivity, Culture-Crossing, and White Womanhood from Mary Rowlandson to Patty Hearst* (Chicago: University of Chicago Press, 1996).

57. Films such as *A Red Man's Love* (Columbia, 1909), *Chief White Eagle* (Lubin, 1912), *Early Days in the West* (Bison, 1912), *Indian Blood* (1913), *Burning Brand* (1913), *Where the Trail Divides* (Lasky, 1914), *The Half Breed* (Triangle, 1916), and *The Red, Red Heart* (Bluebird, 1918) all proposed and then disposed of the idea of white women partnering with Indian men.

58. On miscegenation laws, see Peggy Pascoe, "Miscegenation Law, Court Cases, and Ideologies of 'Race' in Twentieth-Century America," *Journal of American History* 83 (June 1996): 49. For Jeffersonian race crossing, see Thomas Jefferson, "Letter to Captain Hendrick, the Delawares, Mohiccons, and Munries, December 21, 1808," in *The Complete Jefferson: Containing His Major Writings, Published and Unpublished, Except His Letters*, assembled by Saul K. Padover (New York: Duell, Sloan & Pearce, 1943), 503.

59. On primitivist difference, see Philip Deloria, *Playing Indian* (New Haven, Conn.: Yale University Press, 1998), 95–107; Leah Dilworth, *Imagining Indians in the Southwest: Persistent Visions of a Primitive Past* (Washington, D.C.: Smithsonian Institution Press, 1996); Marianna Torgovnick, *Gone Primitive: Savage Intellects, Modern Lives* (Chicago: University of Chicago Press, 1990);

Elizabeth Hutchinson, "Progressive Primitivism: Race, Gender, and Turn-of-the-Century American Art" (Ph.D. diss., Stanford University, 1998); and Susan Hiller, *The Myth of Primitivism: Perspectives on Art* (New York: Routledge, 1989).

60. "Red Deer's Devotion," *Moving Picture World*, March 25, 1911, 656.

61. For examples in the early films (not discussed here) of "Broncho Billy" Anderson, see Smith, "Shooting Cowboys and Indians," 76.

62. Other examples include *The Redman and the Child* (Biograph, 1908), *The Justice of the Redskin* (Pathé, 1908), *The Squawman's Daughter* (Selig, 1908), *A Broken Doll* (Biograph, 1910), *A Mohawk's Way* (Biograph, 1910), *Red Wing's Loyalty* (Bison, 1910), *A Prisoner of the Mohicans* (Pathé, 1911), *At Old Fort Dearborn* (Bison, 1912), *The Thundering Herd* (Selig, 1914), and *An Indian Hero* (Bison, 1911).

63. "A True Indian Brave," *Moving Picture World*, September 23, 1910, 689.

64. See, e.g., *The Friendless Indian* (Pathé, 1913), *Indian Massacre* (Bison, 1912), *Ramona* (Biograph, 1910), and *Lo, the Poor Indian* (Kalem, 1910).

65. W. Stephen Bush, "Moving Picture Absurdities," *Moving Picture World*, September 16, 1911, 773.

66. Alanson Skinner, "Red Men in Movies," *New York Times*, June 3, 1914, 12.

67. "Report of S. A. M. Young," May 23, 1913, sec. 2, p. 2, NARA, RG-75, 12914, box 45, file "Pine Ridge, 1900–1913."

68. On Willie Boy, see James A. Sandos, *The Hunt for Willie Boy: Indian-Hating and Popular Culture* (Norman: University of Oklahoma Press, 1994).

69. See Smith, "Shooting Cowboys and Indians," 108–9.

70. For the delegation, see "Indians War on Films," *Moving Picture World*, March 18, 1911, 581. For the Cheyenne and Arapaho reactions, see "Indians Say They're Lied About," *Nickelodeon*, February 25, 1911, cited in Smith, "Shooting Cowboys and Indians," 109. For Shoshones, Cheyennes, and Arapahoes and pidgin dialect, see "Poor Lo on the Warpath," *Motion Picture News*, March 4, 1911, 10.

71. For the California protest, see "Indians Grieve over Picture Shows," *Moving Picture World*, October 7, 1911, 32. For John Standing Horse, see "An Indian Criticises Indian Pictures," *Moving Picture World*, November 4, 1911, 398.

72. "News of the Week," *Motion Picture News*, December 16, 1911, 32.

73. Standing Bear, *My People, the Sioux*, 284.

74. "James Young Deer," *Moving Picture World*, May 6, 1911, 999. For industry news involving Young Deer, see *The Rounder*, January 27, 1912, 24, and February 3, 1912, 4. Lillian St. Cyr belonged to a prominent (Ho-Chunk) Winnebago family, and she shows up regularly on the annual census reports filed by Winnebago agents (see "Winnebago and Omaha," NARA, RG-75, M-595, Indian Census Rolls, rolls 664, 665). Her sister, Julia St. Cyr, also a Carlisle graduate, was a practicing Indian attorney during the years Red Wing was in

Hollywood (see "Lawyer Julia St. Cyr and Her Winnebago Folks," *Omaha World Herald*, January 26, 1913, 1M–2M). Young Deer, on the other hand, claimed also to be Winnebago but appears on no census roll between 1910 and 1925. Tribal census roles are generally flawed documents, of course, and it is possible that Young Deer was left off erroneously. It is also possible that he was recorded under a different name. Alternatively, he may have been a mixed blood who did not qualify or did not choose to be recorded. He may also have had another tribal origin or a mixed tribal origin. Or he may have been non-Indian, which would put him in company with a number of other mixed-origin performing couples at this time, in which the nonethnic member simply adopted the ethnic identity of his or her partner. What seems relatively clear is that, at least for a few years, the two worked together to create a body of film that did, in fact, question dominant expectations. The film historian Angela Aleiss (personal communications, September 23, October 20, 2003) suggests that Young Deer and Red Wing did not stay together for very long, as he was apparently forced to leave California after running afoul of the law.

75. On Young Deer and Red Wing, see Smith, "Shooting Cowboys and Indians," 93–105, 116–28. See also Rainey, *Sweethearts of the Sage*, 59–60.

76. "James Young Deer," *Moving Picture World*, May 6, 1911, 999.

77. See, e.g., the nineteenth-century novelistic tradition represented by works such as *Hobomok*, by Lydia Maria Child, and *Hope Leslie*, by Catharine Maria Sedgwick, in which the possibility of white women marrying Indian men is raised and then contained. These plots were revolutionary in the 1830s, and they met with all manner of rebuttals, from James Fenimore Cooper's *Wept of Wish-Ton-Wish*, which aimed to rewrite *Hope Leslie* in patriarchal terms, to their erasure from the American literary canon until the late twentieth century. See Karcher, introduction to *Hobomok*, xxx–xxxviii; and Castiglia, *Bound and Determined*. For a treatment of Young Deer's rewritings of squaw man plotlines, see Smith, "Shooting Cowboys and Indians," 116–28. And, for an African American context, see Jane M. Gaines, *Fire and Desire: Mixed-Race Movies in the Silent Era* (Chicago: University of Chicago Press, 2001).

78. The two messages exist in a bit of tension since cross-race romance also has the Jeffersonian potential for a biological hastening of assimilation, a possibility signified, in this film, through the "mixed-blood" character of Felice.

79. "The Squawman's Revenge," *Moving Picture World*, January 13, 1912, 146.

80. Note that this evocation of violence is read back on the bodies of Indian people. While it undoubtedly reinforces a semiotics of Indian violence, it is also an inversion of sorts of the "defensive" theory of underdog violence so prevalent in American self-representations. Too, the revenge is displaced onto the mixed figure of the squaw man.

81. "Red Eagle, the Lawyer," *Moving Picture World*, November 16, 1912, 696. The

thorough exploration of miscegenation issues and options by Young Deer and Red Wing might lead one to wonder whether they were not in some way exploring dimensions of their own relationship.

82. "Doings at Los Angeles," *Moving Picture World*, January 18, 1913, 251.

83. Contrary to Aleiss's suggestion that Young Deer fled town (see n. 74 above), Brownlow (*War, West, Wilderness*, 334) offers a different (though not necessarily incompatible) narrative, one in which Young Deer first returned to acting, then worked in France as a director for Pathé, returning to the United States in the 1920s and operating an acting school.

84. Louis Reeves Harrison, "The Squaw Man," *Moving Picture World*, February 28, 1914, 1068–69.

85. Frederick Hoxie, "Exploring a Cultural Borderland: Native American Journeys of Discovery in the Early Twentieth Century," *Journal of American History* 79, no. 3 (December 1992): 969–95.

86. On Hazlett, see Hirschfelder, *Native American Almanac*, 182. See also "Navajos Expel Jimmy Walker from Tribe; Indians Demand Film Redskins Be Real Ones," *New York Times*, March 15, 1934, 2. On DeMille, see Kilpatrick, *Celluloid Indians*, 51–52. On War Eagle, see Churchill, Hill, and Hill, "Examination of Stereotyping," 44. On Silverheels, Means, Banks, and Trudell, see Singer, *Wiping the War Paint*, 21. Singer usefully carries this story forward into the more recent world of contemporary film and video production. See also Steven Leuthold, *Indigenous Aesthetics: Native Art, Media, and Identity* (Austin: University of Texas Press, 1998).

87. See, e.g., JoEllen Shively, "Cowboys and Indians: Perceptions of Western Films among American Indians and Anglos," *American Sociological Review* 57, no. 6 (1992): 725–34.

ATHLETICS

1. See Vine V. Deloria Sr., "The Establishment of Christianity among the Sioux," in *Sioux Indian Religion: Tradition and Innovation*, ed. Raymond J. DeMallie and Douglas R. Parks (Norman: University of Oklahoma Press, 1987), 91–111; and Sarah Emilia Olden, *The People of Tipi Sapa* (Milwaukee: Morehouse, 1918).

2. On termination policy, see Donald Fixico, *Termination and Relocation: Federal Indian Policy, 1945–1960* (Albuquerque: University of New Mexico Press, 1986); and Kenneth Philp, *Termination Revisited: American Indians on the Trail to Self-Determination, 1933–1953* (Lincoln: University of Nebraska Press, 1999). For other readings of my grandfather and Deloria family history, see Philip J. Deloria, "Vine V. Deloria Sr.," in *The New Warriors: Native American Leaders since 1900* (Lincoln: University of Nebraska Press, 2001), 79–95; Vine Deloria Jr., *Singing for a Spirit: A Portrait of the Dakota Sioux* (Santa Fe: Clearlight, 1999), 3–87; and Robert Craig, "Christianity and Empire: A Case Study of

American Protestant Colonialism and Native Americans," *American Indian Culture and Research Journal* 21 (spring 1997): 26–29.

3. According to Reamer Kline (*Education for the Common Good: A History of Bard College—the First 100 Years* [1860–1960] [Annandale-on-Hudson, N.Y.: Bard College, 1982], caption of the thirteenth of twenty-four unnumbered photographs following p. 118), the Connecticut Aggies were not beaten but tied by this touchdown.

4. On Wounded Knee as a marker, see, e.g., Ralph Andrist, *The Long Death: The Last Days of the Plains Indian* (New York: Macmillan, 1966); or almost any television documentary, especially Kevin Costner's *500 Nations*. On the Dawes General Allotment Act, see Frederick Hoxie, *A Final Promise: The Campaign to Assimilate the Indians, 1880–1920* (Lincoln: University of Nebraska Press, 1984); and Janet McDonnell, *The Dispossession of the American Indian, 1887–1934* (Bloomington: University of Indiana Press, 1991). On government restrictions and legal decisions, see John Wunder, "*Retained by the People": A History of American Indians and the Bill of Rights* (New York: Oxford University Press, 1994). On boarding schools for Indian children, see David Wallace Adams, *Education for Extinction: American Indians and the Boarding School Experience* (Lawrence: University Press of Kansas, 1995); Tsianina Lomawaima, *They Called It Prairie Light: The Story of Chilocco Indian School* (Lincoln: University of Nebraska Press, 1994); and Michael Coleman, *American Indian Children at School, 1850–1930* (Jackson, Miss.: University of Mississippi Press, 1993).

5. One of the most thoughtful treatments remains James Clifford's *Predicament of Culture: Twentieth-Century Ethnography, Literature, and Art* (Cambridge, Mass.: Harvard University Press, 1988).

6. See Peter Iverson, *When Indians Became Cowboys: Native People and Cattle Ranching in the American West* (Norman: University of Oklahoma Press, 1994); Emily Greenwald, *Reconfiguring the Reservation: The Nez Perces, Jicarilla Apaches, and the Dawes Act* (Albuquerque: University of New Mexico Press, 2002); Frederick Hoxie, "From Prison to Homeland: The Cheyenne River Reservation before World War I," in *The Plains Indians of the Twentieth Century*, ed. Peter Iverson (Norman: University of Oklahoma Press, 1985), 55–75, and "Exploring a Cultural Borderland: Native American Journeys of Discovery in the Early Twentieth Century," *Journal of American History* 79, no. 3 (December 1992): 969–95; and Helen Blish, *A Pictographic History of the Oglala Sioux*, with drawings by Amos Bad Heart Bull (Lincoln: University of Nebraska Press, 1967). See also J. B. Carroll, "The Fourth of July Dishonored," in *The Indian Sentinel* (Washington, D.C.: Bureau of Catholic Indian Missions, 1910), 28.

7. Deloria, *Singing for a Spirit*, 54.

8. See Philip Deloria, *Playing Indian* (New Haven, Conn.: Yale University Press, 1998); and Michael Taussig, *Mimesis and Alterity: A Particular History of the Senses* (New York: Routledge, 1993).

9. See Vine Deloria Sr., "The Standing Rock Reservation: A Personal Reminiscence," *South Dakota Review* 9 (1971): 167–95. See also Luther Standing Bear, *My People, the Sioux*, ed. E. A. Brininstool (Boston: Houghton Mifflin, 1928), 189, where white boys at mixed or integrated schools are described as more apt to learn Lakota than Indian boys were to learn English. My copy of Standing Bear's book, which originally belonged to my Great-Aunt Ella, has her gloss in the margin of this page: "Just like Vine at Kearney!"

10. Iverson, *When Indians Became Cowboys*. My grandfather's accounts of his adventures with Sammy Red Eagle, riding a particularly mean calf named "Calf-Calf," are taken from one of the many tapes of Deloria family oral history in my possession.

11. Still the best work on Indian running is Peter Nabokov's *Indian Running: Native American History and Tradition* (Santa Fe: Ancient City, 1981).

12. Joseph Oxendine, *American Indian Sports Heritage* (Champaign, Ill.: Human Kinetics, 1988), 162–63, 242–43; John Lucas, "Deerfoot in Britain: An Amazing American Long Distance Runner, 1861–1863," *Journal of American Culture* 6, no. 3 (fall 1983): 12–18. On Longboat, see Nabokov, *Indian Running*, 178–79.

13. See Thomas Vennum, *American Indian Lacrosse: Little Brother of War* (Washington, D.C.: Smithsonian Institution Press, 1994); Oxendine, *American Indian Sports Heritage*, esp. 1–156; Stewart Culin, *Games of the North American Indians: Twenty-fourth Annual Report of the Bureau of American Ethnology to the Smithsonian Institution, 1902–1903* (Washington, D.C.: Smithsonian Institution Press, 1907); Edward H. Dewey, "Memoranda and Documents: Football and American Indians," *New England Quarterly* 3 (1930): 736–40; Nabokov, *Indian Running*; Kendall Blanchard, *The Anthropology of Sport: An Introduction* (South Hadley, Mass.: Bergin & Garvey, 1985), esp. 91–120.

14. Kline, *Education for the Common Good*, 79.

15. See Michael Oriard, *Reading Football: How the Popular Press Created an American Spectacle* (Chapel Hill: University of North Carolina Press, 1993), 142–228; Gail Bederman, *Manliness and Civilization: A Cultural History of Gender and Race in the United States, 1880–1917* (Chicago: University of Chicago Press, 1995), 1–42; T. J. Jackson Lears, "From Salvation to Self Realization: Advertising and the Therapeutic Roots of the Consumer Culture, 1880–1930," in *The Culture of Consumption: Critical Essays in American History, 1880–1980*, ed. Richard Wightman Fox and T. J. Jackson Lears (New York: Pantheon, 1983), 1–38; Warren I. Susman, "Culture Heroes: Ford, Barton, Ruth," in *Culture as History: The Transformation of American Society in the Twentieth Century* (New York: Pantheon, 1984), 122–49; Elliot J. Gorn and Warren Goldstein, *A Brief History of American Sports* (New York: Hill & Wang, 1984), 98–182; and Eric Hobsbawm, "Mass-Producing Traditions: Europe, 1870–1914," in *The Invention of*

Tradition, ed. Eric Hobsbawm and Terence Ranger (Cambridge: Cambridge University Press, 1983), 288–90.

16. See Gorn and Goldstein, Brief History of American Sports, 164–69; Richard D. Mandell, Sport: A Cultural History (New York: Columbia University Press, 1984), 187–95; and Oriard, Reading Football, 25–141.

17. Sometimes known as the Harvard-Yale game. The Yale-Princeton game had an even longer tradition and, for a time, an equal cachet.

18. At the same time, as Michael Oriard (Reading Football, 189–91) has shown, such elite competition became the stuff of a fan base that transcended the specific class origins associated with the Ivies. Conducted through newspapers and national magazines, reportage by Walter Camp, Caspar Whitney, and others structured an entire discourse in which football (and, one could argue, other sports as well) became the grounds for male affinities that often transcended class. Race, as Bederman (Manliness and Civilization, 41–42) suggests, was something of a different story.

19. See Kline, Education for the Common Good, 62–85 (on the athletic program generally), 79 (on the 1925 season).

20. Ibid., 78.

21. Stephen I. Thompson, "American Indians in the Major Leagues," Baseball Research Journal 13 (1983): 1–7.

22. See Oxendine, American Indian Sports Heritage; Spotted Dog, "Baseball's Early Greats," Many Smokes 3 (1968): 5; and Thompson, "American Indians in the Major Leagues."

23. John Joseph Mathews, Sundown (1934; Norman: University of Oklahoma Press, 1988).

24. On Indians and modernity, see Deloria, Playing Indian; and Leah Dilworth, Imagining Indians in the Southwest: Persistent Visions of a Primitive Past (Washington, D.C.: Smithsonian Institution Press, 1996).

25. Grantland Rice, The Tumult and the Shouting: My Life in Sport (New York: A. S. Barnes, 1954), 227. See also Spotted Dog, "Baseball's Early Greats," 5–6.

26. For Camp and Whitney, see Oriard, Reading Football, 244–45. On St. Stephen's, see Kline, Education for the Common Good, 79.

27. Oriard, Reading Football, 247.

28. John Bloom, To Show What an Indian Can Do: Sports at Native American Boarding Schools (Minneapolis: University of Minnesota Press, 2000), 15. Oriard (Reading Football, 243) suggests that the popularity of Indians as underdogs when going up against the Ivies may have been produced out of the intersection of class antagonism and the dynamics of race representation.

29. Bloom, To Show What an Indian Can Do, 16.

30. On the development of men from boys, see Oriard, Reading Football, 192–201.

31. See Richard Henry Pratt, Battlefield and Classroom: Four Decades with the Ameri-

can Indian, 1867–1904, ed. Robert Utley (New Haven, Conn.: Yale University Press, 1964), 212–338. See also the Carlisle School's various publications: Red Man and Helper (1880–1904); The Arrow (1904–1917); The Indian Craftsman (1909–1910); and The Red Man (1910–1917).

32. See Adams, Education for Extinction, 184 (Pratt), 187 ("half-wild"), 187 ("race . . . against race"), 188 (on team spirit generally). Adams takes the "half-wild" quotation from Red Man, November 1896, 4, where it is reproduced from the New York Herald. He takes the "race . . . against race" quote from Red Man, December 1898, 5, where it is reproduced from the Philadelphia Press.

33. See Oxendine, American Indian Sports Heritage, 239–55.

34. See Indians of Today, ed. Marion Gridley (Chicago: Indian Council Fire, 1960), 10 (on Bruce), 35–39 (on Jones), 105 (on Key). On Johnson, see The Arrow, September 15, 1904, 4. On Rogers, see Oxendine, American Indian Sports Heritage, 251. For a full biography of Harold Jones, see Mary E. Cochran, Dakota Cross-Bearer: The Life and World of a Native American Bishop (Lincoln: University of Nebraska Press, 2000).

35. See Oxendine, American Indian Sports Heritage, 178–84, 193–201. See also Maury White, "Indian Teams Had Colorful History, Great Athletes," Des Moines Register, 21 January 1990, D1, D9. A great-uncle of mine, Phil Lane (my grandfather's nephew), boxed at Haskell and in Amateur Athletic Union bouts before joining the army and boxing his way to his divisional championship. He won a boxing scholarship to the University of Oregon, which he used to finance an engineering degree.

36. Standing Bear, My People, the Sioux, 124.

37. The Arrow, 15 November 1907, 1. Carlisle had already beaten Penn and lost to Princeton, the other members of the Big Four along with Yale and Harvard.

38. Bloom, To Show What an Indian Can Do, 38–50.

39. "Report of S. A. M. Young," May 23, 1913, sec. 2, p. 2, NARA (National Archives and Records Administration, Washington, D.C.), RG-75, 12914, box 45, file "Pine Ridge, 1900–1913." On Nelson, see Jerry Reynolds, "Sports Is Steady Beat in the Varied Life of Moot Nelson," Lakota Times, December 11, 1991, 16–17.

40. Reynolds, "Sports Is Steady Beat."

41. See "William Conquering Bear," Indian Country Today, October 26, 1994, B5.

42. Maynor quoted in Tim Brayboy and Bruce Barton, Playing before an Overflow Crowd: The Story of Indian Basketball in Robeson, North Carolina, and Adjoining Counties (Chapel Hill, N.C.: Chapel Hill, 2003), 4.

43. See Oxendine, American Indian Sports Heritage, 165, 224; and Sam Borowski, "Oorang Indians—One of the First NFL Teams," Indian Country Today, 5 January 1995, B7–B8.

44. Borowski, "Oorang Indians," B8.

45. Barbara Gregorich, "John Olson and His Barnstorming Baseball Teams," *Michigan History Magazine* 79 (May/June 1995): 38–41; "Report of the Kickapoo School for 1913," p. 10, NARA, RG-75, M–1011, Annual Narrative and Statistical Reports, roll 70.

46. Bloom, *To Show What an Indian Can Do*, 27–30.

47. Ibid., 55–64.

48. Rice (*Tumult and Shouting*, 233) quotes "Pop" Warner's observation that Thorpe gave 100 percent only on certain occasions: "It was difficult to know if Jim was laughing with you or at you." On Tewanima, see Norm Frauenhelm, "Legends of Revered Land Are Long Running," *Lakota Times*, 7 August 1991, B4; and Nabokov, *Indian Running*, 182.

49. On "the dropout phenomenon," see Oxendine, *American Indian Sports Heritage*, 266–67. There were, of course, exceptions—the NBA player Harley Zephier, the University of Washington quarterback Sonny Sixkiller, the baseball players Allie Reynolds and Gene Locklear, and the Olympic runner Billy Mills, among others. See also Larry Colton, *Counting Coup: A True Story of Basketball and Honor on the Little Big Horn* (New York: Warner, 2000). The moving, though problematic, piece of general reportage that has garnered most awareness of the issue is Gary Smith, "Shadow of a Nation," *Sports Illustrated*, February 18, 1991, 60–76.

50. On the contemporary social context of Bennett County, with some historical background, see Paula L. Wagoner, *"They Treated Us Just Like Indians": The Worlds of Bennett County, South Dakota* (Lincoln: University of Nebraska Press, in cooperation with the American Indian Studies Research Institute, 2002).

51. Vine Deloria Sr. to John Collier, 4 February 1956, Yale University, Manuscripts and Archives, John Collier Papers, pt. 3, ser. 1, reel 34, no. 128.

TECHNOLOGY

The subtitle of this chapter is taken from the chorus of Michael Murphey and Charles John Quarto's "Geronimo's Cadillac," *Geronimo's Cadillac* (A&M Records, 1972).

1. This juxtaposition—between Geronimo's Cadillac and Jeep Cherokees— suggests the range of these symbolic systems. Where the Cadillac can't help but evoke class and race distinctions and inversions, the history of the Jeep as a rugged military vehicle translated into a sport and recreational context points its meanings in another direction. Likewise, where Geronimo evokes a more particular history of resistance—which plays powerfully off the meanings evoked by Cadillac—*Cherokee* regretfully functions all too often as a general signifier of Indianness, one well suited to enhance the nature-focused meanings being constructed around Jeeps as sport-utility vehicles. All of which is to say that, in the economy of meaning surrounding Indians and automobiles, specificity matters.

2. "Getting Civilized in a Rush!" *The Indian's Friend* 16 (August 1904): 1.

3. Paul Eldridge, "Gray Roadster," in *The State Anthology* (Oklahoma City: Times-Journal Publishing, for the Poetry Society of Oklahoma, 1936), 106. Thanks to Trisha Yarbrough for bringing this poem to my attention.

4. Angie Debo, *Geronimo: The Man, His Time, His Place* (Norman: University of Oklahoma Press, 1976), 423–24.

5. Michael Murphey and Charles John Quarto, "Geronimo's Cadillac," *Geronimo's Cadillac* (A&M Records, 1972). See also Jan Reid, *The Improbable Rise of Redneck Rock* (Austin: Heidelberg, 1974), 241–75. At the same time, it is worth noting the powerful Native version of the song offered by Mohican singer Bill Miller on *Reservation Road: Bill Miller Live* (Rosebud Records, 1992).

6. *Smoke Signals*, screenplay by Sherman Alexie, directed by Chris Eyre (Miramax Films/Shadowcatcher Entertainment Productions, 1998).

7. My understanding of automotive history is drawn from Michael L. Berger, *Devil Wagon in God's Country: The Automobile and Social Change in Rural America, 1893–1929* (Hamden, Conn.: Archon, 1979); Christopher Finch, *Highways to Heaven: The Auto Biography of America* (New York: HarperCollins, 1992); James J. Flink, *The Automobile Age* (Cambridge, Mass.: MIT Press, 1988), and *The Car Culture* (Cambridge, Mass.: MIT Press, 1955); Allan Nevins, *Ford* (New York: Scribners', 1954); Robert Lacey, *Ford: The Men and the Machine* (Boston: Little, Brown, 1986); John B. Rae, *The American Automobile: A Brief History* (Chicago: University of Chicago Press, 1965); and Vincent Curcio, *Chrysler: The Life and Times of an Automotive Genius* (New York: Oxford University Press, 2000), esp. 127–212.

8. The roots of these words matter. The *auto-* in *automobile* and the *auto-* in *autonomy* have clear resonances, especially in terms of Native people with long traditions of mobility newly restricted by reservation regimes. Mobility and autonomy were mutually constitutive, which suggests at least one aspect of the desire to keep Indian people fixed in space—and the corresponding efforts of Native people to find new ways of making themselves mobile.

9. For the standard early American studies assessment of the relation between technology and culture, still valuable today, see Leo Marx, *The Machine in the Garden: Technology and the Pastoral Ideal in America* (New York: Oxford University Press, 1964). For more specific treatments considering the colonial dimensions, see Michael Adas, *Machines as the Measure of Men: Science, Technology, and Ideologies of Western Dominance* (Ithaca, N.Y.: Cornell University Press, 1989); and Rudolf Mrázek, *Engineers of Happy Land: Technology and Nationalism in a Colony* (Princeton, N.J.: Princeton University Press, 2002).

10. Mary Poovey, *Uneven Developments: The Ideological Work of Gender in Mid-Victorian England* (Chicago: University of Chicago Press, 1988), 1–4; Terry Eagleton, *Ideology* (London: Verso, 1991), 1–31.

11. See, e.g., Frederick Hoxie, *A Final Promise: The Campaign to Assimilate the Indi-*

ans, 1880–1920 (Lincoln: University of Nebraska Press, 1984). Note a distinction between this "soft" social Darwinism, which emphasized not only inferiority but also the possibility of development, and the older ideology of Indian vanishing, which should properly be linked with a "harder" philosophy, one emphasizing the seemingly inevitable result of any competition between superior and inferior peoples. Indian vanishing was, thus, the flip side of the survival and prosperity of the strongest.

12. *The Indian's Friend* 17 (September 1905): 7. Luther Standing Bear (*My People the Sioux*, ed. E. A. Brininstool [Boston: Houghton Mifflin, 1928], 282) recalled living in Sioux City, Iowa, during the last years of the century's first decade by noting that he had his own telephone and would call up friends on the reservation on occasion. Reporting from Pine Ridge in 1913, Indian Office inspector Charles Davis observed: "The reservation is well connected by telephones, which are available to the Indians, so my coming was known" ("Report of C. L. Davis on Trader Matters," September 3, 1913, NARA [National Archives and Records Administration, Washington, D.C.], RG-75, 12914, box 45, file "S. A. M. Young").

13. *The Indian's Friend* 17 (September 1905): 7, and 18 (June 1906): 2.

14. "Report of W. J. Endecott on Sac and Fox," April 11, 1921, n.p., NARA, RG-75, E-953, box 58, "Sac and Fox Iowa, 1910–27."

15. *The Indian's Friend* 17 (September 1905): 7.

16. At the same time, cars have also been gendered feminine, particularly when ownership, communion, and affection have been at stake—of which more later. Likewise, Indian men and women have each been imagined in masculine terms, whether it be the toughness of the warrior or the supposed degradation of Indian women. In other words, genderings of each have been ambiguous and shifting enough that we cannot speak of any sort of typical meaning but must, rather, reflect on the particular circumstances in which certain aspects of this economy of meaning are mobilized and others are deemphasized.

17. Virginia Scharff, *Taking the Wheel: Women and the Coming of the Motor Age* (Albuquerque: University of New Mexico Press, 1991), 15–33, 116–33, 166–75.

18. The reporting forms sent out by the Indian Office in the early twentieth century, e.g., request page after page of information on agricultural practice, ignoring other options, and, thus, creating a discursive lens within which indigenous life could be seen only in terms of a successful (or unsuccessful) transition to agriculture and pastorialism. Reading these forms, I find myself imagining an army of frustrated Indian agents cursing at their charges: "Farm! Damn you, farm!" For Asbury, see "Crow Reservation Report," 1918, p. 16, NARA, RG-75, M-1011, Annual Narrative and Statistical Reports, roll 30.

19. See Debo, *Geronimo*, 400–427. For the exposition as a pageant of progress, see Robert W. Rydell, *All the World's a Fair: Visions of Empire at American International Expositions, 1876–1916* (Chicago: University of Chicago Press, 1984), and *World of Fairs: The Century of Progress Expositions* (Chicago: University of Chicago Press, 1993). See also Warren I. Susman, "The People's Fair: Cultural Contradictions of a Consumer Society," in *Culture as History: The Transformation of American Society in the Twentieth Century* (New York: Pantheon, 1984), 211–30. For Indians as spectacles, see Robert A. Trennert, "Fairs, Expositions, and the Changing Image of Southwestern Indians, 1876–1904," *New Mexico Historical Review* 62 (1987): 127–50; and Leah Dilworth, *Imagining Indians in the Southwest: Persistent Visions of a Primitive Past* (Washington, D.C.: Smithsonian Institution Press, 1996), 47–50.

20. Debo, *Geronimo*, 419.

21. For Geronimo's experiences with glassblowing and other technology, see Debo, *Geronimo*, 415–17. For the buffalo hunt, see ibid., 423–24.

22. On María Martínez, see Alice Marriot, *María: The Potter of San Ildefonso* (Norman: University of Oklahoma Press, 1948), 214. On Marsie Harjo, see Joy Harjo's thoughtful meditation "The Place of Origins," in *Partial Recall: With Essays on Photographs of Native North Americans*, ed. Lucy Lippard (New York: New Press, 1992), 89–93. On Bluebird, see "Report of H. S. Traylor," October 31, 1918, n.p., NARA, RG-75, E-953, box 57, "Rosebud 1909–1917." On Walking Bull, see "Report of C. M. Knight: The Shooting of Charles Walking Bull," January 25, 1917, p. 10, NARA, RG-75, E-953, box 57, "Rosebud 1909–1917." On White, see "Sales," p. 6, NARA, RG-75, M-1011, Annual Narrative and Statistical Reports, Crow, 1912, roll 30. On modernities, see Charles Taylor, "Two Theories of Modernity," 172–96, and Dilip Parameshwar Gaonkar, "On Alternative Modernities," 1–23, both in *Alternative Modernities*, ed. Dilip Parameshwar Gaonkar (Durham, N.C.: Duke University Press, 2001).

23. It is worth pointing out other instances of travel technology. Indian people came to understand railroads rather quickly, not only as an obstacle or a danger, but also as an opportunity. Lakota Ghost Dancers, e.g., took the train when they went to visit Wovoka in Nevada.

24. Flink, *Automobile Age*, 12–24. For a detailed chronology, see Clay McShane, *The Automobile: A Chronology of Its Antecedents, Development, and Impact* (Westport, Conn.: Greenwood, 1997), esp. 22.

25. Nevins, *Ford*; Flink, *Automobile Age*, 42–53.

26. Berger, *Devil Wagon*, 51; Flink, *Automobile Age*, 18.

27. Carolyn Gilman and Mary Jane Schneider, *The Way to Independence: Memories of a Hidatsa Indian Family, 1840–1920* (Saint Paul: Minnesota Historical Society Press, 1987), 269.

28. On South Dakota automobiles, see "Seventeenth Annual Review of the

Progress of South Dakota, 1917," *South Dakota Historical Collections* 9 (1918): 30. On the advantages of a car at Rosebud, see "Report of W. W. McConihe," May 23, 1910, n.p., NARA, RG-75, E-953, box 57, "Rosebud 1909–1917."

29. In 1902, a provision in the Indian appropriations act allowed the sale of inheritance lands—allotments that had been divided among heirs, often into parcels too small to be useful to the individuals who owned them. For the erosion of restrictions on land sales, see John R. Wunder, *"Retained by the People": A History of American Indians and the Bill of Rights* (New York: Oxford University Press, 1994), 44–51. For Sisseton, see Roy W. Meyer, *History of the Santee Sioux: United States Indian Policy on Trial* (Lincoln: University of Nebraska Press, 1967), 318.

30. Meyer, *History of the Santee Sioux*, 302.

31. See Peter Iverson, *When Indians Became Cowboys: Native Peoples and Cattle Ranching in the American West* (Norman: University of Oklahoma Press, 1994), 70, 78–79.

32. "Report of Charles Davis," May 18, 1909, n.p., NARA, RG-75, E-953, box 57, "Rosebud, 1909–1917."

33. On allotment policy in general, see Leonard Carlson, *Indians, Bureaucrats, and Land: The Dawes Act and the Decline of Indian Farming* (Westport, Conn.: Greenwood, 1981); and Emily Greenwald, *Reconfiguring the Reservation: The Nez Perces, Jicarilla Apaches, and the Dawes Act* (Albuquerque: University of New Mexico Press, 2002).

34. On allotment and land loss, see Janet McDonnell, *The Dispossession of the American Indian, 1887–1934* (Bloomington: Indiana University Press, 1991); Hoxie, *A Final Promise*; and Donald J. Berthrong, "Legacies of the Dawes Act: Bureaucrats and Land Thieves at the Cheyenne-Arapaho Agencies of Omaha," in *The Plains Indians of the Twentieth Century*, ed. Peter Iverson (Norman: University of Oklahoma Press, 1985), 31–54. For the Kiowa agent's report, see "Sales," n.p., NARA, RG-75, M-1011, Annual Narrative and Statistical Reports, Kiowa, 1910, roll 37. For the Omaha, see Judith A. Boughter, *Betraying the Omaha Nation, 1790–1916* (Norman: University of Oklahoma Press, 1998), 184–204, 186 (quotation).

35. "Section IX, Sales," n.p., NARA, RG-75, M-1011, Annual Narrative and Statistical Reports, Crow Reservation, 1912, roll 30.

36. Howard Echo-Hawk, e.g., bought a Hudson two-seater in 1920 using the proceeds from leases on his allotments (Owen Echo-Hawk Sr., interview with Roger Echo-Hawk, January 2, 1982, near Pawnee, Okla.). My thanks to Roger Echo-Hawk for sharing this material. See McDonnell, *Dispossession of the American Indian*, 101, 106, 113–14. For Round Valley, see "Report of H. G. Wilson," n.p., NARA, RG-75, E-953, box 58, "Round Valley, 1910–1924." For Klamath, see "Report of C. H. Asbury," p. 27, NARA, RG-75, M-1011, Annual Narrative and Statistical Reports, Klamath, 1917, roll 73. For Frank Shane,

see "Section VII, Sales," p. 13, NARA, RG-75, M-1011, Annual Narrative and Statistical Reports, Crow Reservation, 1917, roll 30. For Bonesteel, see *The Indian's Friend* 16 (August 1904): 1. For reports on other auto purchases linked to unethical behavior on the part of dealers and local officials, see "Report of C. L. Ellis," November 19, 1920, NARA, RG-75, E-953, Inspection Reports, Rosebud, 1909–1931, box 57, "Rosebud 1909–1917," file "Rosebud, 1919–1931"; and "Report of Frank E. Brandon," March 15, 1921, NARA, RG-75, E-953, Inspection Reports, Rosebud, 1909–1931, box 57, "Rosebud 1909–1917," file "Rosebud, 1919–1931." It is important to note that, while I will argue that automobility was more widespread on the northern plains and other reservations than one might expect, it was not until the later 1930s, when New Deal programs brought Native people more completely into the cash economy, that cars became fairly common and not until the postwar period, when returning veterans brought cash infusions to the reservations, that automobiles became widespread. Even today, the proportion of Native people possessing automobiles is below the national average. See, e.g., Dowell Harry Smith, "Old Cars and Social Productions among the Teton Lakota" (Ph.D. diss., University of Colorado, 1973).

37. Ironically, their practice (opening Indians lands to non-Indians) worked to achieve the exact opposite—the liquidation of Indian capital.

38. See, e.g., historical recollections in *70 Years of Pioneer Life in Bennett County, South Dakota, 1911–1981* (Pierre, S.D.: Bennett County Historical Society, 1981), 32, 47, 493; Gladys Whitehorn Jorgensen, *Before Homesteads in Tripp County and the Rosebud* (Freeman, S.D.: Pine Hill, 1974), 47–50, 94–101; and Standing Bear, *My People, the Sioux*, 231–47.

39. On White, see "Sales," p. 6, NARA, RG-75, M-1011, Annual Narrative and Statistical Reports, Crow, 1915, roll 30. On 101 actors, see L. G. Moses, *Wild West Shows and the Images of American Indians, 1883–1933* (Albuquerque: University of New Mexico Press, 1996), 265. As Tara Browner (*Heartbeat of the People: Music and Dance of the Northern Pow-Wow* [Urbana: University of Illinois Press, 2002], 150 n. 1) points out, the question of powwow origins is open to multiple interpretations. Among the many elements to be considered in narrating the powwow are tribal dance traditions, cross-tribal dance traditions, Wild West and medicine show performances, and federal restrictions on dancing that forced music and dance into white performative venues, among others. Browner notes several instances in which individual tribal powwow events date back to the nineteenth century but concludes that the earliest "intertribal pow-wow is Crow Fair at the Crow Agency in Montana, which began in 1918." See also the useful discussion in ibid., 19–32. On powwow more generally, see William K. Powers, *War Dance: Plains Indian Musical Performance* (Tucson: University of Arizona Press, 1990), 50–60; Susan Applegate Krouse, "A Window into the Indian Culture: The Powwow as Per-

formance" (Ph.D. diss., University of Wisconsin, Milwaukee, 1991); Gloria Young, "Powwow Power: Perspectives on Historic and Contemporary Intertribalism" (Ph.D. diss., University of Indiana, 1981); and Ann Marguerite Axtmann, "Dance: Celebration and Resistance—Native American Indian Intertribal Powwow Performance" (Ph.D. diss., New York University, 1999).

40. The linguist Allan Taylor (personal conversation, September 9, 1994) suggested the possibility of the direct translation of *automobile* into various Indian languages. I would like to thank the following linguists and speakers for assistance with these terms: Douglas Parks for Arikara and Pawnee; Ray DeMallie and Jan Ullrich for Lakota; Allan Taylor for Lakota and Blackfeet; Roger Echo-Hawk for Pawnee; and Laurel Watkins for Kiowa.

41. The joyriding story comes from an oral history interview tape in my possession recorded at a family gathering in the early 1970s. The Wanblee story comes from an oral history interview I conducted with my grandmother in December 1989.

42. Jaime de Angulo, *Indians in Overalls* (San Francisco: City Lights, 1990), 47, 48.

43. Jim Robb, "George Johnston: Trapper, Photographer, Merchant," *The Colorful Five Per Cent Illustrated* (Whitehorse, Yukon Territory) 1, no. 1 (1984): n.p. My thanks to Roy Hohn of the Denver Westerners for pointing me toward Johnston.

44. See Peggy Albright, *Crow Indian Photographer: The Work of Richard Throssell*, with commentaries by Barney Old Coyote Jr., Mardell Hogan Plainfeather, and Dean Curtis Bear Claw (Albuquerque: University of New Mexico Press, 1997), 35–42, 132–33.

45. John Joseph Mathews, *Sundown* (1934; Norman: University of Oklahoma Press, 1988), 294, 296 (see generally 281–301); Leslie Marmon Silko, *Ceremony* (New York: Viking, 1977), esp. 249–74; Ray A. Young Bear, *Black Eagle Child: The Facepaint Narratives* (New York: Grove, 1992), 109; and Sherman Alexie, *The Lone Ranger and Tonto Fistfight in Heaven* (New York: Atlantic Monthly Press, 1993), 63; *Powwow Highway*, dir. Jonathan Wacks (Hand Made Films/Warner Bros., 1988).

46. On Arthur Amiotte, see John Day, ed., *Arthur Amiotte: Retrospective Exhibition Continuity and Diversity* (Pine Ridge, S.D.: Heritage Center, Red Cloud Indian School), esp. Christina Burke, "Ledger Art Collages of Arthur Amiotte," 31–34. I would like to thank Arthur Amiotte for his generosity in allowing me to spend time with a number of the powerful images in this series and to use them in this book.

47. Dan Cushman, *Stay Away, Joe* (New York: Viking, 1953); William Saroyan, "Locomotive 38, the Ojibway," in *Best Stories of William Saroyan* (London: Reader's Union, 1944), 309–18.

48. On conflicts over change, see Flink, *Automobile Age*, 140; and Robert S. Lynd

and Helen M. Lynd, *Middletown: A Study in American Culture* (New York: Harcourt, Brace, 1929), 251, 259–60.

49. See, e.g., Warren I. Susman, "Culture Heroes: Ford, Barton, Ruth," in *Culture as History*, 122–49, and "The People's Fair." For a powerful treatment of consumerism in the later twentieth century, see Lizabeth Cohen, *A Consumer's Republic: The Politics of Mass Consumption in Postwar America* (New York: Knopf, 2003).

50. On credit and finance, see Flink, *Automobile Age*, 144–47. Note, however, the class and economic constraints that prevented larger portions of the population from owning automobiles. Almost from the beginning, automobile ownership has been used as a measure of American progress. When one puts the automobile in the context of family, the 1929 statistic "one car for every 4.6 people" sounds impressive (ibid., 140). America's highly unequal distribution of wealth and resources ensured that the actual numbers would be different. In 1927, half of American families had no car (ibid., 142). Indians, of course, figured prominently in the "have-not" half.

51. Lynd and Lynd, *Middletown*, 255–56.

52. See also Scharff, *Taking the Wheel*, 116–31.

53. What activates this gender ambivalence, it seems to me, are the class signifiers embodied in the automobile itself. Like golf and skiing, which offer a class-based license for women's participation in male sporting circles, this particular form of automobility seems to belong to the elite rancher's daughter, who has, not only the means, but the cultural encouragement to rethink gender boundaries built on leisure rather than labor.

54. For a comprehensive historiographic discussion, see Flannery Burke, "Finding What They Came For: The Mabel Dodge Luhan Circle and the Making of a Modern Place, 1912–1930" (Ph.D. diss., University of Wisconsin–Madison, 2002).

55. Philip Deloria, *Playing Indian* (New Haven, Conn.: Yale University Press, 1998), 95–127. For Dodge and Lujan, see Mabel Dodge Luhan, *Edge of Taos Desert: An Escape to Reality* (1937; Albuquerque: University of New Mexico Press, 1988), esp. 174–334. When Mabel Dodge married Tony Lujan, her New York friends mispronounced Lujan. So, in an attempt to flag for them the correct pronunciation, and perhaps also trying to tone down his exoticism, she began spelling her name *Luhan*. Tony, however, never changed the spelling of his name. Hence the discrepancy between *Mabel Dodge Luhan* and *Tony Lujan*. Dodge's memories of falling in love with Lujan, which parallel her efforts to integrate with and build her local community, are marked by a number of trips on horseback and spring wagon. At the book's climax, the departure of her now-estranged husband Maurice Sterne, Dodge and Lujan set out for the Santo Domingo Corn Dance—in her Ford touring car. The auto

and the ceremony become the twin focal points of the episode, with the automobile getting stuck in sand (Tony frees it) and breaking down (Adolfo repairs it partially, then takes it up to Taos on his own while Dodge and Lujan catch the train!). See also Lois Palken Rudnick, *Mabel Dodge Luhan: New Woman, New Worlds* (Albuquerque: University of New Mexico Press, 1984), 143–56; and Burke, "Finding What They Came For."

56. *70 Years of Pioneer Life*, 106.

57. On the Geronimo Motor Company, see Debo, *Geronimo*, ix. On Pontiac, see http://www.pontiac.com/history/index.jsp?brand=home&pagename=home (accessed October 10, 2003). In 1902, the founders of the Indian Motocycle Company picked that company's name to evoke "a wholly American product in the pioneering tradition." By 1913, Indian controlled 42 percent of the American motorcycle market. On the Indian Motorcycle Company, see http://www.indianmotorcycles.com/company/history/ (accessed October 10, 2003).

58. "Report of C. H. Asbury," p. 2, NARA, RG-75, M-1011, Annual Narrative and Statistical Reports, Klamath, 1917, roll 73.

59. Jimmie Durham, "Geronimo!" in *Partial Recall*, ed. Lippard, 58. As Angie Debo (*Geronimo*, 400, 427) has recounted, Geronimo understood the nature of modernist/antimodernist representational politics. Consider, e.g., his willingness to pose for the artist Elbridge Ayer Burbank as both blanket Indian and U.S Army scout. See Barbara Dayer Gallati, "Blurring the Lines between Likeness and Type," in *American Indian Portraits: Elbridge Ayer Burbank in the West (1897–1910)* (Youngstown, Ohio: Butler Institute of Art, 2000), 27–28. For a similarly evocative example, see Frank Goodyear III, *Red Cloud: Photographs of a Lakota Chief* (Lincoln: University of Nebraska Press, 2003), esp. 6–8.

60. Louis Owens, *Mixedblood Messages: Literature, Film, Family, Place* (Norman: University of Oklahoma Press, 1998), 160–61.

61. Terry P. Wilson, *The Underground Reservation: Osage Oil* (Lincoln: University of Nebraska Press, 1985), 129. See also Lawrence J. Hogan, *The Osage Indian Murders: The True Story of a Multiple Murder Plot to Acquire the Estates of Wealthy Osage Tribe Members* (Frederick, Md.: Amlex, 1998), 38–41. For a sometimes problematic treatment, see Dennis McAuliffe Jr., *The Deaths of Sybil Bolton: An American History* (New York: Times Books, 1994), 233–34. And, for an evocative novelistic reading, see Linda Hogan, *Mean Spirit* (New York: Atheneum, 1990).

62. Vaux quoted in Wilson, *Underground Reservation*, 129.

63. "Rich Indian Picks Hearse Automobile," *New York Times*, November 25, 1917, XII.

64. For a compelling treatment of the material and ideological meetings of Indians and money, see Alexandra Harmon, "American Indians and Land Mo-

nopolies in the Gilded Age," *Journal of American History* 90 (June 2003): 106–33.

65. Indians in cars were often included in the genre of "trick photography" postcards, lumped together with the Jackalope and the fur-covered "beaver trout." See, e.g., Cynthia Elyce Rubin and Morgan Williams, *Larger Than Life: The American Tall Tale Postcard, 1905–1915* (New York: Abbeville, 1990).

66. See Lynd and Lynd, *Middletown*, 251–60. For Asbury, see "Report of C. H. Asbury," p. 27, NARA, RG-75, M-1011, Annual Narrative and Statistical Reports, Crow Reservation, 1918, roll 30.

67. Keith Secola, "NDN Kars" (1987), *Circle* (Akina Records, 1992).

MUSIC

1. Moira F. Harris, *The Paws of Refreshment: The Story of Hamm's Beer Advertising* (Saint Paul, Minn.: Pogo, 2000), 19–23. Harris suggests that the drumbeat underpinning the music is a variant on Haitian rhythms. For an analysis of the commercial's harmonic and melodic origins in Victor Herbert's "Indian opera" *Natoma*, see Michael Pisani, "Exotic Sounds in the Native Land: Portrayals of North American Indians in Western Music" (Ph.D. diss., University of Rochester, 1996), 398–401. Michael Pisani's *Sounds Indian: Imagining Native America in Music* (New Haven, Conn.: Yale University Press, in press) was, unfortunately, not yet available at this writing. For the tomahawk chop, see P. Diddy, Murphy Lee, and Nelly, "Shake Ya Tailfeather," *Bad Boys II Soundtrack* (Bad Boy, 2003). Paul Revere and the Raiders, "Indian Reservation: The Lament of the Cherokee Reservation Indian," words and music by John D. Loudermilk, on *Indian Reservation* (Columbia, 1971), © 1963, 1967, 1971 Acuff-Rose Publications. The Cowsills, "Indian Lake," words and music by T. Romero, on *Captain Sad and His Ship of Fools* (MGM ST4554, 1968). Hank Williams, "Kaw-Liga," words and music by Hank Williams (MGM K11416 [backed with "Your Cheatin' Heart"], 1953).

2. *Shanewis: The Robin Woman*, music by Charles Wakefield Cadman, libretto by Nelle Richmond Eberhardt (1918). For a synopsis, the performance history, and the libretto, see http:rick.stanford.edu/opera/Cadman/Shanewis /history.htm (accessed September 15, 2003). All quotations of the libretto of *Shanewis* are taken from the text available at the Stanford website. The *New York Times* covered the preparation and performance of *Shanewis* in some detail: see, e.g., "News of the Musical World," March 10, 1918, XII; "Home Talent Gets Its Innings at Last," March 17, 1918, 59; "'Shanewis,' Indian Opera, Captivates," March 24, 1918, 19; "Shanewis Pleases Again," March 29, 1918, 9; "New Native Operas Foreign in Scene," March 9, 1919, 50; and "Opera Season Ending: A War Season's Record," April 13, 1919, 52.

3. *Shanewis*, 12. The Osage song had rhythmic accompaniment from the percussion section.

4. Though Cadman was an Indianist composer, he himself chose to characterize the opera, not as "Indian," but as "American." See "News of the Musical World," *New York Times*, March 10, 1918, XII.

5. For a superlative chronological list of Indian-sound music, see Pisani, "Exotic Sounds," 526–57. See also Deborah Osman, "The American 'Indianist' Composers: A Critical Review of Their Sources, Their Aims, and Their Compositional Procedures" (D.M.A. diss., University of South Carolina, 1992), 77–80. Tara Browner ("Transposing Cultures: The Appropriation of Native North American Musics, 1890–1990" [Ph.D. diss., University of Michigan, 1995], 91) suggests that the first Indian opera written by an American was, in fact, Henry Waller's *Ogallala*, performed in Chicago on February 20, 1893.

6. Charles Wakefield Cadman, "The American Indian's Music Idealized," *Etude* 38, no. 10 (October 1920): 659.

7. Charles Wakefield Cadman, *Four Indian Songs Op. 45*, with lyrics by Nelle Richmond Eberhardt (Boca Raton, Fla.: Masters Music, 1962), n.p.

8. For Cadman's philosophy of idealization and an accompanying discussion of *Shanewis*, see Cadman, "The American Indian's Music Idealized," 659–60. See also Charles Wakefield Cadman, "The 'Idealization' of Indian Music," *Musical Quarterly* 1 (1915): 387–96. For a detailed treatment of Cadman's practice of idealization, see Frederik E. Schuetze, "The Idealization of American Indian Music as Exemplified in Two Indianist Song Cycles of Charles Wakefield Cadman: An Historical and Stylistic Analysis to Aid in Their Performance" (D.M.A. diss., University of Missouri–Kansas City, 1984). Schuetze argues that Cadman tended to select Native melodies that conformed most closely to the melodic canons of the art-music tradition in which he composed. In part because of this selection bias, his music can sound less exotic than that of other Indianist composers.

9. On Farwell and others, see Barbara A. Zuck, *A History of Musical Americanism* (Ann Arbor, Mich.: UMI Research, 1980), 64; Arthur Farwell, *Wanderjahre of a Revolutionist* (Rochester, N.Y.: University of Rochester Press, 1995), 97–126, 133–45; and Pisani, "Exotic Sounds," 84–90. On Cadman, see Schuetze, "Idealization of American Indian Music," 6–23; and Tsianina Blackstone [Tsianina Redfeather], *Where Trails Have Led Me* (Burbank: Tsianina Blackstone, 1968), 25–34. (A second edition of *Where Trails Have Led Me* appeared in 1970 under the same title and from the same publisher. The 1970 edition is roughly twenty pages longer than the 1968 edition and includes testimonials and additional memories of experiences during World War I. Subsequent citations will specify the edition to which I am referring.) For Troyer, see Carlos Troyer, *A Lecture-Recital on Indian Music* (Philadelphia: Theodore Presser, ca. 1913). On Loomis, see Pisani, "Exotic Sounds," 63. On Curtis, see Mick Gidley, *Edward S. Curtis and the North American Indian, Incorporated* (Cambridge: Cambridge University Press, 1998), 202–10. On Lieurance, see

"Thurlow Lieurance Memorial Music Library, Wichita State University," http://library.wichita.edu/music/thurlow_lieurance.htm (accessed June 20, 2002); and, more particularly, Thurlow Lieurance, "The Musical Soul of the American Indian," *Etude* 38, no. 10 (October 1920): 655–56.

10. "American Indian Music," *Etude* 38, no. 10 (October 1920): 667–68. For the most comprehensive recordings of Indianist composers, see Dario Muller, *The American Indianists* (Marco Polo 8.223715, 1994), and *The American Indianists Volume 2* (Marco Polo 8.223738, 1996).

11. On Tin Pan Alley, see David A. Jasen, *Tin Pan Alley: The Composers, the Songs, the Performers, and Their Times* (New York: Donald I. Fine, 1988), 30 and passim. For a detailed chronological list of Tin Pan Alley songs, see Pisani, "Exotic Sounds," pp. 560–62.

12. Alice C. Fletcher, with Francis LaFlesche, "A Study of Omaha Indian Music, with a Report on the Structural Peculiarities of the Music, by John Comfort Fillmore" (1893), in *Peabody Museum of American Archaeology and Ethnology, Harvard University, Papers* 1 (1904): 237–382/1–152, 7, 10. Fletcher's study as it appears in the *Peabody Papers* carries the pagination of the 1904 reprinting (237–382) as well as the pagination of the original 1893 version (1–152). I use the latter to document quotations since it is more complete.

13. Ibid., 60. The definitive work on Alice Fletcher is Joan Mark, *A Stranger in Her Native Land: Alice Fletcher and the American Indians* (Lincoln: University of Nebraska Press, 1988). Mark details the extensive and long-lasting collaboration between Fletcher and LaFlesche. On LaFlesche, see Margot Liberty, "Francis LaFlesche: The Osage Odyssey," in *American Indian Intellectuals*, ed. Margot Liberty (Saint Paul, Minn.: West, 1976), 45–59; and Joan Mark, "Francis LaFlesche: The American Indian as Anthropologist," *Isis* 73 (1982): 497–510. See also Pisani, "Exotic Sounds," 316–20.

14. Francis LaFlesche to Susette LaFlesche, October 7, 1894, in Francis LaFlesche, *The Middle Five: Indian Schoolboys of the Omaha Tribe* (1900; Lincoln: University of Nebraska Press, 1963), photograph insert following p. 88.

15. See Browner, "Transposing Cultures," 93–94; and Jarold Ramsey, "Francis LaFlesche's 'The Song of Flying Crow' and the Limits of Ethnography," *Boundary* 2 19, no. 3 (fall 1992): 181.

16. An exceptional collection of the Fletcher/LaFlesche wax cylinder roll recordings is available on-line from the Library of Congress at http://memory.loc.gov/ammem/omhhtml/omhhome.html (accessed June 1, 2002). See also the accompanying materials: Dorothy Sara Lee and Maria La Vigna, eds., *Omaha Indian Music: Historical Recordings from the Fletcher/La Flesche Collection* (Washington, D.C.: Library of Congress, 1985).

17. For an excerpt, see Fletcher, "Omaha Music," 94. To put it another way, the top, melody line fits 180 eighth notes into each minute but the bottom, drumbeat line only 120. This three-against-two dual rhythm pattern, one

should note, represents one of the fundamental features of African musics and helped create the syncopation characteristic of jazz and other African-derived musics. Thanks to David Stowe and Joseph Brown for helping me think about these representations of rhythm. For further treatment of Fletcher, LaFlesche, and Fillmore, framed, in some ways, by Edward Mac-Dowell and the question of nationalism, see Richard Crawford, *America's Musical Life: A History* (New York: Norton, 2001), 382–406.

18. Fletcher, "Omaha Music," 9. ("I have had the Omahas sing me songs of many different tribes," Fletcher recalled, "but they were always credited to the tribe to which they belonged.")

19. On this "conundrum of authenticity," see Jon Cruz, *Culture on the Margins: The Black Spiritual and the Rise of American Cultural Interpretation* (Princeton, N.J.: Princeton University Press, 1999).

20. Fletcher quoted in Mark, *Stranger in Her Native Land*, 17.

21. Zuck, *Musical Americanism*, 1–8. Note that Dvořák's vision of musical nationalism was similarly anti-German and connected with nationalist political aspirations across Europe. Likewise, he would prove naive when it came to sorting out the social relations in the United States that came attached to various vernacular musics. See also Osman, "American 'Indianist' Composers"; and Pisani, "Exotic Sounds," 67–95.

22. Antonín Dvořák, "Music in America," *Harper's New Monthly Magazine* 90, no. 537 (February 1898): 433.

23. Pisani, "Exotic Sounds," 55. For a more detailed discussion, see ibid., 75. Dvořák's tangled relations with Indian people, most visibly in his encounters with the Kickapoo leader Big Moon during the "Spillville Summer" of 1893, have been the subject of a number of writings. See, e.g., John C. Tibbets, "Dvorak and American Indians," in *Dvorak in America*, ed. John C. Tibbets (Portland, Oreg.: Amadeus, 1993). A notable treatment is the reading of Patricia Hampl's *Spillville* (Minneapolis: Milkweed, 1987) in Gerald Vizenor, "A Postmodern Introduction," in *Narrative Chance: Postmodern Discourse on Native American Indian Literatures*, ed. Gerald Vizenor (Norman: University of Oklahoma Press, 1989), 6–8.

24. Alice Fletcher, *Indian Story and Song from North America* (Boston: Small, Maynard, 1900), vii.

25. Theodore Baker, *Uber die Musik der nordamerikanischen Wilden* (Leipzig, 1882), translated as *On the Music of the North American Indians* by Ann Buckley (New York: Da Capo, 1977); Frederick Burton, *American Primitive Music* (New York: Moffat, Yard, 1909); Natalie Curtis, *The Indian's Book* (New York: Harper & Bros., 1907; reprint, New York: Dover, 1968). On music ethnography, see Pisani, "Exotic Sounds," 51–65; and Tara Browner, "'Breathing the Indian Spirit': Thoughts on Musical Borrowing and the 'Indianist' Movement in American Music," *American Music* 15, no. 3 (fall 1997): 265–84, and "Trans-

posing Cultures." On Densmore, see *Frances Densmore and American Indian Music*, comp. and ed. Charles Hoffman (New York: Museum of the American Indian, 1968).

26. For a thorough musicological treatment of these tropes, see Pisani, "Exotic Sounds," 97–269.

27. Arthur Farwell, "Introduction to *American Indian Melodies*," *Wa-Wan Press*, vol. 1, no. 2 (1901), in *The Wa-Wan Press, 1901–1911*, ed. Vera Brodsky Lawrence (New York: Arno Press/New York Times, 1970), 3–4.

28. For the *Wa-Wan Press*, see Gilbert Chase, "The Wa-Wan Press: A Chapter in American Enterprise," in ibid., ix–xv; and Edward N. Waters, "The Wa-Wan Press: An Adventure in Musical Idealism," in *A Birthday Offering to Carl Engel*, ed. Gustave Reese (New York: Schirmer, 1943), 214–33.

29. Farwell, "Introduction," 24.

30. Amy Stillman, personal conversation, November, 2003. My thanks to Amy Stillman, a gifted musicologist, for her invaluable contributions to this chapter and to the project as a whole.

31. The rich scholarship dealing with American cultural productions that seek to produce indigeneity through an imaginative engagement with Indianness includes, among others, Roy Harvey Pearce, *Savagism and Civilization: A Study of the Indian and the American Mind* (Berkeley and Los Angeles: University of California Press, 1988); Leslie Fiedler, *Return of the Vanishing America* (New York: Stein & Day, 1968); Richard Slotkin, *Regeneration through Violence: The Mythology of the American Frontier, 1600–1860* (Middletown, Conn.: Wesleyan University Press, 1973), and *The Fatal Environment: The Myth of the Frontier in the Age of Industrialization, 1800–1890* (New York: Atheneum, 1985); Renee Bergland, *The National Uncanny: Indian Ghosts and American Subjects* (Hanover, N.H.: University Press of New England, 2000); Helen Carr, *Inventing the American Primitive: Politics, Gender, and the Representation of Native American Literary Traditions, 1789–1936* (New York: New York University Press, 1996); Susan Scheckle, *The Insistence of the Indian: Race and Nationalism in Nineteenth-Century American Culture* (Princeton, N.J.: Princeton University Pres, 1998); Shari M. Huhndorf, *Going Native: Indians in the American Cultural Imagination* (Ithaca, N.Y.: Cornell University Press, 2001); and Philip Deloria, *Playing Indian* (New Haven, Conn.: Yale University Press, 1998).

32. The music moved from Native original through layers of simulations, each claiming, not representational accuracy, but an accuracy that was essentialist. Ethnographers who complained about the difficulties of their collecting in ways that called even the initial transcription into question and who failed to question the universality of their representational tools (musical notation, in this case) nonetheless found themselves claiming to have gotten it "essentially" right. Composers privileged their own aesthetic vision as the ground for claiming that their simulations were equivalent to—or perhaps

better than—the originals. Here was a precession of simulacra that operated somewhat differently than that described by Jean Baudrillard, "The Precession of Simulacra," in *Simulacra and Simulation*, trans. Sheila Faria Glaser (Ann Arbor: University of Michigan Press, 1995), 1–42.

33. For singers who were out of tune or otherwise unsuitable, see, e.g., Frances Densmore, "The Study of Indian Music," in *Smithsonian Annual Report*, 1941, reprinted in *Frances Densmore and American Indian Music*, ed. Hoffman, 107–10.

34. Fletcher, "Omaha Music," 152. Mabel Dodge Luhan sensed difficulties in Natalie Curtis's efforts to capture Indian music: "She had caught the simple phrase, she had the time and the tune: but not the feeling! She injected something into it that did not belong there. It became sweet and had a willful virtue in it. . . . 'No,' said Geronimo, very kindly and like a patient teacher. 'Not like that. You make a white man's song'" (*Edge of Taos Desert: Escape to Reality* [1937; Albuquerque: University of New Mexico Press, 1988], 69–70).

35. For a detailed and thoughtful treatment of the question of appropriation, see Browner, "'Breathing the Indian Spirit,'" and "Transposing Cultures," esp. 1–19, 190–209.

36. At this point, we might note some of the key elements in the Indian sound: (1) descending melody lines; (2) tom-tom beats; (3) "short-long" rhythmic patterns; and (4) an emphasis on certain intervals, namely, the minor third and the major second. Following in Fletcher's path, e.g., Frances Densmore (*Teton Sioux Music*, Bureau of American Ethnology Bulletin 61 [Washington, D.C.: U.S. Government Printing Office, 1918], 16–17, 32–33, 46) would chart Lakota and Ojibwe music, showing that the whole step (46 percent) and the minor third (32 percent) made up the vast majority of descending intervals. Even in ascending movements, the whole step (33 percent) and minor third (27 percent) remained critical.

37. Fletcher, "Omaha Music," 61. One should note that, like most tribes, the Omahas already had substantial experience with Christian missionaries, who ensured the presence of pianos and organs on reservations and Western hymn harmony in Indian ears.

38. Ibid.

39. Indeed, without harmony, the elements found in the Indian sound might be located not so far away from African American music as the critics who chortled at Dvořák's conflation of the two might have supposed. The "short-long" rhythmic figure in Indian melody, e.g., is key to the syncopations that characterize jazz rhythm. The three-against-two rhythmic figures found in the relation between drums and voices are not unlike the polyrhythms found in African music, which themselves help create syncopation. Indeed, to those who argued that ragtime and syncopation were the only American musical originals, Cadman would later suggest that "American Indian tunes have also this element developed to the 'steenth degree. Just examine them and see the

wealth of throbbing syncopation found in their outlines" ("The American Indian's Music Idealized," 659). Likewise, the lowered seventh and third degrees of many Indian-sound scales bring to mind and ear the flatted third, fifth, and seventh of the standard blues scale. Black music, particularly jazz and blues, makes familiar use of the pentatonic scales so often attributed to Indian music. Dvořák's failure to separate out these two musics had, as Zuck (*Musical Americanism*, 73) points out, a great deal to do with their otherness for a European observer—an otherness shared by most white Americans as well. It is also the case, however, that, to an ear unshaped by the nuances of American social history, the two sounds might be closer than expected. One of the key elements that sets the two musics apart is harmony. (The simple harmonizations offered by Fillmore did, however, in some senses begin to replicate the process through which African melodies had been brought within—while transforming—a Western harmonic framework. Consider, e.g., the parallel relation between the blues—harmonized using three simple chords—and Fillmore's Indian harmonizations, which often returned to similar chord functions.) Play the similar scales over a dominant seventh chord, and hear the sound of the blues; play them over an open fifth, and hear the sound of Indian.

40. Fillmore's theory was hardly uncontested. For example, Harvard's Benjamin Ives Gilman insisted that Indians had no sense of scale or harmony. On Fillmore's musical debate with Benjamin Ives Gilman, see Mark, *Stranger in Her Native Land*, 225–37; and James C. McNutt, "John Comfort Fillmore: A Student of Indian Music Reconsidered," *American Music* 2 (spring 1984): 61–70.

41. Note, however, that the gesture toward commensurability, which seemingly unites around a common human endowment, was, at the same time, a universalizing gesture of power, one in which the West makes other cultures available for the ongoing production of colonial and colonizing knowledge.

42. On the power and protean character of the idea of development, see Constance Areson Clark, "Mammoths, Museums, and Cave Men: Arguing Evolution in the Decade of the Scopes Trial" (Ph.D. diss., University Of Colorado, 2002).

43. "Jass and Jassism," *New Orleans Times-Picayune*, June 20, 1918, 4, reprinted in *Keeping Time: Readings in Jazz History*, ed. Robert Walser (New York: Oxford University Press, 1999), 8.

44. Fletcher, "Omaha Music," 57.

45. Mason and Howard quoted in Zuck, *Musical Americanism*, 69, 68. For Howard, African American music was far more likely to be useful in creating American composition, if only because of a greater "intermingling."

46. See, e.g., Luke Eric Lassiter, Clyde Ellis, and Ralph Kotay, *The Jesus Road: Kiowas, Christianity, and Indian Hymns* (Lincoln: University of Nebraska Press, 2002); and Michael McNally, *Ojibwe Singers: Hymns, Grief, and a Native Culture in Motion* (New York: Oxford University Press, 2000).

47. John Troutman, "'Playing Indian' in Pitch: Federal Indian Education, American Indian Performers, and the Politics of Music, 1900–1935" (paper presented at the annual meeting of the American Studies Association, Washington, D.C., November 9, 2001). Troutman's important dissertation work at the University of Texas will, when complete, offer the first statement on the pervasiveness and importance of Indian music both inside and outside boarding schools.

48. My thanks to Susan Dominquez (personal correspondence, June 6, 2003), whose extensive research into the life of Zitkala-Sa suggests that, while it is unlikely that she was an enrolled student at the New England Conservatory or Boston University, Richard Henry Pratt did arrange for the federal government to support her music studies in Boston as a "special student," perhaps through private lessons.

49. Lieurance, "Musical Soul," 656.

50. *New York Times*, October 25, 1918, 13. On Eastman, see also *Etude* 38, no. 10 (October 1920): 666. On Princess Pakanli, see Work Projects Administration, *The WPA Guide to 1930s Oklahoma* (1941; Lawrence: University Press of Kansas, 1986). On Angela Gorman, see Dennis McAuliffe Jr., *The Deaths of Sybil Bolton: An American Story* (New York: Times Books, 1994), 208, 218.

51. "American Indian Another Caruso," *New York Times*, November 24, 1912, C5. On Oskenonton, a New York performer who received a great deal of coverage in the *Times*, see, e.g., "Indian in Debut Here Sings to a Tom Tom," *New York Times*, January 23, 1925, 22. Simmons may have been Puyallup rather than Yakama.

52. "Princess Watahwaso Sings," *New York Times*, April 8, 1920, 9. See also Lieurance, "Musical Soul," 656; and Bunny McBride, *Molly Spotted Elk: A Penobscot in Paris* (Norman: University of Oklahoma Press, 1995), 80–83.

53. "Indian Singer Here for Opera Role," *Los Angeles Daily Times*, June 17, 1926, 3; "Throngs at Concert under Tree of Light," *New York Times*, December 26, 1922, 14; "Inkowa Powwow," *New York Times*, November 14, 1915, 5; "The Week's Music," *New York Times*, February 8, 1920, XX6; "Plans of Musicians," *New York Times*, March 6, 1927, X12. In 1938, Yowlache played the Chieftain (the baritone lead) in the New York Light Opera Guild's one-night production of *The Sun Dance* (Susan Dominguez, personal correspondence, June 6, 2003).

54. "Indian Musicians in the Modern World," *Etude* 38, no. 10 (October 1920): 665.

55. On the Indian String Quartet, see "Indian String Quartet," http://sdrc.lib .uiowa.edu/libsdrc/details.jsp?id=Indianstr/1 (accessed May 25, 2002).

56. On the Indian Art and Music Co., see http://sdrcdata.lib.uiowa.edu/libsdrc /details.jsp?id=indianart/1 (accessed May 25, 2002). On the U.S. Indian Band, see http://sdrc.lib.uiowa.edu/libsdrc/details.jsp?id=usib/2 (accessed

May 25, 2002). On Fred Cardin, see *Indians of Today*, ed. Marion Gridley (Chicago: Indian Council Fire, 1960), 57–58.

57. On Childers, Cleveland, and Kilpatrick, see Work Projects Administration, *WPA Guide to 1930s Oklahoma*, 112. On Pepper, see "Jim Pepper," http://www .inmotionmagazine.com/pepper.html (accessed February 15, 2004). On Moore, Stewart, and Stone, see *Indians of Today*, ed. Gridley, 95, 177, 7. On Tecumseh, see John Troutman, "'Indian Blues': The Representation and Participation of American Indians in Popular Music, 1900–1930" (paper presented at the annual meeting of the Western History Association, Portland, Oreg., October 7, 1999). On the Penobscot band, see McBride, *Molly Spotted Elk*, 32–33. I have learned about the Nez Perceans through the exhibit "By Hand through Memory" at the High Desert Museum, Bend, Oreg., and through correspondence with Arthur Taylor, the grandson of H. Pete McCormack, one of the founding members of the band. On David Hill, see John [Robert?] Coon, "Indian Musicians in the Modern World," *Etude* 38, no. 10 (October 1920): 666.

58. On Redfeather generally, see her memoirs: Blackstone, *Where Trails Have Led Me*. See also Blackstone's (i.e., Redfeather's) entry in *Native American Women: A Biographical Dictionary*, ed. Gretchen Bataille (New York: Garland, 1993), 29–30. The chronology recounted in her memoir suggests that perhaps an 1892 birthdate is the more likely, though her Creek enrollment listing suggests 1882. An 1882 birthdate would have had her meeting Cadman around age thirty. Yet her meeting with him came shortly after she had left school in Oklahoma, suggesting a younger age. My appreciation to K. Tsianina Lomawaima for helping me work through the details.

59. Clippings and promotional material can be found in the file "Charles Wakefield Cadman," Charles Lummis Papers, Southwest Museum, Los Angeles (hereafter Lummis Papers). For the reviews, see "What the Critics Say" in the promotional brochure "The American Indian Music Talk." Thanks to Sharyn Yeoman for sharing these with me.

60. Blackstone, *Where Trails Have Led Me* (1968/1970), 27–28.

61. Cadman, *Four American Indian Songs*, n.p.

62. Margaret St. Vrain Sanford, *Denver News*, November 18, 1914, quoted in "What the Critics Say."

63. The Chicago critic is quoted in Blackstone, *Where Trails Have Led Me* (1968/1970), 41–42.

64. Quotations taken from "Tsianina Redfeather" in the promotional brochure "The American Indian Music Talk."

65. Ibid.

66. Carol B. Storrs, *Minneapolis Tribune*, October 19, 1913, quoted in "What the Critics Say."

67. Lulu Sanford-Tefft, *Little Intimate Stories of Charles Wakefield Cadman* (Holly-

wood: D. G. Fisher, 1926), 34–35, quoted in Browner, "Transposing Cultures," 95. The claim of Tsianina as inspiration was frequently made by Cadman, Tsianina, and Eberhardt in all the promotional materials surrounding the opera.

68. On the other hand, her memoir may be reflecting the image crafted by the opera.

69. See Blackstone, *Where Trails Have Led Me* (1968), 18–19.

70. Ibid., 118.

71. For blood, see *Shanewis*, 13–14. For death, see ibid., 15.

72. For Tsianina's wartime experiences, see Blackstone, *Where Trails Have Led Me* (1970), 85–103. For Yowlachie, see ibid., 125. For Oskenonton, see "Indian Singer Here for Opera Role," *Los Angeles Daily Times*, June, 17, 1926, 3.

73. Blackstone, *Where Trails Have Led Me* (1968), 36.

74. Dorothy McAllister, "The Santa Fe Fiesta," *El Palacio* 11, no. 6 (September 15, 1921): 81.

75. On the chautauqua circuit, see http://sdrcdata.lib.uiowa.edu/libsdrc/details .jsp?id=usib/2 (accessed May 25, 2002). On Oskenonton, see "Plans of Musicians," *New York Times*, March 6, 1927, X12. On Tsianina's fund-raising activity, see "Republican Fund Reached," *New York Times*, January 3, 1929, 5. On her further career, see Blackstone, *Where Trails Have Led Me* (1970), 111–37; and Troutman, "'Indian Blues,'" esp. 13 (on the Foundation for American Indian Education).

76. On the powwow, see Tara Browner, *Heartbeat of the People: Music and Dance of the Northern Pow-Wow* (Urbana: University of Illinois Press, 2002); William K. Powers, *War Dance: Plains Indian Musical Performance* (Tucson: University of Arizona Press, 1990), 50–60; Susan Applegate Krouse, "A Window into the Indian Culture: The Powwow as Performance" (Ph.D. diss., University of Wisconsin, Milwaukee, 1991); Gloria Young, "Powwow Power: Perspectives on Historic and Contemporary Intertribalism" (Ph.D. diss., University of Indiana, 1981); and Ann Marguerite Axtmann, "Dance: Celebration and Resistance—Native American Indian Intertribal Powwow Performance" (Ph.D. diss., New York University, 1999).

77. On the beach as "in-between," see Greg Dening, *Islands and Beaches: Discourse on a Silent Land, Marquesas, 1774–1880* (Melbourne: Melbourne University Press, 1980).

78. Michael Pisani, "The Romantic Savage: American Indians in the Parlor," in *The Voices That Are Gone*, ed. Jon W. Finson (New York: Oxford University Press, 1994), 268–69.

79. J. S. Zamecnik, *Sam Fox Moving Picture Music* (Cleveland: Sam Fox, 1913), vol. 1. Michael Pisani's forthcoming *Sounds Indian* promises to deal with Indian film music in its final chapter.

80. Kathryn Kalinak, "'The Sound of Many Voices': Music in John Ford's West-

erns," in *John Ford Made Westerns: Filming the Legend in the Sound Era*, ed. Gaylyn Studlar and Matthew Bernstein (Bloomington: Indiana University Press, 2001), 181. See also *John Ford's "Stagecoach*," ed. Barry Keith Grant (Cambridge: Cambridge University Press, 2003); and, more particularly, Kathryn Kalinak, *Settling the Score: Music and the Classical Hollywood Film* (Madison: University of Wisconsin Press, 1992).

81. On the war chant, see http://community-2.webtv.net/The-Johnz/THEHISTORY OFTHEWAR/ (accessed September 13, 2003). Citing a 1984 origin, the fan who operates this website proudly notes: "The chant continued among the student body during the [Florida State Seminole's] 1985 season, and by the 1986 season was a stadiumwide activity. The Marching Chiefs refined the chant, plus put its own brand of accompaniment to it. And to this day continue to change it. Other sports teams like the Atlanta Braves and the Kansas City Chiefs, have adopted one or both, the chant, or the arm motion called 'The Chop.' And every year more sports teams are doing The Chop. It has been seen in stadiums for the Washington Redskins, among others not even associated with Indians. But it was first 'The Seminole Chop'!!"

CONCLUSION

1. P. Diddy, Murphy Lee, and Nelly, "Shake Ya Tailfeather," *Bad Boys II Soundtrack* (Bad Boy, 2003).

2. The definitive treatment of the SAI remains Hazel Hertzberg, *The Search for an American Indian Identity: Modern Pan Indian Movements* (Syracuse, N.Y.: Syracuse University Press, 1971). See also Peter Iverson, *Carlos Montezuma and the Changing World of American Indians* (Albuquerque: University of New Mexico Press, 1982); and Joy Porter, *To Be Indian: The Life of Iroquois-Seneca Arthur Caswell Parker* (Norman: University of Oklahoma Press, 2001).

3. Essanay Film Co. advertisement, *Moving Picture World*, October 21, 1911.

4. I choose the word *cohort* for its multiple inflections. As one of the divisions of a Roman legion, *cohort* carries with it connotations of conflict and struggle, which, in my mind, are constantly underpinning the activities of the people I've been discussing. There's a sense of enclosure, of boundary surrounding a cohort that I want to draw on in arguing that these people make up a category of their own. At the same time, I want to be aware of the differences in their histories, motivations, and experiences. And, in that sense, I want *cohort* to evoke the related word *cohere*, which brings with it a sense of things— not necessarily the *same* things—finding a congruence, which allows one to perceive a commonality, a coherence.

5. See Bunny McBride, *Molly Spotted Elk: A Penobscot in Paris* (Norman: University of Oklahoma Press, 1995); Lili Cockerille Livingston, *American Indian Ballerinas* (Norman: University of Oklahoma Press, 1997); Charles C. Eldredge, Julie Schimmel, and William H. Truettner, *Art in New Mexico, 1900–1945: Paths*

to *Taos and Santa Fe* (New York: Abbeville; Washington, D.C.: Smithsonian Institution, for the National Museum of American Art, 1986); Bruce Bernstein
and W. Jackson Rushing, *Modern by Tradition: American Indian Painting in the
Studio Style* (Santa Fe: Museum of New Mexico Press, 1995); James Slotkin,
The Peyote Religion; A Study in Indian-White Relations (Glencoe, Ill.: Free Press,
1956); Peter Iverson, *When Indians Became Cowboys: Native Peoples and Cattle
Ranching in the American West* (Norman: University of Oklahoma Press, 1994),
and Iverson, *Carlos Montezuma*; Porter, *To Be Indian*; Raymond Wilson, *Ohiyesa:
Charles Eastman, Santee Sioux* (Urbana: University of Illinois Press, 1983); L. G.
Moses and Raymond Wilson, eds., *Indian Lives: Essays on Nineteenth- and Twen-
tieth-Century Native American Leaders* (Albuquerque: University of New Mexico
Press, 1985); Margot Liberty, ed., *American Indian Intellectuals* (Saint Paul,
Minn.: West, 1978); R. David Edmunds, *American Indian Leaders: Studies in Di-
versity* (Lincoln: University of Nebraska Press, 1980); R. David Edmunds, ed.,
The New Warriors: Native American Leaders since 1900 (Lincoln: University of Ne-
braska Press, 2001); and Frederick Hoxie, "Exploring a Cultural Borderland:
Native American Journeys of Discovery in the Early Twentieth Century," *Jour-
nal of American History* 79, no. 3 (December 1992): 969–95.

6. See, e.g., Alexandra Harmon, "American Indians and Land Monopolies in
the Gilded Age," *Journal of American History* 90 (June 2003): 106–33; David
Kamper, "Introduction: The Mimicry of Indian Gaming," in *Indian Gaming:
Who Wins?* ed. Angela Mullis and David Kamper (Los Angeles: University of
California, Los Angeles, American Indian Studies Center, 2000), vii–xiv; Paul
Pasquaretta, "On the 'Indianness' of Bingo: Gambling and the Native Ameri-
can Community," *Critical Inquiry* 20, no. 4 (summer 1994): 694–714; Thomas
A. Britten, *American Indians in World War I: At War and at Home* (Albuquerque:
University of New Mexico Press, 1997), esp. 99–115; Alison Bernstein, *Ameri-
can Indians and World War II: Toward a New Era in Indian Affairs* (Norman: Uni-
versity of Oklahoma Press, 1991), esp. 40–63; and Tom Holm, *Strong Hearts,
Wounded Souls: Native American Veterans of the Vietnam War* (Austin: University of
Texas Press, 1996).

7. The transformation that goes by the name *modernity* has a long reach back
into the past and an uncertain run forward into the present, which makes locating a specific moment of modernity difficult, if not impossible. In this
particular formulation, aimed at the late nineteenth century and the early
twentieth in the United States, I use *modernity* to reflect several transformations: new aesthetic practices (which some might name modernism), which
sought to represent and experience the "newness" and fluidity of the societies created by industrial capitalism, urbanization, and mass consumption.
At the same time, this modernity also relies on notions of scientific rationalism and a trajectory of human progress. It rejects (even as it embraces) ir-
rationality and superstition and, thus, argues for social and self-awareness

of the ways in which individuals and collectives—rather than gods and angels—act to shape history. It that sense, modernity aims toward liberation, freedom, autonomy, enlightenment, and reason. Linked to changes in the structures of capitalism but not solely determined by them, modernity offers spaces and rationales for the making of new identities and practices. As a global structural sequence of events, however, this idea of modernity has usually been narrated from a Eurocentric perspective: liberation and freedom for some came at the expense of forced labor and dispossession for others. For a useful overview, see Stuart Hall, David Held, Don Hebert, and Kenneth Thompson, eds., *Modernity: An Introduction to Modern Societies* (Oxford: Blackwell, 1996). See also Dilip Parameshwar Gaonkar, ed., *Alternative Modernities* (Durham, N.C.: Duke University Press, 2001); and Néstor García Canclini, *Hybrid Cultures: Strategies for Entering and Leaving Modernity*, trans. Christopher L. Chiappari and Silvia L. López (Minneapolis: University of Minnesota Press, 1995).

8. In "Exploring a Cultural Borderland," Frederick Hoxie has offered the most persuasive reading of Indian cultural production in this moment. Among the many useful cautions against an overstated agency argument, I have taken most to heart those found in the subtle readings offered by Arnold Krupat in *Red Matters: Native American Studies* (Philadelphia: University of Pennsylvania Press, 2002).

9. See, e.g., Vine Deloria Jr., *Behind the Trail of Broken Treaties: An Indian Declaration of Independence* (1974; Austin: University of Texas Press, 1985); Vine Deloria Jr. and Clifford Lytle, *The Nations Within: The Past and Future of American Indian Sovereignty* (New York: Pantheon, 1984); John R. Wunder, ed., *Native American Sovereignty* (New York: Garland, 1996); David E. Wilkins, *American Indian Sovereignty and the U.S. Supreme Court: The Masking of Justice* (Austin: University of Texas Press, 1997); Robert Williams Jr., *The American Indian in Western Legal Thought: The Discourse of Conquest* (New York: Oxford University Press, 1990); and Taiaiake Alfred, *Peace, Power, and Righteousness: An Indigenous Manifesto* (Toronto: Oxford University Press, 1999).

10. I'm referring here largely to Bhabha's notion of mimicry, which suggests a "difference that is almost the same, but not quite" (Homi Bhabha, *The Location of Culture* [London: Routledge, 1994], 86). See also Ann Laura Stoler, "Tense and Tender Ties: The Politics of Comparison in North American History and (Post) Colonial Studies," *Journal of American History* 88 (December 2001): 829–65, and *Race and the Education of Desire: Foucault's "History of Sexuality" and the Colonial Order of Things* (Durham, N.C.: Duke University Press, 1995).

11. One could ask for no better example of a social-cultural-political assertion of difference that takes full account of both indigenous ('akota) and modern sensibilities than the brilliant and fantastic volume by Iktomi (the 'akota

trickster), *America Needs Indians* (Denver: Bradford-Robinson, 1937). Of course, there is a voluminous literature on the history and strategy of African American integration efforts. See, e.g., John Kirk, *Redefining the Color Line: Black Activism in Little Rock, Arkansas, 1940–1970* (Gainesville: University Press of Florida, 2002); Bruce Adelson, *Brushing Back Jim Crow: The Integration of Minor-League Baseball in the American South* (Charlottesville: University Press of Virginia, 1999); Charles K. Ross, *Outside the Lines: African Americans and the Integration of the National Football League* (New York: New York University Press, 1999); Michael W. Homel, *Down from Equality: Black Chicagoans and the Public Schools, 1920–41* (Urbana: University of Illinois Press, 1984); Timothy J. Minchin, *Hiring the Black Worker: The Racial Integration of the Southern Textile Industry, 1960–1980* (Chapel Hill: University of North Carolina Press, 1999); Allan Keiler, *Marian Anderson: A Singer's Journey* (New York: Scribner, 2000); and Pearl Bowser, Jane Gaines, and Charles Musser, eds., *Oscar Micheaux and His Circle: African-American Filmmaking and Race Cinema of the Silent Era* (Bloomington: Indiana University Press, 2001). Particularly evocative is the broad canvas offered by Thomas C. Holt, *The Problem of Race in the Twenty-first Century* (Cambridge, Mass.: Harvard University Press, 2000).

12. One should note that each of the major social groups defined in the United States by race and ethnicity has had distinct experiences with regard to colonialism, inclusion, mimicry, and subjection to the American civil order. Many Mexican Americans, e.g., retained a memory of political difference, if not autonomy, and certainly of a land base, supposedly protected under the Treaty of Guadalupe Hidalgo, but often stripped through mechanisms not dissimilar from those through which Indians lost land under allotment. In Puerto Rico, the Insular Cases, the 1917 Jones Act, and the 1952 Commonwealth Constitution can be seen in terms of long-term Spanish and, later, American colonialism, but also in terms of the existence of a coherent land base. We might see some of the differences in the character of black, Indian, and Chicano nationalism (which lay claim to the land base of Aztlan, to which it had little hope of acquiring) through the lens of different approaches to and experiences with the tensions between colonial inclusion and rights-based integration.

13. *Cherokee Nation v. State of Georgia*, 30 U.S. 1 (1831). In addition to the many texts cited that treat the Cherokee cases, see John R. Wunder, *"Retained by the People": A History of American Indians and the Bill of Rights* (New York: Oxford University Press, 1994), 24–27.

14. *Lone Wolf v. Hitchcock*, 187 U.S. 553 (1903); U.S. Constitution, art. 6: "This Constitution, and the laws of the United States which shall be made in pursuance thereof; and all treaties made, or which shall be made, under the authority of the United States, shall be the supreme law of the land."

15. On Long Lance, see Donald B. Smith, *Long Lance: The True Story of an Imposter*

(Lincoln: University of Nebraska Press, 1982); and Laura Browder, *Slippery Characters: Ethnic Impersonators and American Identities* (Chapel Hill: University of North Carolina Press, 2000).

16. While the IRA governments set up during the Indian New Deal were (and, some would argue, are) colonial structures, it is also true that they became key sites for Native political aspirations, and they certainly helped emphasize the idea, if not always the reality, of self-governance, autonomy, and sovereignty. For two revealing studies, see Thomas Biolsi's *Organizing the Lakota: The Political Economy of the New Deal on the Pine Ridge and Rosebud Reservations* (Tucson: University of Arizona Press, 1992) and his *Deadliest Enemies: Law and the Making of Race Relations on and off Rosebud Reservation* (Berkeley and Los Angeles: University of California Press, 2001).

17. See Holt, *Problem of Race*, esp. 77–85.

18. On black music, modernity, and cultural politics, see Paul Allen Anderson, *Deep River: Music and Memory in Harlem Renaissance Thought* (Durham: Duke University Press, 2001).

index

Irving, Henry, 70
Ives, Charles, 198

Jeep Cherokee, 138, 166, 265 n.1
Jefferson, Thomas, 85
Jeffries, Jim, 125, 237
John Olson Cherokee Indian Baseball
    Club, 130
Johnson, Emma, 227
Johnson, George, 155
Johnson, Jack, 125, 237
Johnson, Jimmy, 126, 127
Jones, Harold S., 127
Jordan Motor Company, 164–**65**

Kalinak, Kathryn, 222
Kawbawbam, Carlisle, 206
"Kaw-Liga," 184
Kelley, William, 36–37, 39–40
Keokuk, 71
Key, Ted, 127
Kickapoo Medicine Show, 68
Kicking Bear, 22, 28, 43, 64, 69, 71
Kiowa, 150
Klamath, 151
Knowlton, Bruce, 186

LaFlesche, Francis, 205, 228, 229
    ethnography, 188–92
    notation, 191–94
LaFlesche, Joseph, 25
Lakota. See Sioux
Langtry, Lillie, 217
Lanier, Sidney, 194–95
Last of the Line (film), 90
"Last Stand," 20, 27, 35, 48, 49
Latino Americans, 61, 125, 235–37,
    287 n.12
Levi, John, 128
Lieurance, Thurlow, 187, 205–6,
    207, 218

Lightning Creek, 52
    and expectations, 45–49
    killings, 15, 19, 24,
    as trope, 20–21, 41
Little, Edward, 78
Little Big Horn, 20, 45
Little Thunder, 78
Lone Star (film), 90
Lone Wolf, 71
Lone Wolf v. Hitchcock (1903), 112, 236,
    248 n.60
Longboat, Tom, 115
Loomis, Harvey Worthington, 187, 197
Low Neck, John Burke, 63–64
Luhan, Antonio, 87, 166, 272 n.55
Luhan, Mabel Dodge, 166, 272 n.55,
    279 n.34
Lumbee basketball, 129
Lynd, Helen and Paul, 163

McAllister, Dorothy, 218
McClintock, Anne, 242 n.1, 245 n.24
McDonnell, Janet, 150
McDowell, Edward, 187, 196
McGillycuddy, Valentine, 38–39, 41
McLain, Mayes, 128
McLaughlin, James, 23
Marshall, John, 236
Martinez, Maria, 148
Masculinity, 65, 118–19, 124–25, 146,
    164–65, 248 n.61, 263 n.18
    and sexuality, 124, 256 n.18
Mason, Daniel, 204
Mathews, John J., 120, 156
Maynor, Ken, 129
Means, Russell, 105
Melodrama, 83–85, 96–100
Melovidov, Alex, 207, 209
Mended Lute, The (film), 94
Mesquite's Gratitude, The (film), 88
Meyers, John, 120, **227–28**